EPISCOPAL VISITATION OF MONASTERIES IN THE THIRTEENTH CENTURY

EPISCOPAL VISITATION OF MONASTERIES IN THE THIRTEENTH CENTURY

BY

C. R. CHENEY

SECOND, REVISED, EDITION

PORCUPINE PRESS
MANCHESTER UNIVERSITY PRESS

First published 1931 by Manchester University Press
Second, revised, edition 1983

© copyright 1983 by C. R. Cheney

Published in the United States of America by
PORCUPINE PRESS INC
1317 Filbert Street
Philadelphia PA   19107
ISBN 0 87991 638 9

and in Great Britain by
MANCHESTER UNIVERSITY PRESS
Oxford Road, Manchester M13 9PL
ISBN 0 7190 0748 8

Library of Congress Cataloging in Publication Data

Cheney, C.R. (Christopher Robert), 1906-
   Episcopal visitation of monasteries in the thirteenth
century.
   Bibliography: p.
   Includes index
   1.   Visitations, Ecclesiastical—Europe-History.
2.   Monasticism and religious orders—History—Middle
Ages, 600-1500. 3. Monasteries—Europe. 4. Church
history—Middle Ages, 600-1500. 5. Bishops—Europe.
I. Title
BX2590.C44   1983   282' .09'022   83-2339

MANUFACTURED IN THE UNITED STATES OF AMERICA

PREFACE
TO THE FIRST EDITION

THIS study does not profess to explore unfamiliar ground or arrive at unexpected conclusions. I have been mainly concerned to collect as much evidence as I could for the practice of episcopal visitation of monasteries in the thirteenth century, to observe the details of procedure and to examine, unaffected by outside evidence, the value of the visitations in a small area over a limited period of time. If the notes have become cumbersome with many references, it is because the value of the study seemed to depend on fullness of documentation for each statement.

Matters of monastic discipline, which were the main subject of these visitations, present the most striking features of the records. Here they have only been incidentally mentioned. It is to be hoped that with increased knowledge of administrative details we shall be in a better position to appreciate the tendency of episcopal work and the character of monastic life in the thirteenth century.

Several modern historians have made important contributions to the study of visitation of monasteries. Dom Berlière, in his important essays on the Benedictines, has shown how much material may be found in the papal registers. Professor Hamilton Thompson and Dr. Coulton have established canons of criticism and offered interpretations of the actual visitation documents, the former in his editions of various episcopal registers, the latter in the *English Historical Review* and *Five Centuries of Religion*. Dr. Frere, in an introductory volume to *Visitation Articles and Injunctions of the Period of the Reformation*, has given an admirable survey of the development of visitations in the Western Church. This is the only comprehensive work of its kind, and it is much to be regretted that the book is scarce and little known.

My debt to these scholars will be apparent throughout the following pages. I also wish to express my profound gratitude to my teacher, Professor F. M. Powicke, for his continual guidance and kindly help. My mother has read the whole of the book in manuscript, and Professor G. W. Coopland and Mr. R. V. Lennard have read portions of it. I am very grateful to them for their advice and criticism. I am also much obliged to Dr. Rose Graham for her loan of transcripts from Archbishop Winchelsey's register and from the British Museum MS. *Cotton*, Galba, E. IV.

In the preparation of the bibliography (Appendix III.) I have not attempted to include all the printed books and manuscripts mentioned in the course of the book. The list gives those which are most commonly quoted, and provides an index to the abbreviated references in footnotes.

C. R. CHENEY.

Oxford, *May*, 1931.

INTRODUCTION
TO SECOND EDITION

This short monograph, dealing with a strictly limited subject, was first published in 1931. Were the author to re-write it now, it would undoubtedly look very different, but he cannot now make an entirely new approach to the subject. Since no single study has appeared to replace the original edition, long since out of print, I have been encouraged to think that its revision may be useful. When it was first published, almost all the substantial thirteenth-century accounts of episcopal visitations came from England or Normandy, and some readers inferred from its contents that the author had of set purpose restricted himself to those regions. This was not in fact true : dearth of sources accounted for the geographical limitations. I did indeed make use of papal letters to illustrate the practice of visitation in other parts of Europe, but this kind of material did not, and does not, redress the balance for regions where local evidence is scarce. Even now, fifty years on, the numerous records of visitations which have come to light in the intervening time include relatively few within the scope of this book. For the most part they are too late in date, or they touch Orders exempt from diocesans and concern visitations by Order visitors, or they are diocesan visitations of parishes, not monasteries. Other thirteenth-century visitation records have, to be sure, come to light in England and in Italy, but the harvest in France and Spain, Germany and Scandinavia is meagre. On the other hand, sources of later date published in recent years are valuable for comparison ; and if thirteenth-century records are still in short supply, there has been great advance throughout Europe in the critical approach to the study of monasticism and episcopal government in the Middle Ages. Students of these topics nowadays are much better equipped than we were equipped fifty years ago with books on administrative themes and notable prelates, with specialized bibliographies, repertories of records, topographical guides, and maps. The field is too vast to be charted here, but one may note how for England the masterly survey of monastic history by David Knowles has added to and refined the earlier judgments of G. G. Coulton and Hamilton Thompson on the efficacy and the problems of the visitatorial system. Finally, Noël Coulet has recently provided a precious aid to the evaluation of the records and a guide to the bibliography for Europe as a whole in *Les visites pastorales*.[1] This is " essential reading," and exonerates me from enlarging on general background literature.

The changes which I have made in this edition are as follows :

(1) The original text has been slightly modified in scores of places to correct minor factual errors and to insert in the footnotes up-to-date references to better editions of documents which were formerly cited in manuscript or in inadequate editions. I have also altered a few of those ill-advised generalizations of a novice which may cause a scholar to blush in later life.

---

[1] Typologie des sources du moyen âge occidental. Directeur : L. Genicot. Fasc. 23. A–IV.1*. Brépols. Turnhout, Belgium, 1977.

(2) Some amplification and up-dating of a bibliographical sort was needed, at certain points, which could not be conveniently accommodated in the revised body of the original text. A few addenda therefore form an Appendix to this introduction, with references to the pages of the book which they concern. Cross-references to them are set in the margin of the main text.

(3) In the remaining pages of this introduction I indicate the chief points at which I see need for change of emphasis and room for further study.

The chronology of episcopal visitation given in chapter II needs some qualification. This account underestimated the extent to which prelates were coming to adopt the visitation of monasteries as an occasional expedient from the second half of the twelfth century onwards. The practice had certainly sprung up in many regions long before the mid thirteenth century, to judge by scattered evidence in papal letters, chronicles, judicial settlements, and so on. The significance of these bits and pieces is enhanced when we consider, not only their wide distribution, but also how much their survival has depended on chance. The practice was in keeping with the trend of the times. It was a part of the elaboration of diocesan government which was so notable a feature of the history of the Church in the century after 1150— no less notable than the dramatic growth of papal authority with which it was connected. From the mid twelfth century, bishops were increasingly concerned with the patronage and ministry of parish churches. Along with this, the diocesans naturally made vigorous attempts to protect the material and moral condition of monasteries and to tighten diocesan control over them.

As part of this general development, monastic visitation, even if only spasmodically undertaken, gradually came to be recognized—from late in the twelfth century—as a serviceable means of reform in the hands of a zealous prelate.

The English evidence for the early period is more copious than appears in chapter II. References there to occasional monastic visitations by Archbishops Richard, Baldwin, and Hubert of Canterbury and by some of their suffragans by no means exhausted the available indications. I discuss this part of the subject again, using additional material, in more recent works.[1]   Here I carry my account down to the middle of the thirteenth century.

The picture at the beginning of the thirteenth century is one in which episcopal visitation is recognized as a possible remedy for monastic ills of all kinds—more widely recognized than could be inferred from the evidence I took into account in 1931. The diocesan or metropolitan is ready to accept the responsibility for intervening in this way and monasteries are not so generally resistant as a few acts of violent opposition would suggest. Inspection by the diocesan might even be solicited, either by a community discontented with its head or by the head of a house plagued by insubordination. A community seeking reform might even secure the diocesan's attention by order of the king. Bishop Jocelin of Bath visited the Cluniac priory of Montacute after the subprior and monks had complained to King John against their prior, and the king had requested the

---

[1] *From Becket to Langton* (Manchester, 1956), 139–41 and, in a broader setting, *Pope Innocent III and England* (Päpste und Papsttum, 9. Stuttgart, 1976), 179–236.

bishop to investigate and, if need be, deprive him.[1] Moreover, if a bishop was admitted as visitor without demur, the legal implications of his action might be uncontested and the consequences unforeseen. It required a contentious and expert advocate, Mr Thomas of Marlborough, to persuade his fellow monks of Evesham in 1202 that the visiting bishop plotted the total subversion of their liberty. Not all monks were so sensitive.

Visitations were not undertaken universally, nor repeated at fixed intervals, nor conducted according to a single pattern. The first three successors of St Thomas at Canterbury probably invoked their legatine power during the years when they enjoyed it, but when they could not claim it, they undoubtedly used their metropolitan right of visitation. At least twice, Archbishop Hubert joined forces with a diocesan to visit a monastery, with the bishop of Worcester at Cirencester, with the bishop of Lincoln at Ramsey. It was a tactful measure, when the canon law was far from explicit about a metropolitan's rights in a suffragan's diocese. At other times one sees Hubert authorizing ordinances for a monastic house which he has agreed with the convent, at Lanthony[2] and at Christ Church, Canterbury. So might the rigour of outside discipline be masked.

Ordinances made for a monastic cathedral after consultation between the prelate and the community may be ambiguous in character. They may or may not result from a formal visitation, with all the authoritarian

---

[1] *Rotuli lit. patentium*, ed. T. D. Hardy, 78*a* (21 Dec. 1207); cf. *Pipe Roll* 9 *John* (Pipe Roll Soc.), 60, *Pipe Roll* 10 *John*, 110, *Rotuli de Oblatis*, ed. T. D. Hardy, 420.

[2] *CPR*, 42.

claims of the prelate which that implies. English monastic cathedrals present a special situation, in that the bishop " vicem gerit abbatis," as Innocent III told the monks of Durham in 1198.[1] Archbishop Hubert promulgates ordinances or injunctions for Christ Church in 1203 by which he declares the suppression of certain conventual offices, having secured the express approval of the monks. Archbishop and convent both put their seals to the ordinance.[2] This sort of collaboration is also found in later times. When Bishop Alexander holds his visitation at Coventry in 1236 and finds irregularities in the procedure for admitting monks, an agreed formula is devised for making profession before the bishop and the prior, to be recorded in a chirograph carrying the seals of the bishop and the prior and the convent.[3] Ely cathedral archives yield two mid thirteenth-century ordinances which illustrate the possible diversity. The initiative for the first seems to have lain with the monks : " Hec sunt provisa a conventu Eliensi " (1241 x 1254) by the consent and wish of Bishop Hugh Northwold ; bishop and chapter add their seals. The other ordinance is framed as formal injunctions in the name of Bishop Hugh Balsham (1262), made after careful discussion with the prior and senior monks and the consent of the whole chapter. Both the episcopal and capitular seals are attached, and the bishop excommunicates transgressors with the prior's assent.[4]

---

[1] Innocent III, I. 459.

[2] Lambeth Palace MS. 1212 f. 43r. The archbishop says : " de eorum consilio et consensu unanimi ... ministeria quorumdam servientium suorum ... nos auctoritate qua fungimur cassavimus ...". Cf. Cheney, BIHR LVI (1983).

[3] *Magnum registrum album of Lichfield* (Wm Salt Soc., 1926), 343–4.

[4] *Camden Miscellany XVII*, pp. vi–vii, 1–5.

As the thirteenth century advanced towards its middle years, the practice of visitation increased in England until—at least in some dioceses—it no longer seemed extraordinary, even if it was sometimes resented. Richard Poore, as bishop of Salisbury, left injunctions at Abingdon Abbey in 1219 (Hubert Walter had been there before him as bishop c. 1190), and in 1245 the abbey received a later bishop's official. Besides the visitation of Gloucester Abbey by Bishop Walter de Cantilupe (below, p. 34), he and his predecessor visited Great Malvern Priory several times between 1233 and 1237, and other religious houses besides. His friend and contemporary Robert Grosseteste is celebrated as a visitor (below, pp. 34–5) but he has left us no full records. A letter of his Franciscan friend, Adam Marsh, in 1251, speaks of the good results expected of a visit by the bishop's deputies at Godstow Abbey. Grosseteste himself told the pope at Lyons that bishops of Lincoln before him had always been used to visit the subject religious houses of their diocese, and to take procurations from them by reason of visitation. These visitations, he said were approved and become tolerable by long custom. Other prelates of Grosseteste's circle leave minimal vestiges of their visitations : William Raleigh, bishop of Winchester, Roger Weseham of Coventry, Richard Wich of Chichester. Striking evidence of the common disciplinary policy of these prelates is seen in their diocesan statutes.[1]

[1] Chatsworth House MS. 71 ff. 5v–9v. Giffard, *Worc.*, I. 198 and *Ann. Mon.*, IV. 429. For Grosseteste see *Councils & Synods ... of the English Church*, Vol. II, ed. F. M. Powicke and C. R. Cheney (Oxford, 1964), 261–5 and *Monumenta francisc.* (Rolls series), I. 117. For Lichfield (1246) see *Magnum reg. album*, 193, for Winchester (? 1244) see *HMCR Var. Coll.*, IV. 144, for Chichester (1245–53) see *Acta SS. Bolland. Aprilis*, I. 289–90, 293.

Meanwhile, in the province of York, Archbishop Walter Gray visited religious houses in his diocese, and the mighty cathedral priory of Durham formally recognized its bishop's visitatorial rights in the statesmanlike settlement, " Le convenit," negotiated in 1229 by Bishop Richard Poore.[1]

As for early visitations in France, there is no sign that any French prelate conducted regular circuits of all monasteries under his care before Eudes Rigaud started his journeys in 1248 ; but a combing of local sources, published and unpublished, brings to light isolated records of visits, as in England. Eudes was not the first archbishop of Rouen to visit monasteries of his diocese and province, and to keep a written record. The copy of a visitation-roll of Archbishop Thibault d'Amiens contains the injunctions he addressed to the abbey of S.-Ouen at Rouen and other houses in 1222–3. A manuscript from Le Mont S.-Michel contains the same archbishop's injunctions delivered to that great abbey in 1224.[2] De Bascher points to a series of occasions when archbishops of Bourges from Pierre le Châtre (d. 1171) to Simon de Sully (d. 1233) are said to have visited the province of Bordeaux and received papal mandates to correct religious houses of their province.[3] Archbishop Juhel of Tours had his right to visit the

---

[1] *Feodarium Dunelmense* (Surtees Soc., 1872), 212–17 at p. 214.

[2] The " rotulus cuiusdam visitationis " was copied into the s.xiv cartulary of the see, Archives Seine-Maritime G 7 ff. 176v–179v and edited by C. R. Cheney, " Early Norman monastic visitations : a neglected record ", *Journal of Eccl. History*, XXXIII (1982). The injunctions for Le Mont S.-Michel are preserved in an abbey manuscript (Avranches, Bibl. mun. 149), printed by E. Martene and U. Durand, *Thesaurus novus anecdotorum* (Paris, 1717), I. 911–12.

[3] *Revue de l'hist. de l'Eglise de France*, LVIII (1972), 75. Cf. below, 141.

cathedral of S.-Brieuc recognized by the bishop and chapter in 1233.[1]

In other regions, too, bishops visited monasteries early in the thirteenth century. That emerges from the many papal letters cited in chapters II and VI below from the registers of Innocent III and his successors, directed to many parts of Europe ; and in Italy the visitors themselves have left a few records. Robert Brentano has unearthed a neglected " quaternus visitationis " of 1230 in the bishop's register of Città di Castello. The evidence it provides of pastoral activity in this little Umbrian diocese raises the possibility, at least, that some contemporary bishops in other parts of Italy were equally active, though their registers have perished or are undiscovered.[2]

A reader of this book will form the impression that by the second half of the thirteenth century the practice of visiting monasteries had become normal and accepted (if still irregular) in the better-disciplined dioceses of England and France ; and the importance of this period for visitations in England was confirmed by David Knowles's findings.[3] If we look beyond England and France, few comparable records are forthcoming from the rest of Europe. The remarkable discovery by Robert Brentano of the bishops' books of Città di

---

[1] L. d'Achery, *Spicilegium* (2nd ed., 1723), III. 612–13.

[2] " The bishops' books of Città di Castello," *Traditio*, XVI (1960), 241–54 at 246 ; cf. Brentano, *Two Churches* (Princeton, 1968), 126, 130–2. Visitations are recorded by the bishop of Pistoia, *c*. 1225–1250, and by the archbishop of Brindisi in 1245 (*Two Churches*, 107, 124–5), but for Pistoia the report is imprecise, making no mention of monasteries : the bishop " visitò con esatissima diligenza tutta la Diogesi " ; while the record from Brindisi is simply concerned with the archbishop's vindication of his right to visit the abbey of Sant' Andrea.

[3] *Religious Orders in England* I (Cambridge, 1948), 78–112 at 80.

Castello shows that in this Italian diocese, by the 1270s, under a vigorous bishop, the pastoral visit was an established institution.[1] Whether visitations were then common in other parts of Italy is still a matter for conjecture. In Spain and Portugal no records have been brought to light to suggest that episcopal visitation of monasteries was anything but rare. The Germanic lands still yield little evidence, though Albert Hauck found more activity than in earlier times. He noted that Conrad of Cologne, after visiting his diocese on the order of the pope, legislated for his clergy in 1261, and he produced nearly a dozen instances between 1271 and 1300 of metropolitan visitations undertaken by the archbishop of Mainz—and sometimes resisted.[2] Hauck's evidence hardly ever discloses whether or not the metropolitan visits included, or were meant to include, the regular clergy. Othmar Hageneder has supplied a handful of references to monastic visitations by the bishops of Passau and their deputies, 1258–1301.[3]

To determine the nature and procedure of these visitations or estimate the pastoral concern of the visitors is excessively difficult. The evidence cannot compare with that for England and Normandy. But what conclusion can be drawn from this fact? What we have is almost exclusively occupied with recording legal and

[1] " The bishops' books " and *Two Churches*, 125–32. As Brentano records, their existence had been briefly noted by Paul Kehr.

[2] *Kirchengeschichte Deutschlands*, IV (1913), 20, 799, V (1911), 150, 184. Following Hauck (V. 180 n. 4), I treated the Cologne statutes for religious houses (1261) appended to the statutes for seculars as evidence of prior visitation of the Benedictine monasteries (p. 30 below); but the preamble to them does not establish this beyond doubt.

[3] *Die geistliche Gerichtsbarkeit in Ober- und Niederösterreich* (Linz, 1967).

financial aspects of the relations between bishops and monasteries. It is impossible to say whether these visits were most often undertaken mainly to secure legal and pecuniary advantage for a diocesan or metropolitan. The problem was touched on below, in my pages on the visitations of Simon de Beaulieu (pp. 11–3), where the adverse judgment upon Simon which Coulton had recently expressed was contested. There is no easy answer, but the matter has to be viewed in the light of local conditions : the ambitions, territorial or political, of certain prelates, the history and traditions of particular monasteries, the habits of record-keeping of bishops and monasteries.

Only in the last section of the last chapter of this book (pp. 161–7) was the reader invited to focus his attention briefly on administration and finance. The recent literature of monasticism has a good deal to say about the efforts of monastic reformers in this direction. When diocesans and metropolitans visited the religious with a view to reform, they brought with them the experience of their own household- and estate-management. Many of the faults they found in religous observance and regular discipline stemmed from economic disorders, over-staffing, lack of supervision, waste of resources, general improvidence. Archbishop Winchelsey's articles of enquiry have a section " Circa temporalia " which shows the range of topics. From England throughout the century we can point to injunctions made for particular houses on these matters. Archbishop Hubert, working in each case with the diocesan, made regulations for the management of Cirencester and Ramsey Abbeys, which may be compared with injunctions left a little later by a papal legate at St Mary's Abbey, York, and the measures taken by Hubert to reduce the staff of the obedientiaries of Christ Church have already been mentioned (p. 6). Throughout the thirteenth century, and beyond, visitors are as much concerned with the economic stability of religious houses as with the moral and spiritual welfare of the inmates. They regulate the powers of obedientiaries, provide for the appointment of treasurers, order the audit of accounts, and restrain the granting of leases and corrodies. In these fields of reform a businesslike visitor might well hope for more concrete, visible success than in the area of monastic *mores*.[1]

The scope of this book was deliberately restricted to visitation of monasteries. This meant the isolation of a topic which is best understood in the context of the bishop's whole pastoral office and of his role in the increasingly complex structure of ecclesiastical law and administration. His various duties were interconnected, and so were the classes of people who needed his guidance and discipline. The unreformed Benedictines and the Austin canons who submitted to his visitation were only a small part of the flock for whom the bishop was answerable ; and although in certain important respects they formed a class apart, they were none the less deeply involved in the world around them. They had interests and obligations innumerable outside their

[1] English studies, later than Snape's book, are: R. A. L. Smith, *Canterbury Cathedral Priory* (Cambridge, 1943) and his *Collected papers* (1947), 23–73 (three important essays on monastic finances) ; D. L. Douie, *Archbishop Pecham* (Oxford, 1952), 170–81. I edited the injunctions of Cardinal John of Ferentino for St Mary's, York, 1206, in *EHR*, XLVI (1931), 443–52.

cloisters. Once episcopal visitation had become common, from the bishop's point of view many factors favoured a combination in one circuit of his monastic visits with his pastoral oversight of the secular clergy and laity. By combining inquiry into the parochial life of the deaneries and the conduct of communities, a bishop was likely to get better insight into the behaviour of both parts of his flock. The legal and practical problems arising from monastic patronage of parish churches, service of parishes by regular canons, incompatible claims of the religious and the parochial clergy to tithe, all favoured a single circuit. It saved time and money. Whether the bishop visited parish by parish or, as more often, deanery by deanery, the monastery must provide a better chance that the visitor would find board and lodging sufficient for his staff and suitable to his state.

So, as visitation became customary, it became usual for the bishop to visit monasteries when he visited the rest of his flock. This has not been stressed in the following pages, and a prelate's itinerary is seldom full enough to show his movements; but the records of Rouen in the middle of the thirteenth century and those of Hereford _c._ 1290 show clear examples of a practice which must have been widespread. The records of Città di Castello show the bishop visiting parishes and religious houses on one tour in the 1270s.

The glimpse of the bishop simultaneously facing several tasks emphasizes an important aspect of the visitation. It brings out the utility of the visitatorial system in providing opportunity for transactions of many kinds. Pastoral care did not only consist in enforcing moral standards and auditing accounts. Just as, in the twelfth century, the bishop in his synod gave publicity to the endowment of monasteries and to settlements of conflicting claims to lands and possessions, so the bishop of the thirteenth century performed a part of his duty as visitor by clearing up a great deal of legal business, contentious or otherwise. It was noted on page 148 below that " in archbishops', as in bishops', visitations business was often transacted which was not concerned with discipline." This statement hardly did justice to the amount of other work which fell to visitors and their staff in investigating privileges, verifying and ratifying title-deeds, composing differences between monastic rectors and their vicars, and adjusting claims to tithes and dues. The register of Eudes Rigaud provides many examples. When Bishop Roger Meuland of Coventry in 1266 visited Lapley, Staffordshire, where the little alien priory of S.-Remi of Reims was rector of the parish, he found the vicarage inadequate. He established new terms, with the " cordial concurrence " of the monks and after taking expert advice ; the ordinance was sealed by the bishop and the convent.[1] English evidence for business of this sort is commonly, though not exclusively, found in the records of metropolitan visitations of Canterbury. From the time of Robert Kilwardby onwards, archiepiscopal charters certify that at the visitation of a religious its original titles to lands and appropriated churches were inspected, sometimes on the demand of the visitor, sometimes at the request of the house. When John Pecham visited Norwich Cathedral in 1281, he asked to see the evidences bearing on the church's ecclesiastical property in the diocese. The

---

[1] *Magnum registrum album Lichfield*, 154–5, no. 318.

monks took the opportunity to get a comprehensive inspeximus charter from him, because some of their ancient charters were frail and others damaged in recent riots in Norwich (p. 148, below). Even monasteries whose exemption debarred the ordinary from a disciplinary visit might be summoned to defend their claims when a visitor passed their way. So Kilwardby inspected the privileges of Sempringham during his visitation of the diocese of Lincoln in 1277; and a proctor of Malmesbury Abbey waited on John Pecham, when he visited in Wiltshire in 1285, to receive a certificate that the titles to the abbey's portions and pensions which he exhibited were in order.[1]

The lengthy document (170 cm. long) in which Pecham recited the charters of Norwich was drawn up in the form of a notarial exemplification by his clerk, John Alani of Beccles. Following the archbishop's example, English bishops were beginning at the end of the thirteenth century to realize the value of employing notaries public on visitations as their clerks. The practice was encouraged by a judgment in the Curia in 1302, when Boniface VIII ruled that the bishop of Durham might introduce a secular, when he visited his cathedral priory, in the person of a notary public (below, pp. 68–9). Notaries public were qualified to make authentic copies of legal instruments, and their presence at visitations must have increased the demand for their products. Moreover, we find other signs of their activity as inspectors of deeds at visitations. It is not unusual to

---

[1] Bodleian MS. Laud misc. 642 f. 9v and *Reg. Malmesbury* (Rolls series), I. 268. Cf. *Darley Cartulary* (Derbyshire Archaeol. Soc., 1945), II. 626 and *Burton Charters* (Staffs. Hist. Collections, 1937), 80 (both dated 1280).

find that a notary public of this period has endorsed with his customary mark an original charter of the twelfth or thirteenth century by which a bishop had authorized an appropriation or ordained a vicarage or approved a layman's gift to a monastery. Most often, the notary can be found to be in the employment of an archbishop or bishop, and most likely the occasion is a visitation.[1] In the later Middle Ages the multiplication of authenticated certificates in every type of business provided the notary with more work of this routine sort. We must remember that even the most zealous bishop's pastoral visit always had about it an element of authoritarian display. If zeal and tact were wanting, legal formalities might be more conspicuous than pastoral care.

Two topics related to visitation which find place in this book deserve particular mention here on account of more recent studies : exemption and procuration. Monastic exemption from the diocesan, discussed in chapter II, was examined in a more fundamental way with reference to the English evidence by Dom David Knowles in 1932. He showed, among other things, how the immunity of an exempt house might be won in the twelfth century by virtue of the king's patronage with the help of spurious royal charters, without much regard for the principles of canon law. More recently Eleanor Searle has illustrated this by exposing the whole story of forgery at Battle Abbey, and J. H. Denton has shown the limits to the canonical exemption of that house in the

---

[1] Cf. below, 148 and C. R. Cheney, *Notaries public in England* (Oxford, 1972), 34–7.

changed conditions of the thirteenth century.[1] Other scholars have addressed themselves to the history of exempt houses in other regions. For Germany I might have referred to the classic treatment by Georg Schreiber in his *Kurie und Kloster*. Hans Goetting later questioned the applicability of Schreiber's definition of exemption in twelfth-century Germany and stressed the territorial and political aspects of papal protection. J. F. Lemarignier studied the nature of exemption in northern France in the eleventh–twelfth centuries.[2] These studies have more than local importance. They point to central questions of the legal and political theory of the Church in the Gregorian age. Lemarignier has shown how often the monastic immunity of the early Middle Ages had nothing to do with the special papal protection which became all-important by the end of the twelfth century. Moreover, since canonical visitation was seldom attempted in the period before 1140 with which he deals, exemption from episcopal visitation is seldom counted among the immunities in question in earlier days. Within the limited scope of the present work, study could profitably be directed to a more thorough examination of the formulas preferred by the papal chancery in the time of

---

[1] D. Knowles, " The growth of exemption ", *Downside Review*, L (1932), 201–31, 396–436 ; he returned to the subject in *The Monastic Order in England* (Cambridge, 1940). E. Searle, " Battle Abbey and exemption : the forged charters," *EHR*, LXXXIII (1968), 449–80. J. H. Denton, *English Royal Free Chapels* 1100–1300 (Manchester, 1970), 82–8.

[2] G. Schreiber, *Kurie und Kloster im 12. Jh.* (Kirchenrechtliche Abhandlungen, 65–68. Stuttgart, 1910). Hans Goetting, " Die klösterliche Exemtion in Nord- und Mitteldeutschland vom 8. bis zum 15. Jh.", *Archiv für Urkundenforschung*, XIV (1936), 105–87. J. F. Lemarignier, *Étude sur les privilèges d'exemption et de juridiction ecclésiastique des abbayes normandes depuis les origines jusqu'en* 1140 (Archives de la France monastique, XLIV. Paris, 1937).

Alexander III and after to express the various categories
of privilege granted to the new religious Orders and to
express in new terms the immunities of some ancient
foundations. It was an age of profound change in
juridical thought, when canonists were making a new
approach to the relations of bishops, lay rulers, and
monks, and an age when freedom from canonical visitation
by the bishop became a matter of practical importance.

Chapter IV gives a brief account of the law and
custom by which a bishop-visitor was provided with
hospitality. The evidence adduced is enough to show
that the popes of the twelfth and thirteenth centuries
supported firmly the bishop's right to recompense for
his labour, but that they did not as a rule countenance
the exaction of money in lieu of hospitality. It was
Innocent IV who first enacted in so many words the rule
that money payments for procuration were forbidden,
and this was renewed in the second Council of Lyons.
Despite the prohibition, some visitors still took money.
The *novella* of Boniface VIII of 1298 (*Sext*, III. 20. 3)
which allowed the practice in fact made no innovation.
The *Codex Iuris Canonici*, c. 346, leaves the matter open :
" servetur legitima locorum consuetudo." Recent study
of procuration has chiefly arisen from an interest in its
bearing on papal finances from the twelfth century
onwards. In an important and wide-ranging essay
Carlrichard Brühl underlines the political significance of
the institution as applied to papal legates and other
envoys.[1] The demands for *procuratio* of nuncios and

---

[1] C. Brühl, " Zur Geschichte der Procuratio canonica vornehmlich
in 11. und 12. Jh.", *Papato, cardinalato ed episcopato* (Atti della va
settimana internazionale di studi, Mendola, 1971. Milan, 1974). U.
Berlière gave a characteristically comprehensive account of " Le droit

collectors, which became common in the thirteenth century, transformed it into a mere pecuniary tax for the benefit of the pope or of his envoys, and divorced the word from its original association in the canon law : it was no longer necessarily a concomitant and recompense for the pastoral visit. In the fourteenth century that association was weakened more seriously when the pope reserved a part of episcopal procurations or prohibited the exaction of procurations by episcopal visitors ; but that topic lies outside the bounds of this essay. There is still room (as Brühl suggests, p. 429) for study of the canonists' commentaries to throw light on thirteenth-century attitudes.

In concluding this Introduction I wish to make grateful acknowledgment of the help I have had from my wife in framing it. While I hope that the book, as revised, will be useful to a younger generation of historians, I hope that its imperfections will encourage some scholar to carry this study further.

C. R. CHENEY

CAMBRIDGE, *September* 1982.

---

de procuration ou de gîte : papes et légats " in *Bulletin de la Classe des Lettres et des Sciences morales et politiques*, Académie royale de Belgique, 1919, 509–38. See also R. Naz, "Droit de procuration ou droit de gîte" in *Dict. Droit canonique*, VII (1965), 314–24. W. E. Lunt gives a general account in *Papal Revenues in the Middle Ages* (Columbia Univ. Records of Civilization, 1934), I. 107–11, and details of procuration of papal envoys in *Financial relations of the Papacy with England to* 1327 (Mediaeval Academy of America, 1939), 532–70.

ADDENDA TO THE FOLLOWING TEXT

p. 3   Some of the principal publications since 1930 of relevant English ecclesiastical records must be noted. The only two known registers of thirteenth-century archbishops of Canterbury, Pecham and Winchelsey, are now printed in full (see below, pp. 180, 182) and the important edition of *The Rolls and Register of Bishop Oliver Sutton*, 1280–99 for Lincoln, by R. M. T. Hill (Lincoln Record Soc., 7 vols, to date, 1948–75) is nearly complete. Besides finishing the editions of early fourteenth-century registers noted in the bibliography below, the Canterbury and York Society has published *Registrum Henrici Woodlock, dioc. Wintoniensis*, 1305–16 (2 vols. 1940–1), edited by A. W. Goodman. The Surtees Society published, 1931–40, in five volumes, *The Register of William Greenfield, Lord Archbishop of York*, 1306–15, edited by A. Hamilton Thompson.

    "Ely Chapter Ordinances and Visitation Records 1241–1515 ", edited by Seiriol J. A. Evans, *Camden Miscellany XVII* (Camden 3rd series vol. lxiv, 1940, Royal Hist. Soc.), includes episcopal injunctions as early as 1262, 1300, and 1307, found in a cathedral register. Documents about Bishop Antony Bek's important battle with the convent of Durham over visitatorial rights in 1300 are edited from cathedral archives by C. M. Fraser, *Records of Antony Bek* (Surtees Soc. 1953) and the episode is studied in detail in her *History of Antony Bek* (Oxford, 1957). Robert Brentano, *York Metropolitan Jurisdiction and Papal Judges Delegate* 1279–96 (Univ. of California Publications in History, 58. 1959) prints and discusses documents from Durham cathedral archives on Archbishop William Wickwane's fruitless efforts to hold metropolitan visitations at Durham between 1281 and 1285.

p. 5   There are other examples of injunctions copied by registrars, either from their own archives or from the originals in the hands of the visitand, which were issued by earlier diocesans. Bishop Walter de Cantilupe of Worcester's ordinances for the collegiate church of St Mary, Warwick, are in Giffard, *Worc.*, I. 6. In 1308 Archbishop Greenfield's registrar at York copies injunctions for Blyth Priory issued by Archbishop Godfrey, 1261, approving and supplementing injunctions of Archbishop Walter Gray, and also later injunctions by Archbishop Walter Giffard, 1276 (*Reg. W. Greenfield*, IV, 41–5).

p. 6   Other registers besides Bronescombe's note special records of visitations, and a few registers in the decades on either side of 1300 contain separate quires with injunctions addressed to particular monasteries. Cf. C. R. Cheney, *English Bishop's Chanceries* (Manchester,

1950), 109. Miscellaneous registers yield formulas for the use of visitors. " Liber Evidenciarum C " of Salisbury has the form of notice for canon Thomas of Bridport, preparing to visit Milton Abbey in July 1284 to exercise the chapter's right *sede vacante* ; and in B.L. MS. Royal 12 D xi f. 69r (a letter-book from Salisbury) the same letter is accompanied by other documents for visitations, including articles for enquiry in a monastery.

p. 6   The register of Archbishop Eudes Rigaud has been the object of substantial studies since 1931, notably the elaborate and useful, if un-critical, monograph of Mgr. P. L. R. Andrieu-Guitrancourt, *L'archévêque Eudes Rigaud et la vie de l'église au xiii*e *siecle, d'après le Regestrum visitationum* (Paris, 1938) ; see Coulet, pp. 14, 57–8 (" Les présupposés politiques transparaissent fréquémment "). O. G. Darlington, *The Travels of Odo Rigaud, Archbishop of Rouen* (Philadelphia, 1940) is a slighter work. The register was translated by Sydney M. Brown, edited after his death by Jeremiah F. O'Sullivan, *The Register of Eudes of Rouen* (Columbia Univ. Press, Records of Civilization, LXXII. 1964) ; the translation is uneven, and pp. 649–802 of Bonnin's edition are omitted.

p. 11   L. de Lacger returned to the visitations of Simon de Beaulieu, archbishop of Bourges, in " La primauté d'Aquitaine du viiie au xive siecle," *Revue d'hist. de l'Église de France*, XXIII (1937), 29–50, at 42–6. Cf. J. de Bascher, " La chronologie des visites pastorales de Simon de Beaulieu," *ibid.* LVIII (1972), 73–89. Baluze printed from a thirteenth–fourteenth century register in the archiepiscopal archives which he borrowed and failed to return. It passed with his manuscripts to the Bibliothèque Royale in 1719 and is now B.N. MS. lat. 5536. De Bascher gives details about the visitations of the province of Bordeaux supplementing p. 141 below. Archbishop Simon de Sully was ordered by Honorius to visit and correct conventual houses as early as 1218. Cf. p. xiv above.

p. 14   The archives of Cirencester Abbey preserved injunctions appar-ently imposed by Bishop William or Bishop Walter of Worcester between 1218 and 1266, which concern the abbey's treasury, accounting, and auditing. *Cartulary of Cirencester Abbey*, ed. C. D. Ross and Mary Devine (Oxford, 1964–77), I. pp. xi, xx.

p. 17   On Innocent III and the monasteries see, in addition to Dom Berlière's study of 1920 (" Innocent III "), M. Maccarrone, *Studi su Innocenzo III* (Italia Sacra 17. Padua, 1972) : " Riforme e innovazioni di Innocenzo III nella vita religiosa ", 223–337, and my *Pope Innocent III and England* (Päpste und Papsttum, 9. Stuttgart, 1976), 179–236.

p. 108, footnote 3   Matthew Paris's account is tendentious and confused. For the bishop's complaints at the Curia in these years see below, p. 138, and W. E. Lunt, *Financial Relations of the Papacy with England to* 1327

(Mediaeval Acad. of America, 1939). Cf. *Councils & Synods ... of the English Church*, Vol. II, 264 n. 1, 447–8.

p. 120 In 1277 Archbishop Kilwardby stayed at Dunstable Priory for five days. " Procuravimus ipsum ad omnes sumptus unico tantum die ; reliquis diebus invenimus boscum et foenum et xennia omni die. In correctionibus suis regulariter et curialiter se habebat, et correctiones suas reliquit in scriptis." *Ann. Mon.*, III. 276.

p. 144 Other English cases to add to those cited on pp. 142–3 are as follows : Archbishop Boniface visited Burton Abbey by deputy, the see of Coventry being vacant, 21 Jan. 1257 (*Burton Charters*, Staffs. Hist. Collections, 1957), 157. In 1259 he visited Exeter diocese (Bronescombe, 41, 42). Kilwardby visited Dunstable (*supra*) and Ramsey (*Ramsey Cart.*, I. 104 nos. 484–5). He sent injunctions after visitation to Abingdon, dated at Sonning, 5 May 1278 (Chatsworth House, MS. 71 ff. 4v–5v). Pecham is recorded at an uncertain date at Barnwell Priory (*Ecclesie de Bernewell liber memorandorum*, ed. J. W. Clark (Cambridge, 1907) 72). A good account of his monastic visitations is given by Decima L. Douie in *Archbishop Pecham* (Oxford, 1952), 156–91. References to Winchelsey's visitations will be found here at pp. 60–2, 73–4.

CONTENTS.

CHAPTER I.

THE SOURCES AVAILABLE FOR THE STUDY OF EPISCOPAL VISITATION.

Our knowledge of episcopal visitation in the thirteenth century is extensive but fragmentary. As with many other parts of medieval administration, we may be misled by the mass of evidence into supposing that we can form a complete, detailed picture of the system. But this is far from being true ; for not until a later period was the visitatorial system comprehensively surveyed, and only in the fifteenth century do we meet with the full records of particular visitations.

The canon law contains scraps of information on the subject, without providing any single set of authoritative pronouncements. It leaves many legal questions unsolved, so that we often have to turn to the commentators for enlightenment. The legal evidence is swelled by the records of provincial councils and monastic chapters, but these add little of importance. As for the details of procedure and the evidences of practice, these are scattered among many sorts of official records, local chronicles and edifying literature. At no point can the inquirer imagine that he has explored every possible road to new discoveries. For always the evidence is fragmentary, and new fragments are always appearing in unexpected quarters—in a sermon or a formulary, or a cartulary concerned with other business.

If we examine the references to visitation in the *Corpus Iuris*, we see that they fall into two groups. There are the somewhat vague pronouncements on bishops' duties culled by Gratian from early councils and decrees ; and there are the up-to-date practical rescripts and decrees, the work of recent popes, embodied in the

Extravagantes of Gregory IX and in the *Liber Sextus* of Boniface VIII. Of the latter class some were due to the Lateran Councils and the Second Council of Lyons, but most had been in response to particular inquiries or needs, and decretal letters of this kind achieved wide publicity in unofficial collections or in the official *Compilatio III* before their inclusion in *Extra*. They form the background to thirteenth-century visitations.

Other kinds of evidence come up for consideration with these legal records. It should be remembered that the boundary of canon law and practice is indeterminate in the thirteenth century. Contemporary visitors relied, not only on the exiguous stream of authoritative papal statements in the decretals, but also on the accumulation of glosses, which circulated in legal circles. It is hard to gauge precisely the authority of a Hostiensis or a Durandus ; but at least Cardinal Henry of Susa, and the celebrated lawyer and bishop of Mende, can be trusted to represent a learned opinion of the recognized practice of their day. At the same time, the papal registers for the thirteenth century provide us with considerable material relating to, and governing, the visitation of particular monasteries and dioceses. Both the policy of the popes and the aspirations of regulars caused a great deal of papal correspondence on the subject of visitations. Here are found orders for prelates to visit, and letters protecting the exemption of particular houses. Thus Honorius III writes to Stephen Langton, archbishop of Canterbury, complaining that he does not visit his province.[1] The compromise between the abbey of St. Mary at York and the archbishop of York is to be found in the Regesta of the same pope, as well as in the registers of two archbishops.[2] In the register of Innocent IV we first meet with that pronouncement (in the judgment " Romana ecclesia ", often attributed to the Council of Lyons) which constitutes the only comprehensive legislation of the Curia on episcopal visitation.[3]

---

[1] Honorii III, 3891.   [2] *Ibid.*, 5850, 6254.   [3] *Infra*, 135–7.

For the best source of information after the law and its commentators, we turn naturally to episcopal records. Here we may expect to trace the whole of the visitatorial process from the sending of notice to the final despatch of ordinances by the bishop. Briefly the procedure of the clerks was this : notice of a coming visitation was sent to a monastery and upon the arrival of the visiting bishop a certificate of its receipt was sometimes demanded. As each regular was examined, his depositions were noted down. The clerks then re-arranged this evidence, which then provided the basis of the bishop's verbal admonitions and of the written injunctions which he might send to the monastery after his departure. At every stage, be it noted, written records had to be made. So we may look for very valuable evidence from the bishop's chancery.

It is no accident that the age which saw the greatest development of the administrative machinery of the Church was also the age from which we first have official episcopal records in profusion. But we must not suppose, on account of this profusion, that all bishops' registers are alike, or that any one of them contains all possible materials for the study of a bishop's visitations.

Let us illustrate this from the English records of the *
thirteenth century. England possesses an unrivalled series of bishops' registers, which perhaps reflects the comparative order and good government of her dioceses in this period. But for visitations of monasteries these registers are somewhat disappointing. The bishops' clerks did their work so well—separated so carefully what was of permanent value from the transitory things—that we hardly ever find a full record of a visitation process. The visitation records of thirteenth-century English bishops vary considerably, but they are alike in their scrappiness. Sometimes a bishop recorded his injunctions; at other times he merely made memoranda on such visits as were memorable ; or he might note simply where he had been received. What Professor Hamilton Thompson has said of the Lincoln register of Bishop Gray in the fifteenth century applies equally well to registers two hundred years

older : " the fact that a large number of injunctions to religious houses remain in his register does not even prove special activity in visitation. It merely indicates that his registrar was industrious in copying injunctions for inclusion in the register." [1]

The form of the register, in spite of some common usages, remained very largely a matter for individual selection. Unlike the delegates of the monastic Orders who visited in England, the episcopal visitors had to make no reports for superiors to inspect. They completed the process themselves, and they preserved such records as they thought to be useful to themselves and their successors. Thus the series for the see of York in the second half of the thirteenth century shows distinct varieties of arrangement. Here we need only notice their peculiarities in recording visitations. Archbishop Giffard sometimes had his injunctions written down and sometimes noted the evidence he collected. Occasionally he did what his successors hardly ever did—recorded the injunctions of preceding visitors.[2] Archbishop Wickwane, on the other hand, registered a long series of his own injunctions and seldom troubled to record the antecedent proceedings. But John le Romeyn made far more visitations, in person or by deputy, than appear from the nine existing injunctions in his register : this is proved by his regular record of letters announcing visitation despatched to religious houses, and of commissions to deputies. Corbridge's register likewise shows much more activity in visiting than would be suspected from the paucity of injunctions. Turning to another region, we find that the Lincoln registers, so fruitful at a later date, yield practically no information about visitations. The rolls of Bishop Hugh de Welles have a single entry on the subject,[3] while Gravesend's register only mentions visitation once *en*

----

[1] *Linc. Visit.*, I. xvii.

[2] Giffard, *York*, 203, 212, 213, 215, 216, 217 ; cf. Romeyn, I. 70.

[3] Welles, II. 51. The records for Tickford and Brooke Priories, referred to in *VCH Bucks.* (I. 361) and *VCH Rutland* (I. 160), are not in the printed register.

passant: " Declinante dom . . . episcopo apud Caude-well causa visitationis . . ." [1] For an account of Grosse-teste's celebrated circuits we search his register in vain.

The full record of visitations was not indeed a neces-sary part of a bishop's register ; and it is very rarely found. There would be little reason for its preservation. All that was necessary for enrolment were the common forms of usual documents concerned with visitatorial business—the framework of citations, injunctions, mandates. The rest had to be put in writing, but it was not required for long. We must therefore always be ready to admit the possibility of injunctions where no injunctions have survived, and of visitation minutes like those of Bishop Alnwick of Lincoln (1436-49) out of which injunctions may have been composed. This admission is further justi-fied by the fact that the bulk of evidence is increased by mere chance entries, out of their proper places in the registers. Archbishop Giffard copied into his register two sets of injunctions which date from the time of Gray (1215-55) : yet they are not in Gray's register.[2] Similarly, we find the " ordinationes W. Giffard " (1277) for Blyth priory printed by Dugdale *ex registro nuncupato Grene-feild* ; [3] and the metropolitan injunctions of Archbishop Winchelsey for certain houses in London diocese are only found in the register of Bishop Baldock.[4] Archbishop Rigaud, re-visiting Petit-Quevilly in 1250, registered for the first time the ordinance " quam fecimus ibidem in alio anno." [5] Archbishop Pecham left in his register a copy of injunctions for the nunnery of Holy Sepulchre, Canterbury ; but only from a letter addressed to Martin, his commissary, do we learn that Pecham had found the prioress incompetent and ordained that she should have two coadjutresses.[6] Slight indications such as these show that even the most business-like of bishops' registers are probably incomplete on the matter of visitation.

[1] Gravesend, 196.   [2] Gray, xxxiii ; cf. 327-8.
[3] Dugdale, IV. 624.
[4] *Register of Ralph Baldock*, etc. (Canterbury and York Society, 1911), 26, 31, 34, 60, 77, 84, 85.   [5] Rigaud, 101.   [6] Peckham, II. 706-9.

While the term Register is usually applied to the permanent collection in which clerks recorded those privileges and agreements which were of permanent value to the diocesan, it is obvious that every bishop's registry must have kept far more than one register, some of them being specialized temporary records, such as the visitation books which have occasionally accidentally survived. Archbishop Gray's register contains no visitation records : the editor says : " it is plain that there must have been books set apart for matters of correction and discipline which have not been preserved." [1] It may be noted, moreover, that these less formal collections are often of far more use to the student of visitations than are the registers intended for a longer life. Regarding the later Lincoln records Professor Hamilton Thompson observes : " it is useful to remember that, had the manuscript of Bishop Alnwick's visitation minutes not survived, the only record of this side of Alnwick's work would have been one set of injunctions in his register." [2]

The fifteenth-century records of Lincoln and Norwich dioceses yield very important material of this sort, but we cannot point to any comparable English survivals from * the thirteenth century. In the register of Bronescombe of Exeter is the following note : " Facta fuit Visitacio in Ecclesia de Brigidedestow, sicut in Rotulo Visitacionis plenius continetur " ; [3] but the visitation roll has never come to light. A note, jotted on the back of an odd document, is stitched into Archbishop Pecham's register : [4] it relates to a visitation of Battle Abbey, and, though scrappy, is illustrative of procedure, for it forms part of the *detecta* ; but no injunctions arising out of this evidence have been traced, in Pecham's register or elsewhere.

Normandy, however, provides us with a thirteenth-century register of unequalled importance for the study * of visitations. The *Regestrum Visitationum Odonis Rigaldi archiepiscopi Rothomagensis* is remarkable both on account

---

[1] Gray, xxxiii.   [2] *Linc. Visit.*, I. xvii.

[3] Bronescombe, 280 ; cf. Giffard, *Worc.*, II. 233 and f. 11 *recto*.

[4] Peckham, 198-9. For the meaning of *detecta* see *infra*, 95.

of its form and on account of the great man for whom it was compiled. Rigaud was made archbishop of Rouen in 1248, and the register continues from that year to the end of 1269. In the course of these twenty-one years it records hundreds of visitations of monasteries and deaneries, and records them with a fullness which is—for this early period at least—unique. We hear little of forms and ceremonies, it is true, but we hear a great deal about actual inquiries and monastic discipline. No other record gives such a mass of detailed information on the life of Norman monks as this does : it is concerned with both their spiritual and their temporal welfare, and here are materials for judging the state of both. But the importance of the register is not altogether due to those characteristics which certain historians have stressed. We cannot assign a face-value to each statement isolated from the rest ; to appreciate the document properly we must compare and interpret. Before we go to the details for evidence, it will be best to discover the reason for its compilation, and to see in what ways it differs from other episcopal registers.

At the outset it should be remarked that it is not only, as its title suggests, a journal of pastoral visits. The additional matter includes the acts of synods,[1] papal letters, the statutes of Pope Gregory IX for the Black Monks, the Premonstratensians' privileges, a treaty of the English and French kings, grants of farms by the archbishop and the record of other privileges and rights.[2] Nevertheless it differs from the majority of surviving bishops' registers in the small proportion of its contents devoted to non-visitatorial matters.

As regards the visitations themselves, and documents directly resulting from them,[3] the book obviously affords a marvellous and unparalleled series of records. The archbishop's register is arranged as a journal extending from the 17th July, 1248,[4] to the 16th December, 1269. In the

---

[1] Rigaud, 286, 356, 387, 481.   [2] *Ibid.*, Appendices, pp. 643-802.
[3] *Ibid.*, Diffamationes, 649-74 (cf. *infra*, 79), and Ordines, 675-732.
[4] One folio on a lost leaf was earlier than this.

original the visitations of the various dioceses were begun on new sections, causing a break in the continuity which does not appear in the printed text.[1] This does not, however, detract from the chronological character of the work. It is true that the journal was not written up invariably from day to day ;[2] but the general character of the entries make it probable that it was kept as regularly as most diaries are. The visitations were usually recorded in concise notes, neither the abundant and overlapping depositions which the visitor would collect from separate inquiries, nor the elaborately prepared injunctions which it was customary to send to a visited house for permanent observance. Both these types of record do occasionally occur in Rigaud's register,[3] but most often the *corrigenda* remarked by the archbishop and his orders are placed side by side ; " invenimus . . . iniunximus " is the usual formula.

The question arises, whether or not such records as this were common in the thirteenth century. Was Rigaud's register one of a type frequently employed, was chance alone responsible for the survival of this solitary example ?

[1] Professor Jenkins suggests that the editor has lost a document in the rearrangement (*CQR*, 86 note 1). It is printed on p. 776 of the register. The editor has given a reference to f. 377 *verso* instead of f. 381 *verso* (p. 282).

[2] The injunctions for Villarceaux in 1249 occur immediately after the account of the visitation, but they are directed from Sausseuse, which the archbishop did not reach for another two days (Rigaud, 44). An examination of the manuscript reveals conclusive proofs that the register was not *strictly* a journal. The fact that consecutive entries are bracketed together : " cum expensis . . . " suggests that they were entered into the book together (e.g. Rigaud, ff. 5, 6, 14). On f. 14 *verso* later insertions are evident. The entry for VIII. Kal. Aug., 1248, was first entered immediately after the first short notice of the preceding day. This has been crossed out to make room for the documents which follow ; then the entry for VIII. Kal. Aug. is re-copied (Rigaud, f. 2 *verso*). Spaces frequently occur in the earlier part of the manuscript, where the scribe left room for documents which did not occupy so much space as he had anticipated. A considerable gap, for example, is left at the head of f. 4 *recto* in the account of Bival, before the entry : " Ipsa die abbatissa . . . " (p. 6).   [3] Rigaud, 43 (detecta), 44, 56, 81, 90 (injunctions).

Most of the records which we possess are either sets of injunctions preserved in the bishop's register, like so many other classes of documents, to illustrate a form of writing ; or else they are, as Professor Hamilton Thompson says, " the memoranda upon which the bishop and his clerks relied to carry the visitation from stage to stage." [1] Once the injunctions had been compiled and despatched, there was no further use for this unsorted collection of scraps. Only a lucky chance has preserved Bishop Alnwick's memoranda—perhaps merely the fact that the injunctions were not copied into the register, which was not kept up to date.[2] But Rigaud's register, as we have seen, contains very few sets of injunctions and very few entries which can be construed as Professor Hamilton Thompson construes the Alnwick records. Its whole character is that of a journal, and its material seems intended, not so much " to carry the visitation from stage to stage " as to provide memoranda for future visitations and to serve as the archbishop's diary.

The manuscript bears few corrections or inter-lineations ; and although several hands have been at work the book is fairly neat throughout. It is definitely a personal journal. This point is less exaggerated by its editor than it is under-estimated by Professor Jenkins ; and Dr. Coulton rightly complains when the latter says : " As a matter of fact the volume is an Episcopal Register in exactly the same sense as any of the others which we have." [3] True, it is not written in the archbishop's handwriting, but it contains matters which interested none but the archbishop, and which would not have been written except at the archbishop's dictation. What use could it be to the officials of his household to have recorded the fact that on such a day the archbishop went on pilgrimage or journeyed to comfort the king in his illness ? Who but the archbishop would think it necessary to make excuses for not visiting in person, and comment on his stomach-ache ? On what other assumption than

---

[1] *Linc. Visit.*, II. xlvi.   [2] *Ibid.*, II. xxxi.
[3] Jenkins, *CQR*, 84 ; cf. Coulton, *Five Centuries*, II. 207 note 2.

that it was meant to be a personal diary as well as a record
of visitations can we account for the introduction of such
matters as these ?

There is no register dealing with monasteries in the
thirteenth century which is comparable in form with
Rigaud's, but we may compare it with several contemporary parochial visitation books and some later records
of monastic visitations. The dean and chapter of St.
Paul's in the thirteenth century preserved the proceedings
of visits in their area of jurisdiction ; and some of the
visitation records of an archdeaconry in Bayeux diocese
date from Rigaud's time.[1] These documents at least
resemble the register of Rigaud in their form, and clearly
had much the same object. The same may be said of the
diocesan visitations of Hereford, lately brought to light
by Canon Bannister.[2] Among monastic visitation records
we have the important series of Grenoble registers for the
fourteenth and fifteenth centuries,[3] and the Norwich
registers of the fifteenth and sixteenth.[4] In all these we
see the same intention as in Rigaud's register, carried out
less systematically. They differ from the Lincoln " minute
books " in suggesting a desire for permanency. They
record visitations day by day, and nothing else, and they
allowed of reference from one visitation to another, on
personal matters not usually covered by written injunctions. That Rigaud used his register for reference is
certain. Apart from information which he might obtain
from his own earlier injunctions deposited in a monastery,
there are some specific references to points which would

[1] *Visitations of churches belonging to St. Paul's cathedral* (1249-52),
(Camden Society Miscellany, IX. 1895) ; *Visitations of churches belonging to
St. Paul's* (1297 and 1458), (Camden Society, 1895) ; *Visites pastorales
de Maître Henri de Vézelai, archidiacre d'Hiémois* (1267-8), Bibliothèque
de l'école des chartes, LIV. (1893).

[2] *Visitation returns in the diocese of Hereford in* 1397 (*English Hist.
Review*, XLIV., XLV. (1929-30)).

[3] *Visites pastorales et ordinations des Evêques de Grenoble* (14e-15e
siècles), Docs. histor. inédits sur le Dauphiné, 4e livraison (1874).

[4] Edited with a misleading introduction by A. Jessopp (Camden
Society, new series, XLIII. (1888)).

never be embodied in written injunctions, or would at least be generalized first.[1] Moreover, on various occasions the scribe writes : " Invenimus prout in alia visitatione contenta in . . . folio." [2]

But if the form of Rigaud's register, so different from the most usual type of episcopal register, can be paralleled by a few later examples, it is none the less certain that no other known record approaches it for its wealth of material and its personal value. The register of Rigaud differs not only in magnitude but in kind from all other episcopal registers which survive. It was not merely the product of a peculiarly well-organised staff of officials : it was the journal of an exceptionally active, pious and efficient prelate, used by him for frequent reference. Dr. Coulton has painted an attractive picture of this great man, and the register testifies to the accuracy of the colouring.

There remains to be considered one notable record of monastic visitations from an archbishop's chancery, totally different from all the foregoing episcopal documents. The *Acta Visitationis Provinciarum Burdegalensis et Bituricensis* (1283-91) is an elaborate official record, drawn up for Simon, archbishop of Bourges, by one who had accompanied him on his visitations.[3] As primate of Aquitaine the archbishop visited both the province of Bordeaux and that of Bourges ; his visitations of the two provinces were made with great state, which is all recorded in this fulsome narrative. Dr. Coulton has given a sample

---

[1] e.g. Rigaud, 132, 206, 207, 362.

[2] e.g. *ibid.*, 47, 59, 98, 98, 98, 104, 105, 166, 166, 227.

[3] This is contained in a register of the archbishopric of Bourges (Archives du Cher, G. 1), which has various other valuable materials, including the procès-verbal of a primatial visitation of 1265 (see Lacger, *RHE*, 63). Archbishop Simon de Beaulieu's visitations were published by Hardouin in his *Acta Conciliorum* (Paris, 1714), VII. cols. 963-1066, while Mabillon gave excerpts from them in his *Vetera Analecta* (Paris, 1723), 338 *sqq.* They may also be found in the *Miscellanea* of Baluze and in Mansi's *Nova et Amplissima Collectio*. Parts relating to visitations of the diocese of Albi appear in the *Bulletin de la comm. des antiquités de la ville de Castres et du départ. du Tarn*, 1880, and for the diocese of Cahors in the *Bulletin de la soc. des études . . . du Lot*, 1900.

of the evidence contained therein.[1] It is extremely detailed on certain points of ceremony, copies legal documents in full, and is precise about the procuration charges which the visitor occasioned where he stayed. But if the painstaking description of rights and ceremonies leads us to expect much information about the visitor's disciplinary work, we are disappointed. Very scanty are the references to the archbishop's inquiries. Indeed, so scanty are the references (some fifteen in fifty folio pages of narrative) that we must assume that the record is incomplete. The compiler was concerned only with the rights of visitation and hospitality to which the archbishop laid claim. For these matters he has provided posterity with ample and valuable records. But if in his narrative the questions of rights are especially prominent, are we entitled to argue from the document as to the seriousness and value of Archbishop Simon's visitations ?

The fact that much is omitted would not of itself lead to the conclusion of Dr. Coulton that Simon was " mainly concerned with his own privileges and fees ".[2] Not even the fact that his chronicler noted appreciatively where he was well fed proves that the archbishop cared unduly for meat and drink ; for the embellishments of this business record may have been the choice of the chronicler himself. The insistence upon privileges is remarkable ; [3] but even the zealous Rigaud of Rouen and Pecham of Canterbury were very jealous for their rights. The large retinue with which Archbishop Simon travelled, and the heavy expenses of his visits certainly show that he was a more worldly man than the Franciscan Rigaud ; but even Simon remitted fees [4] (if sometimes for base reasons), and was no more careful than the scrupulous archbishop

---

[1] Coulton, *Five Centuries*, II. 230-2.

[2] *Ibid.*, II. 232. Grosseteste stresses the importance of bell-ringing to announce the bishop's presence in a place (Grosseteste, *Epistolæ*, 426-8).

[3] " Comme Eudes Rigaud, archevêque de Rouen, avec lequel il a tant de rapport au point de vue du zêle apostolique, il rencontrait parfois de vives oppositions." Feret, *La Faculté de Théologie* (Paris, 1894), II. 189 ; cf. Coulton, *Five Centuries*, II. 210.

[4] e.g. Baluze-Mansi, I. 282*b*, 292*b*, 293*b*, 296*a*.

of Rouen to reserve his rights on these occasions.[1] The material side only of his duty as visitor stands recorded in these *Acta*. It is, however, compatible with efficiency and even a keen interest in maintaining discipline. We hear of Simon of Bourges from other sources ; they suggest that he was, if not a saint, at least a very worthy prelate, talented, energetic and reforming.[2] We find no trace of this in the *Acta* ; but the compiler of a book of rights was not bound to speak of monastic reform. Dr. Coulton himself has taught us to put no faith in the completeness of episcopal registers.[3] Archbishop Simon may have had more interest in monastic reform than his chronicler had.

Having briefly reviewed the records which come from the legal authorities and the visitors, we may turn to the traces of visitation in the records of the visitands. Here we find a surprising dearth of material. Monastic annals contain some references to the subject, but these are remarkably few and far between. The collection of English chronicles edited in the Rolls series under the title *Annales Monastici* gives the barest of comments on bishops' visitations. In the other monastic chronicles of the same period, at home and abroad, visitations are only exceptionally commented on ; [4] only when the visitor is a particularly anxious disciplinarian does the chronicler change his usual colourless tone to a note of anger and alarm.[5] Monastic registers and cartularies are equally disappointing. Wilkins printed in his *Concilia* a description of procedure culled from the register of a prior of Canterbury,[6] whence also come the articles for Archbishop Winchelsey's inquiries ; another important series of articles of inquiry is placed in his chronicle by the Burton

---

[1] e.g. Baluze-Mansi, I. 301*a* ; Rigaud, 117, 193, 260, 557-8.

[2] *Hist. litt. de la France*, XXI. 20-40 ; Feret, *op. cit.*, II. 184-92.

[3] *Five Centuries*, II. 239, 268 *sqq.*, 485-6.

[4] This is partly explicable by the fact that many of our best monastic authorities come from houses which were exempt from the diocesan's jurisdiction.

[5] e.g. *Ann Mon.*, I. 146, II. 94, III. 152, 178 ; Matt. Paris, V. 380

[6] Wilkins, *Concilia*, II. 217 ; Winchelsey, II. 1303-4, cf. 1289-1303. See also below, 60-61.

annalist, *s.a.* 1259.[1] Canon Wilson illustrates procedure from the Worcester *Liber Albus*;[2] while Archbishop Kilwardby's visitation of the diocese of Ely in 1277 finds an interesting record in the *Vetus Liber Archidiaconi Eliensis*, where the archbishop's premonitory letter is entered, along with the proposed itinerary of the visitor.[3] A cartulary at Chichester contains contemporary verses on the visitations of Archbishop Pecham,[4] and other documents are extant in the various cathedral muniments.

The injunctions which visitors intended to be permanent additions to the statutes of a house have rarely survived among the archives of monasteries. Dugdale prints some early ones from a register of Nun Coton Priory,[5] and the Swaffham cartulary at Peterborough contains " statuta Hugonis episcopi per visitacionem factam pro episcopo apud Burgum." [6] At his primary visitation of the cathedral in 1300, Bishop Ralph de Walpole of Ely examined his predecessors' injunctions and left others with them which were preserved in a register of the priory.[7] Monastic letter-books, as yet insufficiently explored, occasionally yield injunctions and other items of visitation procedure. Thus the fifteenth-century Launceston book which Mr. Salter uses for the history of Augustinian chapters, contains the *decreta* (1306-10) made by Thomas, bishop of Exeter, after his visitations of the priory ; and a book from Lanthony by Gloucester several letters relating to the bishop of Worcester's visitation.[8]

---

[1] *Ann. Mon.*, I. 484-6.   [2] *Worcester Liber Albus*, 36.

[3] *Vetus Liber Archidiaconi Eliensis* (Camb. Antiq. Society, 1917), 18-19.

[4] Quoted *infra*, 143.   [5] Dugdale, V. 677.

[6] f. 105r (formerly f. xciiii). I owe this reference to Miss K. Major. The injunctions followed visitation by two archdeacons and clerks of the bishop, 10 Aug. 1231. Cf. *VCH Northants.*, II. 88.

[7] *Camden Miscellany XVII* (Royal Hist. Soc., Camden 3rd Series, vol. LXIV 1940), 6–23.

[8] Bodley MS. *Tanner* 196, f. 210 ; C.C.C. Oxon, MS. 154, p. 386 (cf. *infra*, 63 note). A fourteenth century MS. of Reading Abbey at Cambridge has a formula relating to a monastic visitation by the bishop of Llandaff (1297-1323), (*Notices et Extraits des MSS*. XXXIV. 2e ptie. 20). A Premonstratensian formulary at Soissons contains a description of visitation-procedure, a form in which to recommend Order visitors to a foreign prince, and specimen injunctions (*ibid.*, XXXIV. 1e ptie. 312 *sqq.*).

We seldom find the actual copy of injunctions sent by
the visiting prelate,[1] but we do occasionally get early
references to their preservation. In a list of Ramsey
Abbey deeds is the note : " In saccella picta : Visitatio
Oliveri anno suo quinto "; this was Oliver, bishop of
Lincoln, who visited Dunstable also in 1284.[2] In 1389
the library of Dover Priory contained " constituciones
R. archiepiscopi monachorum douorre [sic]," as we know
from the catalogue of that date; [3] if the archbishop was
Robert Winchelsey it is particularly interesting to find
his injunctions still preserved at this time; for when he
visited the monastery ninety years before he expressed
his surprise that he had found no injunctions of his predecessors, although he believed that they had made
ordinances for the house.[4]

But it must be admitted that, besides the examples
quoted, monastic records on this topic are scanty. No-
body could fail to remark the lack of interest in episcopal
visitation which their usual silence suggests.

We leave the official records of jurists, bishops and
monks to glance at the vast literature of sermons, stories
suitable for the use of preachers, and disputations of the
schools. It cannot be said that we are rewarded by any
remarkable discoveries. Some sermons exhorting prelates
to visit come from the church of Tours,[5] and an elaborate
discourse intended for a visitation, now in the British

[1] British Museum, Charter *Addit.* 19632 seems to be the original sent
by Pecham to Leominster Priory in 1283 (as in his register, Peckham, II.
505-7) ; the seal is missing. Cf. some injunctions of William of Wykeham,
1387 (*Cal. of charters and documents relating to Selborne* . . . ed. W. D.
Macray (Hants. Record Soc., 1891), I. 95-108).

[2] *Ramsey Cart.*, I. 63 ; cf. *ibid.*, I. 104, II. 204 ; *Ann. Mon.*, III. 313.

[3] *Ancient Libraries of Canterbury and Dover*, M. R. James (1903),
464, no. 213 ; cf. *ibid.*, no. 203 (probably Kilwardby's injunctions).

[4] Winchelsey, II. 848. Pecham's injunctions of 1283 are in
Peckham, II. 612. Cf. Baldock, 26.

[5] Bibliothèque Nationale, Paris, MS. *Latin* 10455, ff. 37-68, "Tractatus
de visitatione." (Delisle, *Notices et Extraits*, XXXI. 1e partie (1883),
234.) Manuscript of the end of the thirteenth century. It is described according to its title (written in a 16th-century hand) by Delisle as a treatise
on the visitation of prelates. Upon examination it proves to be nothing more

Museum, may have belonged originally to St. Werburg's Abbey, Chester.[1] From the *exempla* of the age, the work of preachers of the new Orders, we may glean some illustrative tales and moralizings; and some of the moral questions involved in bishops' inquiries are discussed by the quodlibetists. Even in a manual of letter-writing we may meet with useful statements of the law—commonplaces at the time, no doubt, but difficult to seize upon after seven centuries.

The fragmentary character of these various records of bishops' visitations makes it almost impossible to give a general view of this important side of ecclesiastical administration in the thirteenth century, and very difficult to form any estimate of the extent of either its operation or its efficacy.

than a collection of ten sermons, of which numbers 1-4, 9 and 10 relate to visitations and were accordingly marked by the scribe " In visitatione ", " Item in visitatione ", etc. (ff. 37 *recto* b, 39 *verso* a, 43 *recto* a, 46 *verso* a, 61 *recto* a, 64 *verso* b). The sermons at ff. 39 *verso* and 46 *verso* are also contained in the Bib. Nat. MS. *Latin* 14952, ff. 210, 213. There also they are anonymous, and Hauréau cannot give the authorship. The MS. is of the thirteenth century, after 1274. (*Notices et Extraits*, XXXII. 2ᵉ ptie. 1888, 336-7.) The text of the first two sermons in MS. *Latin* 10455 is used for a different sermon on the same topic in Bodley MS. *Ashmole* 1398, f. 262, also late thirteenth century.

[1] Royal MS. 8, F. IX. ff. 73 *sqq.*

CHAPTER II.

THE PAPACY AND THE EPISCOPAL VISITATION OF MONASTERIES IN THE THIRTEENTH CENTURY.

At the beginning of the thirteenth century monachism in Western Europe, though not desperately unhealthy, was suffering in many places from the consequences of a diminishing enthusiasm joined to increasing material comfort and complacency. A vigorous general reform was needed. The world had invaded the cloister. Even the new Orders were seriously tainted with the sins of simony and luxury and overmuch care for mundane things. A pope of splendid ability and great ambition, Innocent III, tried to cope with the situation. He included in his ✳ great scheme for the regeneration of Christendom a comprehensive plan of monastic reform. With his unfailing energy he kept himself informed of monastic affairs in every part of Europe, beseeching and commanding in all quarters that justice might be done, order restored, irregularities suppressed. Yet when Innocent III died, his successor encountered the same problems. Honorius III had to combat the same apathy in the cloister, the same inadequacy of instruments to enforce his will. After him Gregory IX devoted himself earnestly to reforming the monasteries ; later popes throughout the century are occupied with the same task. But their efforts are not crowned with success. Dom Berlière writes : " Toujours, ce seront les mêmes efforts de Sisyphe, qui n'arrive jamais à escalader la montée. C'est que les papes ne portèrent pas la cognée à la racine du mal : le recrutement était assez souvent déplorable, laissé à la merci des influences séculières et des convoitises intéressées,[1] la formation

[1] See Berlière, *Recrutement.*

défectueuse et incomplète, la vie trop souvent réduite à
une exonération fatigante d'offices multipliés à l'infini, ou
à l'administration matérielle de propriétés étendues ; les
chapitres provinciaux et les visiteurs étaient désarmés en
face des résistances locales ; il manquait un idéal nette-
ment défini, approprié aux besoins de l'époque et con-
séquemment un programme." [1]

The efforts of the popes in this uphill struggle are
instructive. They show the comprehensive centralizing
policy of the Curia in the thirteenth century, and reveal
the weakness as well as the strength of that policy. In a
number of remarkable essays [2] Dom Berlière has examined
the relations of the papacy to the Benedictine Order in
this period. He has shown that Cîteaux was the model [3]
chosen by the papacy and that provincial chapters and
Order visitations were the instruments proposed for the
reform. [4]

All this was in accord with the rest of papal policy and
was undoubtedly the foremost feature in the movement
for monastic reform as envisaged by the popes. But it
was not this work of centralization which had the chief
effect on the Benedictine Order in the thirteenth and
fourteenth centuries. The Benedictine houses did not
rise or fall together—there was no uniformity in their
fate. To quote Dom Berlière once more : " On verra
dans une même ville des monastères assez rapprochés l'un
de l'autre, présenter l'étrange spectacle d'un niveau
différent de vie religieuse et intellectuelle. C'est leur
indépendance qui les sauve, au même titre que leur
autonomie peut être une cause de faiblesse." [5] The
centralizing work of the papacy failed to have much effect
on the Benedictines, but another external instrument of
reform was made important in the thirteenth century—
the bishop visitor.

While Dom Berlière does take account of this (" c'est
surtout par l'épiscopat," he says " qu' Innocent III veut

[1] Berlière, *Honorius*, 250.   [2] Berlière, *RB ; Innocent ; Honorius*.
[3] *Honorius*, 245 ; *RB*, VIII. 255.   [4] *Honorius*, 249.
[5] Berlière, *Recrutement*, 66 ; cf. *Innocent*, 25.

mener à bonne fin le relèvement des monastères " [1]), the system of episcopal visitation has only been slightly indicated in his main theme of papal relations with Benedictine houses. Only incidentally do we find reference to episcopal visitation in the papal registers, only occasionally do the popes seem to take a lively interest in its work for monastic reform. Yet this was to be the most efficient machinery of reform for the next two centuries, whatever its defects ; and though the popes might favour other machinery more, they were bound to take some notice of the work of individual diocesans, to stimulate, supplement or supersede them.

It was natural to suppose, in the Middle Ages, that the very wide powers of the bishop in his diocese ordinarily extended over regulars as well as seculars. For monachism in the West had no special status in the ecclesiastical hierarchy ; in its early days certainly a large proportion of the monks never came to the priesthood, and up to the time of the Roman Council of 826 it was not necessary for an abbot to be a priest. It was perfectly natural, therefore, for the Church to place religious houses under the care and authority of the diocesan. Even where the seclusion of their life had at first given monks a certain amount of autonomy, they began to lose their privileged position early in the Middle Ages. " The independence which the monks enjoyed had produced many irregularities which, from the beginning of the fifth century, the Councils in Gaul set themselves to correct. . . . The discipline of all religious houses is to be under the inspection and control of the bishop. The abbots are under his spiritual power." [2] The extension of the bishop's power was effected, as Mr. O. M. Dalton remarks, " by the decrees of episcopal councils, which naturally took the bishop's point of view rather than that of the abbot ".[3] Although it might be expected that the bishop would in

---

[1] Berlière, *Innocent*, 147 ; cf. *ibid.*, 27-33.
[2] S. Dill, *Roman Society in Gaul in the Merovingian Age* (1926), 393
[3] Gregory of Tours, *The History of the Franks* (Oxford, 1927), I. 354 ; cf. 357.

practice have little occasion for supervising, in theory he did possess the power : we find that expressed throughout the Middle Ages, from the time when Gregory the Great wrote to the acting bishop of Palermo : " We allow that the monasteries, if there be any founded in the diocese, shall be in your care and disposition until its own bishop be ordained." [1] The same pope ordained that a monastery united to one in another diocese should remain subject to its original diocesan " so that we may preserve inviolate the rights of each bishop ".[2]

Gratian adduces a large number of early ordinances to the same effect : " Monasteries and the discipline of monks belong to the bishop in whose territory they are founded." [3] He gives the letter of Gregory the Great to the bishop of Agropoli, bidding him see that the religious of his diocese lead a regular life,[4] and the letter regretting that the bishops of Campania are said to be wanting in proper care (*solicitudinem*) of monasteries.[5] Other chapters state the general subservience of monks to bishops.[6] Gratian does, indeed, quote Gregory I, writing to the bishop of Ariano, who says : " Nec audeat ibi [in monasterio] cathedram collocare Episcopus, vel quamlibet potestatem exercere imperandi, nec aliquam ordinationem, quamvis levissimam, faciendi, nisi ab Abbate loci fuerit rogatus ; quatenus Monachi semper maneant in Abbatum suorum potestate : ut remotis vexationibus, ac cunctis gravaminibus, divinum opus cum summa devotione animi perficiant." [7] But this is explained and qualified by the letter of Gregory incorporated in the Decretals which says that the diocesan should not molest (*aliquid molestiae inferre*) monasteries except for the purpose of correcting discipline.[8] The same quaestio in the Decretum shows that the bishop is by no means to be supplanted. On one chapter Gratian remarks : " Hinc etiam constitutum

---

[1] *Decretum*, I. LXI. 16.
[2] *Decretales*, III. xxxvi. 2.
[3] *Decretum*, II. XVIII. ii. 17.
[4] *Ibid*., II. XII. i. 14.
[5] *Ibid*., I. LXXXIV. 2 ; cf. *ibid*., II. XVI. i. 12 (Conc. Chalc.).
[6] *Ibid*., II. XVI. i. 9-10.
[7] *Ibid*., II. XVIII. ii. 6.
[8] *Decretales*, III. xxxv. 1.

est, ut clerici singulorum monasteriorum sint in potestate Episcoporum, nec alicui liceat extra eorum conscientiam monasteria edificare ".[1]

Moreover, the monks may always remain in the power of their abbots, as Gregory demanded, but both are ultimately governed by the bishop. The great canonist Hostiensis leaves the matter uncertain in one place where he discusses the obligations of the monk : among which he at first includes " to do obedience to the bishop, unless he be exempt ".[2] He bases this on the Decretum I, xciii. 8, which says : " Nulla ratione clerici aut sacerdotes habendi sunt, qui sub nullius episcopi disciplina et providentia gubernantur "—such have earned the name of *acephali*. But then, says Hostiensis, " dic quod illud intelligitur de clericis secularibus regulares autem suo maiori, scilicet abbati, vel priori, ipsam praestabunt . . . sed hoc verum est quod religiosus tenetur esse obediens." This uncertainty, however, can only concern the question of immediate superiority, for in a passage of his Commentaries, Hostiensis says : " Salva regula in omnibus, de iure communi subiacent episcopis monachi et abbates," [3] and quotes Gratian as his authority : " Abbates pro humilitate religionis in Episcoporum potestate consistant, et si quid extra regulam fecerint, ab Episcopo corrigantur." [4] This particular passage is taken from a very early council—that of Orleans, 511 A.D. There are various other equally ancient citations.[5] In the Carolingian age, when ecclesiastical legislation occupies an important place in imperial capitularies, abbots and monks are enjoined to be subject to their bishops with all humility and deference, " sicut canonica constitutione mandat. . . . Et monachi ab episcopo provinciae ipsius corripiantur " ; [6] again, " ut monachi per verbum episcopi et per regimen

---

[1] *Decretum*, II. XVIII. ii. 10 ; cf. Hostiensis, *Summa*, III. de relig. dom. I. (f. 219 *verso*).   [2] *Summa*, III. de regular. (f. 211 *verso*).
[3] *Comment.*, I. XXIII. x. 11 (vol. I. f. 127 *verso*).
[4] *Decretum*, II. XVIII. ii. 16.
[5] *Ibid.*, II. XVI. i. 12 and 17 ; II. XVI. ii. 7 ; II. XVII. iv. 40.
[6] Mon. Germ. Hist., *Capitularia* (ed. Boretius), I. 94.

abbatis et per bona illorum exempla regulariter vivant ".[1] About the same time Pope Leo III, writing to the Bavarians, ordered all regulars to submit to their bishops " quorum concilio et doctrinae omnino oboediant."[2] Regino of Prum, in the beginning of the tenth century, drawing freely on early councils; states that the bishop is to go round his diocese at frequent intervals, with a small retinue. He gives articles of inquiry for a parochial visitation and shows the bishop entering monasteries to maintain discipline.[3]

As time goes on examples multiply to illustrate the particular powers of bishops over monasteries. At an early date abbots and priors were ordered to attend diocesan synods each year,[4] and the injunction was repeated in a letter of Innocent III embodied in the Decretals. From the records of these councils it is clear that not only was there much legislation for monasteries, but that the bishops were very often meant to administer the law. At the Council of Rouen (1214) the bishops were ordered [5] to see that monasteries were properly closed ; to restore ill-gotten gains ; to prevent monks from living alone ; [6] to keep the numbers in religious houses at the proper level ; [7] to provide fit confessors for nuns ; and to keep women out of monasteries. The Rouen canons came from a papal legate, Courzon. In England, his countryman Stephen Langton published comparable legislation in the Council of Oxford (1222). Here again is much material for the regulation of monastic

---

[1] Mon. Germ. Hist., *Capitularia* (ed. Boretius), I. 170.

[2] Jaffé, 2503, quoted Vendeuvre, 43.

[3] De eccl. disciplinis. Migne, *Patrol. Latina*, CXXXII. 193-4, etc.

[4] *Decretum*, I. XVIII. 4 and 16 ; *ibid.*, II. XVIII. ii. 16 ; cf. *Decretales*, I. xxxiii. 9

[5] Mansi, XXII. 906-14 (sect. II. caps. 3, 8, 18, 25, 36, 37, 45, 46).

[6] Cf. Innocent III, I. 446, X. 153 (Potthast, 458, 3220) ; Honorii III, 42 (Potthast, 5335), 4913, 5365 ; *Decretales*, III. xxxv. 2 (3rd Lateran Council) ; Hostiensis, *Comment.*, III. de Cap. Mon. 3 and 4 (vol. 2, f. 140 *verso* and 141).

[7] Cf. Honorii III, 3144, 3737, 4823 ; *Autun Cart.*, 265 (temp. Innocent IV).

life, and the control of the bishop is emphasized in several places. The bishop enforces the transference of monks from one monastery to another for purposes of discipline. The sale of corrodies is only allowed with the diocesan's assent. His consent must be obtained before secular women are admitted to nunneries; and he is to appoint confessors for nuns and regulate the numbers in nunneries according to their revenues.[1] At Rouen again, in 1223, the suffragans were exhorted to reform the monasteries subject to them in accordance with canon 12 (second part) of the Fourth Lateran Council.[2] In 1231 the Rouen Council made more legislation specifically for monasteries.[3] The bishop was to control borrowing by abbots; to inspect the fabric of nunneries and keep the monasteries closed; to prohibit private property in nunneries; to supervise appointments to cures; and to control the abbot's power of excommunication.[4]

Episcopal visitation of monasteries followed naturally from such laws as these : it was the natural complement of the synod. While the duty of parish visitation tended to be obliterated by the practice of calling together the clergy, the presence of abbots and priors in synods could never be thought to supersede the visitation in the monasteries ; for monastic affairs were seldom revealed by outside report and were unsuitable for discussion in a synod.

It is often implied, if not directly stated, by modern writers that the development of papal authority in the twelfth and thirteenth centuries caused diocesans to lose their usual authority. In certain respects this is obviously true. The Universal Ordinary not only listened to causes in appeal, but provided a court of first instance which often over-rode the local ordinary's jurisdiction. The exemption of certain monastic Orders and individual monasteries from the diocesan's control was also a limita-

---

[1] *Councils & Synods*, II. 119, 122–4 (cc. 41, 51–5).
[2] Mansi, XXII. 1198 (c. iv.) ; cf. Leclercq-Hefele, V. 1343.
[3] Mansi, XXIII. 213 (cc. 1, 4, 39, 46, 47) ; Martène et Durand, *Thesaurus* (1717), IV. 175.   [4] Cf. Honorii III, 3307.

tion to his power, and papal provisions hampered him in another direction. Nevertheless, it seems necessary to insist that the popes of the twelfth and thirteenth centuries never showed any desire to destroy the disciplinary power of the bishop except where they were influenced by an economic motive, and that when disputes about episcopal jurisdiction arose the Curia judged, on the whole, with impartiality. These matters may be illustrated by the instructions sent out to particular bishops from the Curia, by the treatment in the Curia of exempt houses and disputes about exemption, and by the relations of bishops' synods and visitations to the parallel system set up in the great monastic Orders.

Examples of bishops exercising power in the cloister appear in the law-books of the twelfth and thirteenth centuries. These are very largely composed of papal decisions of the same period. Monks are told to present clerks to the bishop when they want them to be installed in benefices (*diocesanis episcopis clericos idoneos presentetis, qui illis de spiritualibus, vobis autem de temporalibus debeant respondere*).[1] Alexander III tells regulars that they cannot have the patronage of a church without the bishop's recognition of their right.[2] Gratian declares (after Urban II): "Monks shall not take over tithes and churches from laymen without the consent and goodwill of the bishops."[3]

Almost all such injunctions as these, concerning monks, which occur in the *Corpus Iuris*, represent the sympathetic response of the popes to the requests of bishops for additional powers. When the pope tells a bishop that seculars cannot be given the headship of a regular house,[4] we may assume that the bishop had some authority in the matter. When the pope writes to tell the bishop of Worcester that a monk is entitled to accuse his abbot and should be provided from the monastery's funds with the costs of litigation,[5] or to tell the bishop of London that

---

[1] *Quinq. Comp.*, I. III. xxxii. 3 (p. 40).
[2] *Decretales*, III. xxxviii. 11.   [3] *Decretum*, II. XVI. vii. 39.
[4] *Decretales*, I. vi. 49 (a.d. 1227); cf. *ibid.*, I. vi. 27 and 37.
[5] *Ibid.*, V. i. 11 (a.d. 1170 x 1171).

incorrigible monks are to be expelled and replaced by others,[1] we may suppose that these prelates have real control over monastic government.

We commonly find delegated to diocesans powers which were not theirs in common law, but which it was convenient for the pope to entrust to them. Innocent III made it the duty of bishops to protect the religious houses of their dioceses from malefactors, even though the houses might be exempt from their jurisdiction.[2] For this purpose he gave a sop to the bishop of Poitiers, after giving judgment against him for the exemption of the monks of Montierneuf: " ut . . . episcopus favorabilior sit eis et efficacior ad justiciam de suis malefactoribus faciendam ", let him be entertained in the abbey with his retinue, for one day each year.[3] The same pope ordered the bishop of Le Puy, with two abbots, to protect the exempt canons of Brioude " as they frequently suffer wrongs, injuries and violence at the hands of many, because they have no diocesan to whom they may have recourse whensoever they are unduly oppressed ".[4] When the pope sent two abbots to reform the monastery of S.-Josse he bade them ask the bishop of Amiens for advice, since the care of houses in his diocese was his business.[5] Similarly the Poor Catholic brethren were instructed to correct their Order with the advice and authority of the diocesan.[6] The bishop is enlisted to enforce the statutes of a legatine visitor,[7] and of the general council,[8] or to modify the former ;[9] he is told to carry out the pope's sentence of deposition on an abbot of his diocese.[10] Honorius III orders a bishop to transfer a nunnery to another locality, and his register shows another bishop doing the like.[11]

---

[1] *Decretales*, III. l. 7.

[2] Innocent III, I. 163, 268 (Potthast, 196, 282).

[3] *Poitiers Cart.*, 8.   [4] Innocent III, XI. 228 (Potthast, 3633).

[5] *Ibid.*, XVI. 145 (Potthast, 4849).

[6] *Ibid.*, XV. 91 (Potthast, 4508).   [7] Honorii III, 3913.

[8] *Ibid.*, 4602 ; Berlière, *Mélanges d'Histoire Bénédictine*, IVe série (Maredsous, 1902), 158.

[9] Alexandre IV, 1842 (Potthast, 16801).

[10] Honorii III, 5248.   [11] *Ibid.*, 2409, 3401, 3491.

Diocesans are told to unite nunneries ; [1] to remove the inmates of depraved houses ; [2] to see to the disposition of removed monks ; [3] to have vagabond monks reinstated ; [4] to see that monks make their profession ; [5] and to proceed against simoniacal monks [6] and monks holding several offices without dispensation.[7] Alexander IV tells the bishop of Paris to take action, as is his duty, against a brother of Grandmont guilty of homicide, in his diocese.[8] Honorius IV orders the bishop of Burgos to enforce the election of a head for a monastery " which has now been vacant for fifteen years and more ".[9] The bishop of Basel hands over a Benedictine nunnery to a Cistercian house to be reformed, and the pope confirms his act.[10] Sometimes the administration of a vacant or decayed house is committed to the diocesan.[11]

In the appointment of bishops as *papal* visitors it would probably be wrong to see anything more than a disinterested desire on the part of the papacy to get a job done quickly. The examples which occur in the papal registers show the peculiar character of such delegations. The pope most often gave this sort of mandate when he had to deal with a monastery defamed and unreformed by its proper visitors, or with a monastery from which the Curia had received a petition asking for a visitation.

Thus Innocent III orders the bishop of Poitiers to reform a defamed abbey as delegate.[12] The archbishop of Reims is to visit the abbey of S.-Remi, which is much defamed, " vice Papae." [13] A diocesan is sent with two

[1] Honorii III, 3857 (Potthast, 6804), 5754 ; cf. Urbain IV, 1862, 1875 ; Boniface VIII, 2285.
[2] Innocent IV, 780 ; Boniface VIII, 5372 ; cf. Honorii III, 3466 (Potthast, 6684).   [3] Honorii III, 5632.
[4] *Ibid.*, 4740 ; Grégoire IX, 950 ; cf. *ibid.*, 1610 (Potthast, 9340).
[5] *Ibid.*, 4761 (Potthast, 7811 ; *Decretales*, III. xxxi. 22).
[6] *Ibid.*, 2901, 3154.   [7] Nicolas IV, 1320.   [8] Potthast, 17953.
[9] Honorius IV, 509.   [10] Innocent IV, 7487.
[11] e.g. Honorii III, 819, 820, 4832, 5478, 5956 ; Innocent IV, 2627 Alexandre IV, 367 ; Boniface VIII, 409.
[12] With two colleagues. Innocent III, I. 67 (Potthast, 73).
[13] Honorii III, 2148 ; cf. *ibid.*, 5116 (Potthast, 7301).

abbots to a dilapidated Augustinian house, to reform it.[1]
The bishop of Limoges and another are given a second
commission to reform S.-Martial, Limoges.[2] Even in
an exempt house the diocesan sometimes acquires a temporary authority as delegate. The bishop of Nocera is
to visit a decayed exempt house and reform it, without
diminishing its liberty thereby.[3] The archbishop of Arles
is ordered to reform the exempt house of Lérins, which
is decayed, and place Cistercians there if necessary.[4]
Similar mandates are given to diocesans after complaint
by the founder or patron of a monastery that the house
needs reform.[5] At the request of an abbess Honorius III
instructs the bishop of Hildesheim to visit her subject
priories and churches ;[6] and the correction of the monastery of Anagnano is committed to the diocesan bishop
of Arezzo " petente priore ".[7]

The papacy frequently made use of bishops as visitors
in other dioceses than their own. In 1227 two bishops
are sent to the diocese of Calahorra to enforce obedience
to the diocesan and to correct all that needs correction.[8]
A similar case is found among the letters of Urban IV,
where a diocesan has been negligent.[9] The bishop of
Cahors partakes in a visitation of S.-Augustin of
Limoges ;[10] the bishop of Le Mans visits a house in
another diocese, obviously as the pope's delegate, since he
is joined with other officials.[11] These are but a few of
many occasions on which the bishop is employed outside his own diocese to visit a defamed house or remove
an unworthy abbot.[12]

[1] Honorii III, 2220 (Potthast, 6138) ; cf. ibid., 3254 (Potthast, 6619),
3522, 3843, 4274, 5172 (Potthast, 26124) ; Grégoire IX, 2103, 2119, 4102,
4921.   [2] Honorii III, 5927.
    [3] Innocent III, II. 52 (Potthast, 687) ; cf. ibid., IX. 98 (Potthast,
2817) ; Honorii III, 2263, 2442, 2703 ; Honorius IV, 660 (Potthast, 22513).
    [4] Innocent III, I. 273 (Potthast, 281) ; cf. Grégoire IX, 1821.
    [5] Honorii III, 4911 ; Grégoire IX, 1959.
    [6] Honorii III, 4198.   [7] Ibid., 3630 ; cf. 4625.   [8] Ibid., 6195.
    [9] Urbain IV, 529.   [10] Honorii III, 1624.   [11] Grégoire IX, 277.
    [12] Honorii III, 3548, 3553, 3847, 5426, 5637 (Potthast, 26147) ;
Grégoire IX, 1154, 1950, 3161, 2836 ; Innocent IV, 408, 1014 ; Honorius
IV, 171, 474 (Potthast, 22251), 644 ; Nicolas IV, 327 ; Boniface VIII, 5252.

All these mandates concerned defamed houses in which the pope was bound to take direct action, whether they were usually subject to the diocesan or not. In far fewer cases do we find the bishop commissioned to visit where there is no pre-existing ill-fame. These most often occur in comprehensive mandates—to the bishop of Calahorra to visit exempt houses in four provinces of Spain ;[1] to the archbishop of Compostella to visit (not monasteries only) throughout the kingdom of Leon ;[2] to the archbishop of Mainz to visit his and other provinces as legate.[3] Sometimes bishops make such visitations in company with regulars : the bishop of Florence in Tuscany,[4] the bishop of Vercelli in Lombardy,[5] the bishop of Liége in his own diocese,[6] and the archbishop of Cosenza among the Basilian houses in the kingdom of Sicily.[7]

Appointments such as these figure prominently in the papal correspondence relating to monasteries. And this is natural. Only defamed houses and decayed houses and those neglected by the common visitor were likely to be known to the Curia. This system of delegation was designed to counter particular local abuses. It dealt with special cases, and presupposed a regular visitatorial system, which could cope with the commonest requirements, though it might be inadequate in times of stress.

We have seen the diocesans used by the papacy as its own delegates in matters of monastic discipline. Naturally the papal registers throw more light on this than on the diocesan's work as Ordinary ; but from this source we can get enough light to show that the diocesan carried on his usual work with papal approbation. Much of this evidence, as it concerns disputes about exemption, will be considered a little later. For the present it may be remarked that there are many injunctions that bishops are

---

[1] Honorii III, 6241 ; cf. Nicolas IV, 4797.
[2] Grégoire X, 220, and for other countries (Potthast, 20685).
[3] Innocent IV, 627, 653.   [4] Innocent III, XI. 177 (Potthast, 3539).
[5] Honorii III, 1963.   [6] Innocent IV, 3834.
[7] Honorii III, 2788 ; cf. 3367.

to reform the regulars of their dioceses,[1] or to remedy some certain flagrant defects within their jurisdiction.[2] It should be observed that Innocent IV, who gave many particular dispensations from observance of the Gregorian statutes for the Black Monks, looked for their general enforcement to the diocesans.[3] John of Oxenedes says that the statutes were enforced in France by papal command " per visitatores episcopos ", and the English monks viewed with alarm the powers given by the pope to the English bishops in 1253.[4]

The pope may, indeed, according to the theory of himself as Universal Ordinary, regard any action of the diocesan as the outcome of delegated authority. Innocent III tells the bishop of Périgueux that he may visit and correct in the churches of S.-Etienne and S.-Front " quoniam ubique praesentia corporali adesse non possumus, per fratres et coepiscopos nostros, qui sunt in partem sollicitudinis evocati, ad rectum ordinem reduci volumus quae in eis inordinate fuerint attentata." [5] But in relation to this matter it is little more than a figure of speech.

Prelates are told that they may disregard frivolous appeals arising from the discharge of this duty.[6] Sometimes they are taxed with slackness in visiting and told to be more conscientious.[7] After a papal admonition in 1239

---

[1] Innocent III, VIII. 12, 52, 194 (Potthast, 2436, 2495, 2662); Honorii III, 274, 1850, 2041, 2896, 3326, 3871; Grégoire IX, 122, 129 (Potthast, 7963), 521; Innocent IV, 762, 803; Nicolas IV, 1861.

[2] Innocent III, II. 144, X. 212 (Potthast, 771, 3298); Honorii III, 188, 2115, 2180, 4911, 5923 (Potthast, 7568); Grégoire IX, 1766, 2957, 2987, 2393, 2883; Innocent IV, 3776, 5264 (Potthast, 14046); Urbain IV, 713, 2523; Clément IV, 178-9 (Potthast, 19477); Nicolas IV, 3436, 5113, 5925; Potthast, 1342-4, 1359-61, 1639.

[3] Innocent IV, 6544, 7084, 8037; Potthast, 15023; Matt. Paris, V. 380; Rigaud, 143; *Autun Cart.*, 267; cf. Berlière, *Mélanges*, IV. 103 (temp. Gregory IX).

[4] *Chronica Joh. de Oxenedes* (Rolls series, 1859), 197; *Ann. Mon.*, II. 94; Matt. Paris, V. 380.   [5] Innocent III, I. 445 (Potthast, 455).

[6] Canon 7, 4th Lat. Council (Leclercq-Hefele, V. 1335; *Decretales*, I xxxi. 13); Innocent III, I. 445, V. 24, 57, VI. 65 (Potthast, 455, 1665, 1695, 1908); Honorii III, 2022, 3871, 4418, 4567, 4622, 5397, 5590.

[7] Innocent III, I. 483 (Potthast, 495); Honorii III, 3891; Grégoire IX, 3712.

the bishop of Naumburg visits regulars as well as seculars in his diocese, and in 1260 Archbishop Conrad of Cologne says in his synodal statutes that he has visited his diocese at the command of the pope.[1] The bishop of Séez is told that he may correct his subjects " consuetudine iuri contraria non obstante."[2]

Sometimes the episcopal authority is reinforced by papal authority. Thus the archbishop of Nicosia (Cyprus) is told to reform monasteries " que tibi sunt lege diocesana subiecta "[3] : " While it is true (writes Innocent IV) that your jurisdiction as ordinary is considered sufficient for their correction, still, in order that, armed with the force of our own authority, you may proceed more securely, unimpeded by obstacles, we order you . . . with our authority to correct and reform them." This formula is used again by Pope Alexander IV, urging the bishop of Maguelone to correct his chapter.[4] The same mixture of powers is found in a letter addressed by Innocent III to the bishop of Winchester : " Ut igitur super his, quae ad sollicitudinem tuam spectant, sollicitius metiaris quanta necessitate tenearis in dioecesi tua corrigere, quae limam correctionis exposcunt, fraternitati tuae per apostolica scripta mandamus quatenus in monasteriis . . . dioecesana tibi lege subiectis, auctoritate apostolica corrigas . . . quae secundum Deum fuerint corrigenda."[5] Again, Innocent III writes to the bishop of Poitiers in 1198, having heard that the religious houses of the diocese have languished " pro diutina pastoris absentia "—" ut excessus liberius valeas corrigere delinquentium, cum nostra fueris auctoritate suffultus, tibi pagina presenti mandamus "[6] . . . etc.

---

[1] Hartzheim, III. 569, 588 (Conrad had visited the monasteries, *ibid.*, 594).   [2] Honorii III, 2896 ; cf. Grosseteste, *Epistolæ*, 421.

[3] Innocent IV, 2058 ; cf. 5095 ; Grégoire IX, 1604.

[4] *Bullaire de Maguelone*, ed. J. Rouquette and A. Villemagne (Paris, 1911-14) ; II. 358.   [5] Innocent III, VIII. 142 (Potthast, 2594).

[6] *Ibid.*, I. 483 (Potthast, 495) ; it was probably as a result of this that Bishop Maurice of Poitiers obtained (1200) from the convent of Maillezais, which had claimed exemption by papal privilege, an acknowledgment of his full rights in the abbey and its dependencies " sicut in aliis Pictavensis diocesis monasteriis " (*Poitiers Cart.*, 5).

A similar mandate to the archbishop of Sens (" non tam auctoritate tua quam nostra " [1]) has made Luchaire declare : " Encore un demi siècle, et l'on verra les évêques, pour accomplir presque tous les devoirs de leur administration, n'agir plus qu'avec l'autorisation expresse et même par délégation du Saint-Siège." [2] This generalization grossly exaggerates the truth and is most misleading. Dr. Coulton also, commenting on the same case, says that " the papacy had swallowed up the original rights of diocesan bishops and archbishops." [3] We can hardly put this construction on the mandate. Two years later the pope, having ordered the bishop of Paris to visit his diocese,[4] expressly said to the archbishop of Sens that the bishop was visiting, " not as delegate, but as ordinary." [5] We meet with a similar case in the work by Valois on Guillaume d'Auvergne. " On remarquera," says the author, " que Guillaume ne réformait l'abbaye de Lagny, qu'en vertu des pouvoirs extraordinaires qu'il avait reçus du Pape." Yet he had complete episcopal authority over Lagny. Valois continues by remarking " on peut voir par là combien la puissance des papes avait grandi aux dépens de celle des évêques." [6] The extraordinary powers of which Valois speaks were bestowed by a bull of Gregory IX.[7] This letter states that the pope has had complaints regarding the finances of Lagny from the archbishop of Sens and others. The complainants asked the pope to take action : " nos igitur, de discretione tua plenius fiduciam obtinentes, dictum negocium tibi, qui loci diocesanus existis, duximus committendum. . . ."

Important in this connection is the statement of Hostiensis that, if anyone has asked that he may be allowed to correct his subjects both with his ordinary and the

[1] Innocent III, VIII. 52 ; cf. VI. 65 (Potthast, 2495, 1908) ; Alexandre IV, 367.   [2] Le Concile du Latran (1908), 147-8.

[3] Five Centuries, II. 294.

[4] Innocent III, X. 154, 155 (Potthast, 3221-2).

[5] Ibid., X. 171 (Decretales, I. xxxi. 12 ; Potthast, 3249).

[6] N. Valois, Guillaume d'Auvergne (Paris, 1880), 98 note 1.

[7] Ibid., 350 (Grégoire IX, 1163).

Apostolic authority, the consequent mandate neither gives the bishop power over exempt houses,[1] nor prejudices the common law of visitation,[2] " enim ordinarius procurat sibi mandari ea, quae suo iure facere potest, ut magis timeatur." [3] Between such a mandate as this and one despatched without the diocesan's prior request there seems to be no legal difference, though it may signify a policy. In the case of the bishop of Paris which is mentioned above it is possible, though not probable, that the bishop had not himself asked for the mandate.

All this papal correspondence witnesses to considerable activity in visitation. It must be emphasized that the bulk of correspondence on this subject is greater in the first half of the thirteenth century than either before or after ; and that this fact is due to the comparative rarity of visitation in the twelfth century, the disturbance which unwonted activity produced in the following decades, and the final settling down to a fixed administration as the thirteenth century wore on. There can be no doubt that the middle portion of the thirteenth century saw a great advance in the matter of regularity of visitation. This is the opinion of Hauck as regards Germany,[4] and is borne out by the English evidence. The absence of systematic records, the querulous tone of such as we possess, and the notorious need for reform in the English church at the time of the Council of London (1237) certainly point to the general neglect of episcopal visitation up to this period. It seems worth while to collect the references to episcopal visitation in England before 1250, and so to see how the custom came to be regularized.

Archbishop Baldwin, in the course of visiting his province, came to Chester in 1187.[5] His successor, Hubert Walter, visited Christ Church, Canterbury, in 1197, and

---

[1] Cf. *Decretales*, I. xxxi. 19 ; see *infra*, 45.   [2] *Decretales*, I. xxxi. 12.
[3] Hostiensis, *Summa*, I. de off. Ordin. (f. 66 *recto*).
[4] *Kirchengeschichte Deutschlands*, V. (Leipzig 1911), 181-2.
[5] *Annales Cestrienses* (Lanc. and Chesh. Record Soc., 1887), 36, 126.
Archbishop Thomas of York (1108-14) is said to have visited frequently monasteries of his diocese (*The Priory of Hexham*, Surtees Soc., 1864, I. 53).

later, Ramsey Abbey.[1] Archbishop Baldwin was visiting as papal legate. Then, in 1222, the very year of the Council of Oxford, we find the pope complaining that Langton neglects his duty of visitation ;[2] nothing came of this so far as we know. In the diocese of Lincoln Bishop Hugh de Welles visited Dunstable and Tickford in 1220.[3] Later in his pontificate he re-visited Dunstable (1233) by deputy,[4] and visited Brooke Priory (1234).[5] Some time before his death he left injunctions at Nun Coton and at Peterborough,[6] and produced articles for the visitation of parishes.[7]

At York Archbishop Gray came to agreement with the Abbey of St. Mary in 1226, after a dispute about visitation.[8] He left injunctions at Selby Abbey in 1233, and at St Oswald's Gloucester, 1250 and Newstead, 1252.[9] The bishop of Bath in 1235 held several inquiries at Keynsham Abbey, in person and by deputy, prompted by dissension between the abbot and his monks.[10]

In 1232 an important letter was sent to the English archbishops and bishops by the pope. Gregory IX commanded them to visit in person or by deputy all the non-exempt monks and canons of their dioceses.[11] This had some effect. Bartholomew Cotton says that in the next year the bishop of Norwich visited his diocese " per mandatum domini papae," and that other bishops visited elsewhere.[12] It was in virtue of this mandate, says the

[1] *Chron. and Mem. of Reign of Richard I* (Rolls series), II. xciv.; *Ramsey Cart.*, II. 198, 204–7.   [2] Honorii III, 3891.
[3] *Ann. Mon.*, III. 57 ; Welles, II. 51.   [4] Ann. Mon., III. 132
[5] *VCH Rutland*, I. 160, with a reference to Welles's register, which cannot be verified.   [6] *Supra*, 14.   [7] Wilkins, I. 627.
[8] Honorii III, 5850 (*CPR*, 108 ; Gray, 152 ; Romeyn, I. 73).
[9] Gray, 327, 210 ; Giffard, *York*, 203. When he made injunctions for St. Oswald's Gloucester in 1250, Gray referred to his earlier ordinances : and he entrusted the visitation of the defamed Cartmel Priory to a commission in 1248 (*VCH Lancashire*, II. 145, no authority traceable).
[10] *Ann. Mon.*, I. 96.
[11] Grégoire IX, 716 (Potthast, 8947 ; *Ann. Mon.*, I. 243). A tattered copy of the bull serves as flyleaf in a Worcester Cathedral manuscript of Ivo of Chartres (MS. **Q.** 1).
[12] Bartholomæi Cotton *Historia Anglicana* (Rolls series, 1859), 117.

3

Dunstable chronicler, that Hugh de Welles visited the priory in 1233. Disputes settled in the following years probably arose out of the application of the same bull. At Coventry the monks resisted their bishop because they wanted visitors of their own Order ; the case was taken to Rome and decided in favour of the diocesan.[1] To the same years belong the attempt of the bishop of Chichester to visit Battle and the compromise arising out of this attempt.[2] A little later, in 1239, Bishop Walter de Cantilupe was opposed at St. Peter's, Gloucester, and gained formal recognition of his right to examine individuals in the monastery. The same bishop visited Gloucester again in 1242.[3] But if the diocesan bishops could be induced to visit, they saw no reason why they themselves should be visited, and they did not look kindly on a metropolitan visitation. In 1237 the pope ordered the archbishop of Canterbury to visit, notwithstanding the opposition he had aroused among both bishops and abbots.[4] In 1239 the opposition was vigorous : the suffragans inquired in the Curia whether they were liable to metropolitan visitation so long as they were not themselves negligent.[5] The matter was apparently left unsettled, only to be raised again in 1250.[6]

Meanwhile new forces powerful for reform had appeared in the country. In 1235 Robert Grosseteste had been made bishop of Lincoln ; in that year and in 1237 the pope issued his statutes to be observed by the Benedictines ;[7] and in 1237 the Legate Otto presided over a council at London in which the bishops were exhorted to visit their dioceses at convenient times.[8]

For the next twelve years we hear of hardly any English episcopal visitations beside those of Grosseteste. If Bishop Hugh de Welles had earned the title which John of Oxenedes gives him, of " omnium religiosorum malleus," [9] his successor far outdid him in arousing the

---

[1] *Ann. Mon.*, I. 89, III. 143 ; cf. *CPR*, 141, 150.   [2] See *infra*, 41-2.
[3] *Ann. Mon.*, IV. 430, 433.   [4] Grégoire IX, 3646 (*CPR*, 162).
[5] *Ann. Mon.*, III. 151.   [6] See *infra*, 138-9.
[7] Grégoire IX, 3045.   [8] Wilkins, I. 654.   [9] *Chronica*, 164.

antagonism of monks. In 1236 he deposed various abbots.[1] Two years later he made a general visitation of monasteries and deaneries.[2] Two years later he was at Dunstable,[3] and again visited there in 1249 and 1251.[4] We also hear of his diocesan visitations in 1246,[5] and of his intervention at Bardney and Peterborough in 1243 and 1249,[6] and by deputy at Godstow about 1251.

The regularity of Grosseteste in visiting his diocese and the strictness of his inquiries certainly helped to make him famous throughout England. Matthew Paris, who often speaks of his severity, says more than once that Archbishop Boniface was fired by the example of Grosseteste when he embarked on the visitations which caused so much bad feeling in 1250.[7] According to the Burton annalist it was by the example of the bishop of Lincoln that the bishop of Coventry and Lichfield made inquiry throughout his diocese in 1252.[8] According to contemporaries, then, Grosseteste influenced other prelates to visit. And if we look for the reason for Grosseteste's visitations, we meet with Matthew Paris' statement that his strict inquiries were " ad suggestum, ut dicitur, Praedicatorum et Minorum "[9]. Thus the chain of influence is usually established : the friars teach Grosseteste the value of visitation, and Grosseteste sets the example for the other English prelates. While this may well represent the contemporary interpretation of the facts, it seems to leave out of account several important factors. In the first place, there were *some* episcopal visitations before Grosseteste's time. Secondly, whatever the imponderable influence of the friars after their arrival in England in the third decade of the century, Pope Gregory IX had given a definite order in 1232, and that order was responded to. Thirdly, this was followed up in 1237 by the Council

---

[1] *Ann. Mon.*, III. 143.   [2] *Ibid.*, III. 147.   [3] *Ibid.*, III. 152.
[4] *Ibid.*, III. 178, 181.   [5] Matt. Paris, IV. 579-80.
[6] *Ibid.*, IV. 245-8, V. 84. Cf. an undated reference to his visitations of Peterborough in Jos. Sparke, *Hist. Angl. Script. Var.* (1723), II. 110.
[7] Matt. Paris, V. 119, 190, 195-6.
[8] *Ann. Mon.*, I. 296.   [9] Matt. Paris, IV. 579.

of London, which had a new code of Benedictine rules to enforce. Finally, we should remember that not only the friars were setting an example to the secular prelates of their day in the work of visitation ; the Cistercian and Premonstratensian Orders had long maintained their systems, and since the Fourth Lateran Council the un-reformed Benedictines and the Augustinian canons had been supposed to hold chapters and visitations triennially. These models, as much as any visitations by one of them-selves, must have inspired the English bishops to visit their dioceses—and particularly their monasteries. We may admit that Grosseteste, who seemed very potent (and very terrible) to Matthew Paris, exercised great influence over his contemporaries, but we cannot ascribe the de-velopment of visitations in England to him alone. Papal admonitions and the example of monastic reformers played a large part in the rousing of the English episcopate.

The visitations of the archbishops of Canterbury in the late twelfth and thirteenth centuries show significant growth. They begin by visiting as legates, but Hubert Walter visits after his legation expired. By the mid-thirteenth century they visit as ordinaries, depending most often on papal stimulus or support. At the end of the century they visit regularly on their own initia-tive and with an authority which is seldom contested.

In connection with the direct action of the papacy on bishop-visitors we should finally take note of the important legislation of Innocent IV on the subject. This formed part of the celebrated constitution " Romana Ecclesia " promulgated in 1246. As it refers in the first instance to metropolitan visitations it will be dealt with more fully in Chapter VI ; here it is merely necessary to emphasize the fact that the rules were applicable to all bishops. " Hanc autem visitandi formam ab universis etiam episcopis aliisque prelatis ordinario jure suos subiectos visitantibus, plene observari precipimus." [1]

The diocesan authority was abrogated in many places because of the exemption which popes had granted to

[1] *Sext*, III. xx. I. § 6.

Orders and individual houses. The desire for exemption persisted throughout the Middle Ages, but the implications of the term alter from age to age. The writer of a formulary near the middle of the thirteenth century gives a broad definition of exemption. " That is properly ' exemption ' (he says) where a conventual church of secular or regular canons, or of monks or nuns, is immediately subject to the Lord Pope : so that although it be situated in the province of an archbishop and the diocese of a bishop, neither metropolitan nor diocesan has right in it, but all things appertain to the pope, to whom such a church appeals without intermediary." [1] This represents the final achievement of " exempt " houses—subjection to the jurisdiction of the pope alone. But exemption had not always implied complete independence from the diocesan's control.

From early times the papacy had granted privileges to monasteries which neither defined the bishop's original power nor altogether removed it ; rarely, if ever, was the right of visitation expressly mentioned. Geoffrey, abbot of Vendôme, considered his abbey exempt, and was certainly never visited by his bishop : but he promised obedience to the diocesan at his election,[2] and the diocesan had certain powers over the abbey's dependencies.[3] In a bull of 1192 the pope declared to another monastery : " Liberum te esse volumus ab omni ditione et potestate dioecesani tui ", but the letter ends with the common proviso " salva sedis apostolicae auctoritate et dioecesani episcopi ecclesiastica vel canonica justitia ".[4] Vendeuvre remarks that the clause reserving the bishop's power tends to drop out of use in the late twelfth century ; [5] till that period salva dioecesana lege was common in charters of

[1] Rockinger, 248.   [2] Compain, Geoffroi de Vendôme (Paris, 1891), 15.
[3] Ibid., 169 note 1.
[4] Migne, Patrol. Latina, CCVI. 951-2 (Jaffé, 16900).
[5] Vendeuvre, 117 sqq. and 104.   For the salva dioecesana lege clause in charters, cf. Innocent III, VIII. 32, XV. 231 (Potthast, 2456, 4625) ; Honorii III, 3805 ; Grégoire IX, 5057 ; Innocent IV, 3541, 3547 (Potthast, 12809).

exemption, and the clause included episcopal jurisdiction
in disciplinary matters.   Up to this time, indeed, exemption from episcopal jurisdiction was rare outside the
Orders of Cluny and Cîteaux.   But when Innocent III
examined the claim of Evesham Abbey to exemption from
visitation (in 1205-6), he rehearsed a bull of Pope Alexander III and said : " In fine vero subiungitur quod salva
sit apostolicae sedis auctoritas, nec dicitur quod diocesani
episcopi canonica sit salva justitia, quum in monasteriis
non exemptis secundum approbatam ecclesiae Romanae
consuetudinem diocesanis episcopis canonica justitia con-
servetur." [1]   Thus an omission which perhaps had seemed
at first to be of slight importance acquired special significance when bishops became more anxious to visit and
monasteries more unwilling to receive them.   Old privileges began to be regarded in a new light.   The change
was slow, and often as imperceptible to contemporaries
as to the modern historians.   " L'exemption de visite,"
says Vendeuvre, breaking into metaphors, " comme les
autres exemptions, est née le plus souvent, peu à peu, de
faibles atteintes aux prérogatives des évêques; végétation
parasitaire, elle a lentement pénétré dans le droit commun,
pour l'étouffer dans la suite." [2]
  By the thirteenth century the great Orders of Cluny,
Cîteaux and Prémontré were all removed from the jurisdiction of diocesans, and Orders instituted after these
nearly always enjoyed similar exemption.   But even in
the great Orders the origin of the privilege is obscure.
To take the example of Prémontré : the Order was allowed
to institute abbatial visitations, but Vendeuvre considers
that this, at the outset, was not so much a matter of
exemption as of internal order. [3]   The abbey was still
subjected to the bishop in extreme cases, according to the
privileges of 1134 and 1144, and in 1188 privileges were
granted saving the bishop's right.   In 1184 the bishop was
conceded the right of reception in the abbey " servato
evectionis numero in Laterano concilio constituto."
Vendeuvre remarks : " limiter le droit de procuration

---

[1] *Evesham Chron.*, 182.   [2] Vendeuvre, 112.   [3] *Ibid.*, 116.

n'est ce pas affirmer le droit de visite ? " [1]   One would, indeed, have thought so, and accepted this as an evidence of visitatorial rights.   Unfortunately for the theory a passage in a Custumal of Bayeux, after describing the bishop's relations with exempt houses, says : " in Premonstratensian houses he has no [right of] visitation or correction, notwithstanding that he has procuration in them ".[2]   We know, moreover, that Archbishop Rigaud of Rouen frequently took procuration fees from houses of the Order, and that not only on account of a first visit.[3]

Elsewhere different customs were observed.   Abbot Gervais of Prémontré complained to Pope Honorius III (1217) that the bishop of Noyon and other diocesans oppressed houses of his Order, illegally seeking to exact procurations from them.   The pope supported the abbot, and the bishop of Noyon finally wrote an apologetic letter to Abbot Gervais, saying that he had not wished to lose the annual procurations which (as he had supposed) his predecessors took ; but now that he found his mistake he wished to make amends.[4]

Exemption in the thirteenth century was not limited to the privileged Orders.   But the exempt houses among the unreformed Black Monks were comparatively rare.   In England, where the proportion was possibly less than in other countries, we can only reckon six Benedictine abbeys with their dependencies totally exempt from episcopal jurisdiction—St. Augustine's, Canterbury, Westminster, Bury St. Edmunds, St. Albans, Evesham, Malmesbury.[5]   In the diocese of Rouen in Archbishop Rigaud's

---

[1] Vendeuvre, 117.

[2] *Consuetudines Ecclesiæ Baiocensis*, ed. U. Chevalier (1902), 322.

[3] e.g. at Ardennes " cum expensis abbacie ".   Rigaud, 94, 261, 575.

[4] Hugo, *Sacræ antiq. Monumenta* (1725), I. 8-9, 10, 46-7.

[5] Malmesbury claimed exemption in the time of Alexander III, and forged bulls for the purpose, it was said (Migne, *Patrol. Latina*, CC. 1457) ; and it was exempt in the next century.   Glastonbury is added by Bishop Frere to the list (Frere, 67-8), but this abbey was certainly visited by both diocesan and metropolitan, after its position in regard to the see of Bath was regularized in 1219.   Statistics compiled for Lincoln diocese in the fifteenth century from Prof. Hamilton Thompson's lists in *Linc. Visit.*, I. 147-71, show 95 houses subject to visitation and 45 exempt.

day forty-five houses of regulars are enumerated by Dom Besse, without the unimportant "prieurés simples ".[1] Of these forty-five Rigaud visited regularly thirty. Fécamp was the only exempt unreformed Benedictine abbey in the diocese. It is noteworthy that the archbishop visited three Cistercian nunneries (although he left three others unvisited) ; nunneries of exempt Orders rarely seem to have escaped episcopal visitation.[2] When in 1238 Bishop Hermann of Würzburg had been asked by the nunnery of Billinkem (O.S.B.) to prescribe reforms, and had prescribed the observance of the Cistercian Rule, he said that he fully reserved (*plenarie retinentes*) " eiusdem loci iurisdictionem et dominium tam in temporalibus quam in spiritualibus . . . Salva in omnibus Cisterciensis Ordinis disciplina ". Similarly he reserved his rights when founding a Cistercian nunnery in the following year.[3] On the other hand Fontevrault and its dependencies maintained exemption. In 1244 the bishop of Poitiers was allowed to participate if necessary in the correction of this nunnery. But next year the archbishop of Reims gave judgment for the abbey when it claimed exemption from the bishop.[4]

" Avec une constance que rien ne put jamais décourager, les moines s'appuyèrent sur le pouvoir royal et sur le pouvoir pontifical, afin de se soustraire au pouvoir épiscopal. L'histoire des conflits aigus et sans cesse renaissants entre évêques et abbés forme un des chapitres les plus originaux de la chicane." [5] Neither visitor nor visitand was uniformly blameless. Abbeys produced forged privileges ; bishops exceeded their powers.[6] The bishop of

---

[1] Beaunier et Besse, 29-76. Rigaud had to neglect 7 Cistercian houses, 4 Premonstratensian, 1 Cluniac, 1 of Grandmont, 1 of Fontevrault, and the Benedictine privileged abbey of Fécamp.

[2] Power, 482. Examples of diocesan visitation of Cistercian nunneries in the diocese of York are given in *Yorks. Archæol. and Topog. Journal*, XVI. (1900-2), 353-4, notes.

[3] Ussermann, *Germania Sacra* (Episc. Wirceburg., 1794), cod. prob., pp. 59, 60.   [4] Innocent IV, 852 ; *Poitiers Cart.*, 22, 27.

[5] H. Leclercq, *Dictionnaire d'Archéologie Chrétienne*, V. 952.

[6] Honorii III, 2284, 2605 (Potthast, 6326), 4181, 4186, 4309 ; Grégoire IX, 1738 ; Alexandre IV, 723 ; Urbain IV, 1213 ; Honorius IV, 171, 461 ; Nicolas IV, 1996, 3600 ; Peckham, I. 192.

Alba was accused of entering violently a monastery, burning its papal privilege and obliterating its royal grant with water.[1] In 1263 an abbot appealed against an inquiry proposed by the excommunicate archbishop of Trèves ; Glastonbury opposed a visitor on the same grounds.[2] From various regions come complaints that the visiting bishop is a " manifest adversary " of the convent, or actually engaged in litigation with it.[3] These were only temporary disturbances, but from such beginnings came exemptions and compromises.

A century's dispute between Battle Abbey and the bishops of Chichester ended with an unusual arrangement in 1235. For a very long while the relations of the diocesan to the abbey had been intensely unfriendly. Successive bishops had tried to obtain full recognition of their jurisdiction. But with royal support the abbots usually triumphed and kept the bishop out of the monastery.[4] While visitation is not mentioned by the monastic chronicler among the questions in dispute, it was obviously involved. Yet in favour of its exemption from visitation Battle Abbey had surprisingly little to show. The king heard the disputes and inspected the abbey's charters ; but royal charters could not dispose of the spiritual jurisdiction of the diocesan. Moreover, it seems doubtful whether the bishop could legally grant—as he is said to have granted—exemption " ab omnibus episcopalibus exactionibus et consuetudinibus." [5] Eventually, when the abbey had refused to admit three delegates of the bishop in 1234, Pope Gregory IX allowed its claim to exemption.[6] But it would seem that the monastery feared that this was too good to last ; the matter was reopened in the next year. This time a papal commission

[1] Honorii III, 4048 (Potthast, 6862) ; cf. Innocent IV, 1476.
[2] J. N. de Hontheim, *Historia Trevirensis* (1750), I. 749, 751, 753, 758 ; Innocent IV, 3720 (*CPR*, 242).
[3] Matt. Paris, IV. 246 *sqq.* (Lincoln diocese) ; Grégoire IX, 4432 (Bari) ; *ibid.*, 2937 (Avranches) ; Urbain IV, 289 ordin. (Arras).
[4] *Chronicon monasterii de Bello* (Anglia Christiana Soc., 1846), 63, 64, 68 71, 77 *sqq.*, 103.   [5] *Ibid.*, 103.
[6] Grégoire IX, 1738, 1776 (*CPR*, 138).

decided that there should be triennial visitation by two
Benedictine monks of Chichester diocese—one appointed
by the bishop, the other by the abbot and convent.
These two were to visit in place of the bishop, acting in
such a way as not to diminish or infringe the ancient
observances of Battle.   If the abbey became notoriously
corrupt, visitors might be reappointed before the expiry
of three years. The bishop himself, with a company of
twenty-five horse, was entitled to entertainment in the
abbey once every three years " qui nichil ibidem corrigat
nec aliquatenus visitet et aliquid ius episcopale ibi vel
infra circumiacentem leugam non exerceat nisi abbatis
and conventus precibus exoratus." [1]

An even more definite assertion of independence had
been made thirteen years earlier by the abbey of Westminster.   Controversy had persisted for a long time when
in 1221 Bishop Eustace of London claimed of the abbey
the usual honours and jurisdiction of a diocesan.   The
abbey claimed contrary privilege, the bishop appealed to
the pope, and the matter was submitted to arbitrators.
As a result, Westminster was conceded total exemption
in 1222.   Its claims, whatever the foundations, had some
very faulty props.[2]

The natural ambitions of both parties certainly led to
many unscrupulous acts, but the constant disputes which
arose were due in part to real uncertainty regarding privileges. Abbot Gervais of Prémontré reproved violently an
abbot of his Order who had allowed himself to be visited

[1] Battle Abbey cartulary (Henry E. Huntington Library, San
Marino, California), ff. 70 *verso-72 verso*. The document is summarized
by Canon Deedes (*Epis. Register of Robert Rede*, part II., Sussex Record
Soc., IX. (1910), 440-2) from the *Liber E* of Chichester. A shorter form,
dated 1255, is given in *Chronicon de Bello*, 191-3. For an account of the
dispute see Graham, *Studies*, 200-1.

[2] Wilkins, I. 598-9 ; Matt. Paris, III. 67, 75 (and see *VCH London*,
I. 438 ; E. H. Pearce, *Walter de Wenlok* (1920), 26-8 ; Frere, I. 60). This
settlement had as one result the notorious case of Great Malvern Priory
—a house dependent on Westminster Abbey.   Consequently neither
Godfrey Giffard nor Archbishop Pecham was able to depose its infamous
prior (see Giffard, *Worc.*, xlii. *sqq.* and Peckham, II. lxxix. *sqq.*).

and judged by the archbishop of Brindisi.[1] The authorities of the same Order were in doubt as to the jurisdiction of Combwell Priory in 1230. This priory was said to have forsaken the Order of Prémontré. After a visitation at the request of the Order, the archbishop of Canterbury decided that the canons there dwelling were Augustinians —and so came under his control.[2] Matters were settled less amicably between Archbishops Wickwane and Romeyn and the Cluniac priory of Monk Bretton. Wickwane visited there and the Cluniac observance was apparently dropped. But Romeyn is found complaining that the earl of Lincoln has abetted certain monks of Cluny in their wicked attempt to visit Monk Bretton ; the priory is described elsewhere in the archbishop's register as " immediately subject to us and our church of York and exempt from the obedience of the Order of Cluny ".[3] About the same time the abbey of Fécamp complained to Nicholas IV that Archbishop Pecham claimed the right of visiting her subject churches in the province of Canterbury, and was too powerful for the abbey to get justice.[4] Cistercian exemption seems an indubitable fact, yet the bishops of Autun tried to visit the abbey of La Bussière, which claimed exemption as a member of the Order. Its exemption was confirmed by Nicholas IV in 1290, but quarrels and complaints were continuing in 1345.[5]

These are a few samples of common misunderstandings. A system which was based on the interpretation of

[1] Hugo, *op. cit.*, I. 27.   [2] H. M. Colvin, *White canons* (1951), 196.
[3] Romeyn, I. 94, 99, 100. An attempted Cluniac visitation of this priory in 1279 is in Duckett's *Visitations of English Cluniac Foundations* (1890), 32-3, and the decision of the General Chapter (1291) regarding its desertion of the Order in *Visitations and Chapters General of Cluni* (Duckett, 1893), 208, 243. Another case of acceptance of episcopal visitation came before this chapter (*loc. cit.*, 208). There was a similar uncertainty regarding the jurisdiction of Tickford, a priory of Marmoutier (*VCH Bucks.*, I. 361-2).   [4] Nicolas IV, 1996 ; cf. Peckham, III. 882 *sqq.*
[5] *Biblioth. de l'Éc. des Chartes*, IV. (1843), 557-8. Over almost exactly the same period, from 1297 to 1346, the chapter of La Chapelle-aux-Riches (a dependency of S.-Bénigne of Dijon) fought the bishops of Langres for exemption from procurations ; the litigation of half a century resulted in the victory of the chapter (*IAD*, Côte d'Or, G. 2090).

doubtful phrases used inconsistently, was bound to cause trouble. There was much to be said for Archbishop Rigaud's method of arriving at the truth—which was to go on visiting until he was countered by an unexceptionable privilege, in black and white. There is no doubt that the development of papal power favoured the exemption of monasteries from diocesan visitation. Dom Leclercq writes [1] : " l'exemption, sous ses différents aspects, concernant le personnel, le temporel et le spirituel, aboutit à une législation, à un droit d'exception, aux dépens du pouvoir épiscopal. La restriction que celui-ci doit subir résulte en accroissement pour le pouvoir pontifical ; ainsi l'exemption a ses destinées associées à celles de l'expansion du Siège romain." Long before the thirteenth century important monasteries had acquired liberties and placed themselves under papal protection. Where these privileges did not include exemption from visitation this exemption came to be most desired ; for it was in such cases that the bishop most anxiously exercised his remaining rights. Vendeuvre shows that the papacy found itself faced with a choice—of reducing the privileges it had already bestowed, or of extending those privileges in the direction of complete exemption.[2] There could be no doubt as to the choice. In the great period of the centralizing popes we find a constant alertness to preserve the privileges of exempt houses. The object is well expressed in a letter of Pope Alexander III to the English episcopate warning them not to excommunicate or interdict an exempt house : " cum autem sententia in parochianos alterius ab aliquo vestrum prolata fuerit, de iure non teneat, *multo minus illa, que in speciales Romanae ecclesiae filios,*

---

[1] *Loc. cit.*, 953. Matthew Paris considered that the growth of papal power was dangerous to monastic houses and favoured anti-monastic policy of the bishops (V. 208). The fact that he was not wholly right does not destroy the significance of his view. Professor Richardson seems to exaggerate when he speaks of the " well-known tendency of the papal-monastic alliance to minimize the power of the local, and exalt that of the universal ordinary " (*Gesta Dunelm.*, viii.).

[2] Vendeuvre, 95.

qui scilicet nullum episcopum preter Romanum ponti-
ficem habent, *profertur, debet ab aliis observari.*" [1]
We see the same attention to privilege in a letter of
Honorius III to the archbishop of Bordeaux, later embodied in the Decretals, bidding the ordinary prevent
monks from living alone in priories ; a proviso is added
" that you extend not your hand to exempt monks by
pretext of this sort of mandate ".[2] Innocent III declares
that exempt houses must not prejudice their right of
exemption,[3] on which Hostiensis comments : " for all
exempt, when they do fealty to the Roman pontiff, swear
that they will alienate nothing without licence." [4] A
letter of Gregory IX embodied in the Decretals declares
that the rescript by which the diocesan is bidden correct
the clergy of his diocese, does not give him jurisdiction
over exempt clergy.[5]

The commissioners of the Curia heard many disputes
between bishops and claimants to exemption and confirmed the exemption of many houses.[6] In granting
privileges to bishops the pope guarded carefully the rights
of monasteries.[7] Innocent IV confirms to a house the
remission of all episcopal rights granted by the diocesan
under the pope's predecessor.[8] In the register of Urban
IV occurs the privilege of temporary exemption from the
diocesan's jurisdiction while the dispute between Anchin
and the bishop of Arras is being tried by the Pope's
commission.[9]

A formidable array of examples could be collected to

---

[1] *Quinq. Compil.*, I. iii. 25. 4 (page 34), (Jaffé, 13741).

[2] Honorii III, 5365 (Potthast, 7820).   [3] *Decretales*, I. xliii. 5.

[4] Hostiensis, *Comment.*, I. xliii. 5, sect. 4 (vol. i. f. 205 *verso*).

[5] *Decretales*, I. xxxi. 19 (Potthast, 9561a).

[6] Honorii III, 2100, 2104-5, 3972, 4177 (Potthast, 6909), 4968-9
(*Decretales*, II. xii. 8 ; Potthast, 7239), 4981, 4983, 5323, 5769 ; Grégoire
IX, 1079, 1578, 1776 ; Innocent IV, 61 (Potthast, 11107), 520, 2542
(Potthast, 12482), 2629 ; Urbain IV, 60, 210 ; Clément IV, 396, 399 ;
Nicolas IV, 469, 1598 ; Boniface VIII, 12 ; *Poitiers Cart.*, 8, 22.

[7] Honorii III, 3622 ; Grégoire IX, 648, 1854 (Potthast, 9432),
1857 (Potthast, 9442), 4843 ; Innocent IV, 2388.

[8] Innocent IV, 153 (Potthast, 11150).   [9] Urbain IV, 289 (ordinaire).

illustrate this fact that the papacy vigorously defended rights of exemption in the thirteenth century. But for the present purpose this recognition of exemption is not so noteworthy as the maintenance of the bishop's rights.[1] It was possible for the papacy to welcome and encourage diocesan visitation as machinery for monastic reform at the same time as it removed certain monasteries from the bishop's jurisdiction. Diocesan visitation would not be wiped out. The bishop's original rights were never in danger of oblivion. Hostiensis, discussing the basis of archidiaconal visitation in custom and that of episcopal visitation in common law, says: " Quid ergo si archidiaconus, qui per consuetudinem acquisivit visitationem, postea amittat eam per desuetudinem, numquid episcopus qui per centum annos stetit, quod non visitavit, volens visitare et veniens admittetur ? Utique . . . convincuntur male sentire, qui dicunt, quod episcopalis visitatio per solam patientiam episcopi praescribatur." [2]

A judgment of Innocent III concerning visitations declared that a monastery is subject to its diocesan unless it can prove exemption.[3] Furthermore, those who could claim the protection of the pope, or show that they paid him the " census " were not *ipso facto* removed from the bishop's jurisdiction.[4] The exemption of a monastery did not necessarily exempt its dependencies ;[5] in 1291 we find an exempt monastery seeking to exchange a church (which it possesses) for the rights of confirmation

[1] Berlière, *Honorius*, 475 *sqq.*

[2] Hostiensis, *Comment.*, I. XXIII. 10, sect. 31 (vol. i. fol. 129 *recto*). Cf. Innocent III, V. 114 (1202) in this sense (*Decretales* II. xxvi. 16), also Innocent III, XV. 87 (quoted *infra.*, 104–5). It is hard to square with this, or to justify, the reported reply of this pope to the bishop of Worcester's proctor in the Evesham case. The proctor had told the pope that according to his teachers prescription did not run against episcopal rights. " Indeed," said the pope, " you and your masters drank deep of English ale when you learnt this from them " (*Chron. Evesham*, 189, transl. Coulton, *Five Centuries*, II. 361).

[3] Innocent III, I. 60 (*Decretales*, III. xxxvi. 8 ; Potthast, 66) ; cf. Honorii III, 3198, 3213, 3716.

[4] *Decretales*, V. xxxiii. 8 and 18 (Alexander III and Innocent III).

[5] Clément IV, 399.

of abbot and of visitation in a subject house (rights which the diocesan possesses).[1] Even where exemption is admitted for a religious house the canonical reverence due to the diocesan and his legal rights in churches and chapels subject to his diocesan authority are to be recognized.[2] A papal legate is instructed to compel the master and brethren of Sempringham to pay due obedience to the bishop of Lincoln, their diocesan.[3] A Cistercian abbess dares to assume the right of imposing the veil of consecration upon nuns—it is strictly forbidden.[4] When the pope grants *insignia* to the abbot of Anchin, he tells the bishop not to molest him, as the grant is not meant to diminish episcopal authority.[5] A religious house cannot without permission deprive its parishes of tithes,[6] nor open interdicted churches.[7]

Even when a house was immune from episcopal visitation, the metropolitan still had the right to visit, unless he, like the bishop, had been specifically excluded. The archbishop's right to visit the house was acknowledged by Evesham Abbey,[8] and enforced by the archbishop of Bourges; of the latter M. Lacger says: " Dans les monastères et chapitres qui sont exempts de la juridiction de l'Ordinaire, mais non de la sienne, non seulement il enquête, mais il réprime les abus de sa propre autorité." [9] At the beginning of the fourteenth century Clement V issued a bull exempting the abbey of Nanteuil from the jurisdiction of the bishop of Poitiers, his diocesan. But he ordained : " ut vos, monasterium,

---

[1] Nicolas IV, 6125.
[2] Innocent IV, 3541 ; *Decretales*, V. xxxiii. 17 and 19.
[3] *CPR*, 189.
[4] Innocent IV, 589-91 (Potthast, 11289).
[5] Honorii III, 2341 ; cf. Grégoire IX, 1853.
[6] *Sext*, III. xiii. 2. 4 (Alexander IV).
[7] Durandus, *Constitutiones*, 130-1 ; *Quinq. Compil.*, I. v. 28. 7 (page 61).
[8] The letters patent appear in the Table of Canterbury Archbishopric Charters compiled in 1330, " Protestacio Abbatis et conventus de Evesham quod archiepiscopus potest per se vel per alios singulis annis visitare ipsos " (p. 14, Camden Miscellany XV., 1929), and see *infra*, 91 note.
[9] Lacger, *RHE*, 295, 301.

persone ac menbra predicta tantum archiepiscopo Burd-
egalensi, qui pro tempore fuerit, subjecti sitis et in
omnibus pareatis." [1]

Finally, against the instances which the papal registers
afford of monasteries receiving confirmation of exemption
we must set the judgments recorded in favour of bishops.[2]
The papal privileges to religious houses, and the appeals
of monasteries to the Curia certainly restricted episcopal
visitations. But the many abuses of exemption should
not blind us to the facts that episcopal visitation continued, its principle was recognized and the popes took
account of it in their schemes for reform.

As regards Provincial Chapters and associations of
abbots for the purposes of discipline, it is clear that in
principle these institutions did not diminish the bishop's
authority. The Benedictines of the province of Rouen
in 1210 decided to meet in annual chapters and send
delegates to the pope every fourth year ;[3] but both they
and the pope specifically reserve the rights of the diocesans—" salvo per omnia iure praelatorum compro-
vincialium ". The Fourth Lateran Council, which introduced these chapters as a universal system for the Black
Monks, ordained that they should be held " salvo iure
dioecesanorum pontificum ".[4] Moreover episcopal visitation is plainly mentioned, and the bishop accepted as a
regular part of the machinery of reform ; as Dom Berlière
says : " Les visiteurs, chargés d'exécuter les réformes,
devaient en référer à l'évêque pour les mesures extrêmes,
c'était respecter le droit de visite inhérent à la charge
épiscopale." [5]

Hostiensis puts the question, whether the visit of
Order delegates prejudices the bishop's right ? and decides
that it does not. " What if these visitors and the bishop

---

[1] 1305, *Poitiers Cart.*, 80.
[2] Honorii III, 4308 (Potthast, 6995), 4840 ; Grégoire IX, 1014 ;
Innocent IV, 6348 ; Alexandre IV, 2061 ; Honorius IV, 461 ; Potthast,
2372, 5151.   [3] Innocent III, XIII. 124 (Potthast, 4067).
[4] Leclercq-Hefele, V. 1342 ; *Decretales*, III. xxxv. 7.
[5] Berlière, *Innocent*, 158.

come [to visit] at the same time ? " he asks. Then it is right and proper that the bishop should give way to them, simply because they have to come from a greater distance and it is less inconvenient for him than for them to postpone a visit. It would seem that he was maliciously impeding them if he did not withdraw, and then he would expose himself to censure from the pope. " *Sed idem iuris est in utroque*," says Hostiensis.[1] When Benedictine visitors came to Durham in 1300, they found an episcopal visitation of the cathedral already begun, the prior excommunicated by the bishop, and the priory blockaded by the bishop's men. In this charged atmosphere they simply made their formal entry into the chapterhouse and then withdrew, recording the fact in the presence of the bishop's officials.

While bishop and Order visitors have equally the right to visit, the bishop's authority at visitation is greater. The Lateran Council orders the bishop to correct houses in such a way that when the Order visitors come they will find more worthy of commendation than worthy of correction. Hostiensis comments : " non tamen intelligas, quod ipsi factum episcopi possint corrigere, . . . sed hoc debent Apostolicae sedi referre ".[3] In another place he speaks of Order visitors as inquiring about the acts of a visiting bishop ; not being able to revise them and correct the visitands themselves, they may report to their superiors. (. . . *Religiosi visitatores . . . qui etiam de visitatione episcoporum inquirunt . . . et tamen corrigere non possunt greges, cum inferiores sint : sed superiori denuntiant . . . Episcopi vero de visitatione religiosorum et inferiorum possunt inquirere et punire.*)[4]

By the formation of a second visitatorial system, then, the papacy had no intention of upsetting the diocesan authority where it was still exercised. Dom Berlière says, indeed, " il semble bien qu'Innocent III la considérait

---

[1] *Comment.*, III. de Sta. Mon. 7 (vol. ii. fol. 134 *verso*).
[2] *Benedictine Chapters*, I. 263–4 and C. M. Fraser, *History of Antony Bek*, ch. VII. [3] *Summa*, III. de Cens. 18 (fol. 224 *recto*).
[4] *Ibid.*, I. de Off. Archid. 5 (fol. 52 *recto*).

comme un contrepoids ou un correctif à l'intervention épiscopale " ; [1] but the Order visitation was regularized for the sake of discipline only : " iudicio meo," says Hostiensis, " plures visitatores admittuntur, ut cautius curentur animae ".[2] Honorius III wrote in 1225 to assure a bishop that the statute for provincial chapters did not diminish his jurisdiction.[3]

Papal letters and the registers of bishops provide us with some indications of the relations of bishops and visitors of the monastic Orders in theory and in practice. Archbishops and their suffragans are told to work with the Provincial Chapters and carry out depositions.[4] The diocesans of Lombardy are ordered to enforce the rulings of the Cluniac chapters in Cluniac houses.[5] The bishops of the Canterbury province are encouraged to visit and reform, saving such ordinances as are made in provincial chapters.[6] At Arbury, in his diocese, the bishop of Coventry establishes the rule of St. Augustine, removing the five dissolute Arroasian canons there dwelling : he takes action at the instance of the prior of Dunstable and his colleague, whom the pope appointed to visit the regular churches of the diocese.[7] A bishop removes an abbess at the request of the Order visitors ; [8] and the visitors of Marmoutier seek the aid of a diocesan in dealing with a disobedient monk.[9] On two occasions Archbishop Rigaud of Rouen records approvingly injunctions by visitors of the Order,[10] and Archbishop Romeyn of York discusses the state of Fountains with the Cistercian

---

[1] Berlière, *Honorius*, 252.

[2] *Summa, loc. cit.* A comparison of the methods of Order visitors and diocesans would be interesting, but it lies outside the scope of this study. A considerable body of visitation records of the exempt Orders remains to provide the needful evidence. The general procedure seems to have been the same in all essentials, though probably more stress was laid by Order visitors than by diocesans upon the economic state of houses.

[3] Honorii III, 5735.   [4] *Ibid.*, 5233, 5708, 5937.

[5] Grégoire IX, 2151.

[6] *Ibid.*, 716 (Potthast, 8947 ; *Ann. Mon.*, I. 243).

[7] Grégoire IX, 2897(*CPR*,149).   [8] *Ibid.*, 1353; cf. Honorii III, 5028.

[9] *IAD, Eure*, H. 844 (a.d. 1239).   [10] Rigaud, 516, 578.

authorities.[1] Incidentally, these examples show that the diocesan's interest in monastic reform was expected to extend to those privileged houses which were normally withdrawn from his direct control.

A note of discord is struck in the register of Bishop Godfrey Giffard of Worcester, in 1278, where we hear that the prior of Worcester has forbidden the sacrist to attend to the bishop's business, by pretext of statutes " lately unreasonably published by the president of the general Chapter of the Benedictine Order." [2] Whoever was at fault here, the presidents of the chapter certainly acted irregularly in 1301, when they relaxed the penances imposed by Archbishop Winchelsey, at his visitation, on a Worcester monk. Dr. Rose Graham surmises that as the archbishop himself absolved the monk a little later, he never heard of the action of the Benedictine authorities ; so no friction resulted from this act of interference.[3]

Archbishop Pecham more than once clashed with the monastic authorities. In 1288 he claimed that the abbey of Faversham was exempt from Order visitors, and he warned the Benedictine Chapter not to interfere ; adding insult to injury, he remarked, " many prudent men doubt whether your visitation, to be undertaken once in three years (even if it were legally your business, which we do not admit), could very well add anything fruitful to our own annual visitation." [4] In Convocation Pecham vigorously opposed the shortening of Church Services which had been ordained by the Benedictine General Chapter, and he denounced it in various injunctions.[5]

Of episcopal relations with the Augustinian Order we have not many notices. The register of Archbishop Giffard of York has three sets of injunctions for Newstead Priory. Two sets come from its diocesan, the third from

[1] Romeyn, II. 79.
[2] *Benedictine Chapters*, ed. Pantin, I. 93-4 (from Giffard, *Worc.*, f. 75).
[3] Graham, *Studies*, 344 (quoting *Worcester Liber Albus*, f. 1 *verso*).
[4] Peckham, III. 959-60. Cf. *Benedictine Chapters*, I. 133.
[5] *Ibid.*, II. lxviii.-lxxii. ; I. 82, 164, 259 ; II. 398 ; *Chronicon Petroburg.* (Camden Soc., XLVII. 1849), 100 ; *Ann. Mon.*, IV. 547 ; and see Graham, *Studies*, 338-9 ; Pantin, *Benedictine Chapters*, I. 60-1.

visitors appointed by the Augustinian General Chapter in 1261.[1] Mr. Salter comments on this, " although the visitors of the Chapter and the bishops performed the same work of visiting, they seem to have ignored each other's work, and this is the only case where there was any collaboration between them." [2] We may note that in 1303 Bishop Halton of Carlisle wrote to the York Provincial Chapter of Augustinian Canons, saying that the customs and observances of the cathedral church of Carlisle (of the Order of St. Augustine), though they differ in some respects from those of other houses of the Order, cannot be altered to the prejudice of the diocesan or without his authority.[3]

Whatever lack of harmony is noticeable in the working of diocesan and Order visitations, it was not due to a conscious policy of the popes. Whatever dispute or disorder is traceable to the existence of exempt houses, it was not the result of a papal scheme to emancipate all monasteries. The popes had bestowed privileges and were obliged to grant more ; but the increase of exemptions is not the only measure of their policy. The increase of exemptions, indeed, does not appear to belong to any disciplinary policy. It arose from the financial needs of the popes and not from a bishop-yoking scheme.[4] In this period we should expect to find the pecuniary motive at work. We see it in another department of ecclesiastical organization : the second half of the thirteenth century witnessed an enormous extension of provisions, also a factor of papal centralization. But here, as in the exemption of monasteries, the purpose of the disciplinary measure was financial.[5] The papacy centralized the

---

[1] Giffard, *York*, 212 *sqq.*

[2] H. E. Salter, *Chapters of the Augustinian Canons* (Oxford Historical Society and Canterbury and York Society, 1922), xxiii.   [3] Halton, I. 181.

[4] On the cost of exemption see Jocelin, 7, 84 ; and for further examples, Snape, 102-4. It is true that the rapacity of certain bishops was sometimes a reason for restricting their jurisdiction. But Richard, Archbishop of Canterbury, who mentions this cause, dismisses it as unimportant (Migne, *Patrol. Latina*, CC. 1459).

[5] Cf. Berlière, *Inventaire des* Libri Obligationum, *etc.* (Rome, 1904), viii.

organization of the Church for financial purposes ; but it did so at a time when the forms of local government were taking shape. The diocesan administration which thirteenth century records reveal was a system too strong and too valuable to be swept away. In the work of monastic reform, therefore, the papacy looked to diocesan visitation as a constant, if a subordinate, instrument.

[1] As a matter of fact, Mr. Salter observes, " the standard of episcopal work became higher rather than lower in the thirteenth and fourteenth centuries, and it was the episcopal visitation, not the monastic visitation, which was carried out with most strictness and was most feared " (*Aug. Chap.*, xliii.).

CHAPTER III.

THE METHOD OF EPISCOPAL VISITATION IN THE THIRTEENTH CENTURY.

WHEREAS the episcopal and monastic records for the fifteenth century are so detailed as to make a description of visitation procedure easy, to see how the system worked in the thirteenth century we have to gather together slight indications from all sides and make up a composite picture which cannot be had from any single narrative. This variety of material, while it denies us the power of precise generalization, gives us a much wider knowledge than we could acquire from documents more stereotyped in form, or records less varying in content. Because references to the visitation system are scanty in the *Corpus Iuris*, we must not suppose that the system had only a slight legal basis. Nor can we assume that the divergences of procedure were as wide as those in the records of procedure. No argument *ex silentio* will suffice to prove that a system adopted in several dioceses did not exist in others. The fact that we have no complete picture of the visitatorial system in any one set of thirteenth-century records both forces us to infer from likeness and justifies us in so doing. We argue from the records of many dioceses to find a common system; for diocesan government was sufficiently advanced in the thirteenth century to make some such system possible and even indispensable. A survey of the papal registers shows this. We may occasionally be directed from the usual by peculiar customs ; but we are more often likely to benefit from a synthesis of various records. It is the only means of obtaining a picture of this part of episcopal administration. For this purpose the English sources are by far the most productive, while Continental records serve to confirm what we learn of English practice in the thirteenth century.

As a prelude to visitation, a bishop customarily sent a warning letter to the visitands. It was important for the success of the visit as a work of inspection that the head of the house and the other obedientiaries should be present. When the bishop of Winchester granted leave of absence to the abbot of Chertsey for a year, the bishop's rights of visitation and correction were safeguarded— "que propter vestri absenciam impediri nolumus etiam vel retardari." [1] This suggests that a visit was not in order unless the head of the house attended. About the same time, Rigaud of Rouen, though he did sometimes visit in the absence of heads, once remarks, "non potuimus visitare propter absentiam prioris," [2] and on other occasions found difficulty in visiting for the same reason (" parum enim potuimus ibi tunc facere, pro eo quod non erat ibi abbatissa " [3]). It is certain that the practice of forewarning prevailed in the dioceses of York, [4] Worcester [5] and Winchester [6]; there is an example in the Salisbury register of Simon of Ghent [7] and others in the registers of Pecham and Winchelsey. [8]

Though we have many references to these warning letters, not many survive from the thirteenth century. Probably no exact formula was maintained; for from the York registers we may quote several entirely dissimilar in wording over the space of only eleven years. Archbishop

---

[1] Pontissara, I, 262-3.   [2] Rigaud, 426; cf. *infra* 58.
[3] *Ibid.*, 575; cf. 78 and *Grenoble Visitations*, 37, 40, 41, 85 (parish priests), 38, 46 (priors).
[4] Giffard, *York*, 302; Wickwane, 2, 20, 22, 28, 54, 79, 97, 98, 127, 153, 312; Romeyn, I. 51, 53, 54, 55, 67, 71, 72, 104, 108, 139, 151, 160, 162, 177, 192, 199, 223, 242, 254, 297, 320, 350; II. 221, 237, 321; Corbridge, I. 30, 42, 50, 52, 53, 76, 108, 112, 123, 125, 145, 154, 163, 174, 198, 210, 261; II. 172.
[5] Giffard, *Worc.*, II. 157, 201, 231, 378, 529; *Chron. Evesham*, 109.
[6] Pontissara, I. 112, 295, 327.   [7] Gandavo, 101.
[8] Peckham, I. 61; Winchelsey, 68.

Giffard wrote to Bolton Priory in 1275 in the following terms : "W., etc., dilectis in Cristo filiis, priori et conventui de Boulton in Cravene, salutem, etc. Quia intendimus et ex causa, Domino disponente, nonis Octobris vestrum tam in capite quam in membris monasterium visitare, et super quibusdam articulis inquirere, ac ulterius facere ut jus erit, vobis mandamus, firmiter injungentes, quatinus omnes concanonicos vestros et conversos faciatis premissis, ut convenit, interesse." [1] Following this is a list of articles on matters for inquiry at Bolton (" intendit dominus archiepiscopus inquirere an Willelmus Hog, prior de Boulton, conjurans aut conspirans fuerit . . ." etc.) ; these are on the dorse of the membrane and may simply be memoranda for the archbishop's private use. In 1286 John le Romeyn, writing to the nunnery of Sinningthwaite, employed a different formula : " Quia intendimus per Dei graciam die Mercurii . . . vos in capitulo vestro de Syningthweit, ad recreacionem animarum vestrarum, personaliter intueri, ac visitacionis et inquisicionis officium apud vos paternis affectibus exercere, vobis tenore presencium injungimus et mandamus quatinus omnes et singule dicto die nobis personas vestras ibidem et votivam presenciam pretendatis, nostra salubria monita, correcciones, et injuncta debita et devota reverencia recepturi, ex quibus fructum Altissimus producat placidum, qui vobis utinam proficiat, sicut pie cupimus, ad salutem. Valete." [2] This form was often used, but in one instance the archbishop prefixed a regretful explanation of his visit to the priory of Thurgarton : the immense deformity of their way of life and the scandal thence arising have decided him to make a personal visit. [3]

Between the letters of Giffard and Romeyn comes a summons of Wickwane to the prior and chapter of Durham, to admit him to a metropolitical visitation. This is in yet another and a more elaborate form. Here a new element occurs : " Vota, igitur, que debite conceperitis in hac parte, nobis per litteras vestras patentes, harum seriem continentes, unacum die recepcionis pre-

---

[1] Giffard, *York*, 302.   [2] Romeyn, I. 51.   [3] *Ibid.*, I. 242.

sencium, citra instans festum Annunciacionis Beate Virginis, sub vinculo et virtute obediencie, evidencius rescribatis." [1] The object of this clause and the demand for a certificate was presumably to prevent contestation of the visitor's rights upon his arrival. At the attempted episcopal visitation of Durham in 1300 the certificate was to be sent to the visitor before the day appointed for visitation.[2] On the other hand, when notices were sent to Canterbury Cathedral Priory in 1296,[3] and Reading Abbey in 1302,[4] the certificate was to be presented to the visitor in the chapter-house. This also was the practice of later times.[5]

The letter of notice which is preserved in Winchelsey's register is reproduced in a document which Wilkins printed " ex registro Henrici, prioris Cantuar." [6] The document is the very certificate presented by the convent at the time of visitation, in accordance with the terms of the archbishop's notice. It is a formal record, of a type well represented in later sources but rare among thirteenth-century remains. It runs as follows : " Venerabili in Christo patri, domino R. Dei gratia Cantuar. archiepiscopo, totius Angliae primati, devoti filii H. prior, et capitulum ecclesiae Christi Cantuar. salutem, et tam debitam, quam devotam in omnibus obedientiam, reverentiam, et honorem. Mandatum vestrum 17. calend. Februarii suscepimus, tenorem continens subsequentem. " Robertus, [. . . etc."] Quod quidem mandatum vestrum juxta tenorem ejusdem in omnibus sumus executi. Datum in capitulo nostro non. Februarii, anno Dom. supradicto."

The usual form of notice used by Simon of Bourges is given by his chronicler.[7] It is brief and peremptory, and asks for no certificate of receipt. Nor, in the elaborate accounts of the archbishop's reception in religious houses, do we read that a certificate was produced.

[1] Wickwane, 155.
[2] *Gesta Dunelm.*, 2 n. 3 ; cf. Giffard, *Worc.*, f. 181 *verso*.
[3] Winchelsey, 69.   [4] Gandavo, 101.   [5] *Linc. Visit.*, II. lxii.
[6] Wilkins, *Concilia*, II. 217 (Cambridge, Univ. Libr. MS. Ee. 5. 31).
Cf. *infra*, 60.   [7] Baluze-Mansi, I, 306b, 307a.

In spite of many indications of the practice of giving notice, bishops occasionally paid surprise visits. On the 5th September, 1284, Oliver, Bishop of Lincoln, visited Peterborough Abbey " nulla premunicione facta." [1] One passage in Archbishop Corbridge's register (which contains many records of notice sent) suggests this : " Mem. quod dominus transiens de Harewod' versus Otteley declinavit apud moniales de Ardington' et ibidem excercuit tunc officium visitacionis." [2] This is not the usual form of entry in Corbridge's register, and no notice of the visitation is recorded. In contemporary Normandy we should expect to find abundant evidence on the matter in Rigaud's register. But nothing certain emerges. We note that in his diocese he visited religious houses seventeen times in the absence of the head. This in itself suggests that his visits were unheralded. The presumption is strengthened by the fact that on one of these occasions he remarked : " displicuit nobis multum quod prior tunc se absentavit, quem quidem credebamus adventum nostrum prescivisse." [3] This looks like an exception. There is also an interesting entry of a visitation of S.-Etienne près Hacqueville, which was undertaken " occasionaliter." [4]

When notice was given, the visitation might be fixed for a day soon after the despatch of letters. Disorderly monasteries often had little time to settle their quarrels or make up their accounts. Simon of Bourges wrote on a Tuesday to the abbey of Angles to announce his arrival on the following Sunday.[5] The warning allowed by Archbishop Corbridge varied from eight weeks to a day ; [6] most frequently it was less than a week. The bishop of Durham gave twenty-four days' notice to his cathedral priory in 1300.[7]

---

[1] *Chronicon Petroburgense* (Camden Soc., XLVII. 1849), 96.

[2] Corbridge, I, 94.

[3] Rigaud, 536. When the archbishop of Bordeaux visited Comblet in 1305, the prior " s'en estant fuy et cache " could not be found on the day appointed. Next day he appeared, submitted and was pardoned (Rabanis, 174).   [4] Rigaud, 530.   [5] Baluze-Mansi, I. 267b.

[6] Corbridge, I. 123, 53.   [7] *Gesta Dunelm.*, 2.

On the day appointed the bishop presented himself
with his retinue at the monastery, to be received rever-
ently by the inmates in procession,[1] and conducted by
them to the chapter-house, where a sermon was preached
before the disciplinary work began.[2] Either before or
after the sermon which was usually given, the head of the
house would present his certificate, if one had been
demanded.

We cannot tell from extant documents whether the
order of events was as systematized as it came to be in the
fifteenth century.[3] We can, however, get a general impression of the procedure from the summaries contained
in certain records. The earliest of the sort is that of
Bishop Hugh de Welles of Lincoln—which has the
additional interest of being the only reference to a
visitation in the rolls of his episcopate. It runs : " Anno
pontificatus domini Honorii tertii quarto, duodecimo
Kalendas Iunii, dominus H. Lincolniensis Episcopus,
veniens apud Prioratum Tikeford extra Neuporte causa
visitationis ibidem faciende, hospitio ibi honorifice et cum
processione sollempni susceptus est eo die, et in crastino,
scilicet, die Veneris, prout moris est, in capitulo facto
sermone ad fratres, officium suum libere et sine contra-
dictione executus, presentibus J. Archidiacono Bede-
fordiense . . . [etc., eight others named] et aliis." [4]
From the annals of Dunstable we learn that Welles's
successor Grosseteste, when visiting monasteries, arch-
deaconries and deaneries in 1238, held general chapters
in each, preached and promulgated statutes.[5]

The fullest account of actual proceedings in the
thirteenth century concerns Canterbury.[6] It describes

---

[1] *Acta* of Simon of Bourges, *passim ;* Rigaud, 307 ; Welles, II. 51 ;
Lanercost, 25.

[2] At S.-Etienne près Hacqueville Archbishop Rigaud examined the
monks " in quadam camera dicti loci," probably because they had no
chapter-house (Rigaud, 530).

[3] Cf. *Linc. Visit.*, I. and II. Introductions ; Coulton, *Five Centuries,*
II. 232 *sqq.*

[4] Welles, II. 51. The exemption of Tickford, a priory of Marmoutier,
was declared in 1290 (*VCH Bucks.*, I. 362).

[5] *Ann. Mon.*, III. 147.　　[6] Winchelsey, I. 68–9, II. 1303–4.

the visitation of Canterbury cathedral by Archbishop Winchelsey in 1296—a visit of which there are other records in the archbishop's and the prior's registers. As it is fairly detailed and precise, it will be useful to present an analysis of it before proceeding to the collection of scattered evidence from other sources.

On the 15th January 1296 the archbishop sent notice of the impending visitation from Godmersham. This was received by the convent on the following day. He proposed to visit on the Monday (6th February) following the feast of the Purification, and ordered a certificate of receipt of this notice to be presented to him then. On the appointed day the archbishop entered the chapter-house and preached (" prout moris est "). Then he ordered all secular persons to leave the building, excepting only his official, his chancellor and his *cruciferarius*. In their presence the certificate of receipt of notice was read.[1]

" Then the archbishop said that he wished to visit the chapter and examine each brother in the presence of the said clerks, and declared that he had a special privilege of Pope Innocent on this matter, which he caused to be read to the brethren and the said clerks. This stated that the archbishop of Canterbury is entitled to visit the chapter in the presence of his clergy. But the chapter caused to be read the rules of archbishops Theobald and St. Thomas and the privileges of popes relative to these rules, which contained the contrary [to Winchelsey's claim] . . . At length, after much altercation on the matter, the aforesaid three clerks, at the command of the archbishop, left the chapter-house." The archdeacon of Middlesex was introduced, however, and also John de Wy, the archbishop's chaplain. In their presence the archbishop examined singly the prior and two brethren, and by common consent the archdeacon wrote down their depositions. This examination only touched on such topics as concerned the community as a whole (*quae communem statum ecclesiae*

---

[1] Cf. Adam de Domerham, ed. T. Hearne (Oxford, 1727), I. 271 a.d. 1313). Cf. I. J. Churchill, *Canterbury Administration*, I. 140–1.

contingebant). When it was completed the archdeacon withdrew, by the consent of archbishop and chapter, and the visitor examined each monk on matters relative to persons, his chaplain writing down their depositions. This apparently ended the business of the day.

A month later, on the 5th March, the archbishop entered the chapter-house and summoned the prior, sub-prior, precentor, penitentiary, cellarer, almoner and *custos feretri*. He made corrections and enjoined penances, beginning with the juniors and ending with the prior, to whom he handed a memorandum of the complaints (*copiam objectorum*). Thereupon the prior replied orally to these complaints, and as a result the inquiry was carried farther with regard to some of them. Concerning brethren who were defamed, the archbishop inquired by six or eight of the convent and acted according to their depositions. Where there was no pre-existing *infamia*, but only the presumption of guilt, the visitor made these suspect brethren purge themselves with three or with six compurgators.

This ended the proceedings,[1] and Winchelsey stopped his visitations temporarily because of the outbreak of war between the English and French kings.

Curiously enough, we have another circumstantial account of Winchelsey's methods—this time in the metropolitan visitation of a secular chapter. On a blank leaf of a book of synodal statutes which once belonged to Chichester cathedral,[2] a contemporary wrote a short description of the archbishop's visitation at Chichester on 12th December, 1299. After the visitor had been received at the city gate by the dean and canons, and greeted by

[1] Undated injunctions in Winchelsey's register (91–3) may be the fruit of this visit. On 28 Aug. 1298 the archbishop addressed a mandate to the monks requiring obedience to temporary injunctions he had made after visitation, which may refer to this (Winchelsey, 280, 1314 ; HMCR Var. Coll. I. 262, dated in error 1297). A long series of injunctions consequent on visitation were sent to the convent on 15 Dec. 1298 (Winchelsey, II. 813–27).

[2] Univ. Coll., Oxon, MS. 148, f. 193, printed in Winchelsey, II. 1306–7.

the bishop at the cathedral with all due ceremony, which is here carefully described, he entered the church. After prayer and blessing of the people, he entered the chapter-house.

Here, as at Canterbury, he delivered a sermon, and his text was from the book of Esdras : " Missus es ut visites Iudeam et Ierusalem " (1 Esdras vii. 14). When the sermon was finished all were excluded from the building besides Winchelsey and his household clerks, the bishop, the dean, and the canons and vicars. The arch-bishop then ordered the certificate of receipt of notice to be read, and then had the recent constitution of Boniface VIII *Quia plerique* recited.[1] Following this came the excommunication of impeders.[2] Then the visitor with-drew with the bishop alone into the treasury, and examined him individually and secretly on many and various *articuli*.

The many fragments of evidence we possess to supple-ment these narratives are consistent with the supposition that Winchelsey's proceedings show the normal stages of an episcopal visitation. In some small priories the visita-tion was no doubt more perfunctory and shorn of cere-monies. Rarely was a visitor in a position to spread his inquiry over a month, as Winchelsey did at Canterbury.

The records of visitations naturally lay most stress upon the legal rights of visitors and their disciplinary work. But it would be wrong to judge the matter merely by mass of evidence. Visitation was undertaken as a pastoral duty, and the good pastor was supposed to teach as well as to correct. The historian finds fewer traces of teaching than of correction, because for administrative purposes only the latter needed to be recorded. Just as

---

[1] As directed in the preamble to the articles, Winchelsey, II. 1290. The constitution nullified all promises to conceal defects (*Sext*, I. xvi. 4). Cf. *infra*, 87.

[2] " Fecit legi cedulam quandam continentem quod monuit omnes et singulos ut super defectibus quos noverint in personis vel in officiis seu in rebus quibuscunque ad ecclesiam pertinentibus meram et liberam patefacerent veritatem sub pena excommunicacionis quam in scriptis promulgavit."

confirmations rarely appear in Archbishop Rigaud's register in the records of parochial visitations, so we seldom hear of his sermons in monasteries before the year 1257, when the scribe began to record them. Nevertheless the obligation to preach was definitely laid down in all legislation for visitors; some few visitation sermons have come down to us from the thirteenth century, and many more texts and references to preaching.

Sermons figure in the accounts given above of proceedings at Canterbury and Chichester. In the province of Rouen there are references to 147 sermons preached during the last twelve years of Archbishop Rigaud's visitations, and the sermon was a regular part of Simon of Bourges' procedure. At S.-Jean-d'Angély, Archbishop Simon preached in the chapter-house " to the clergy and people, both in French and Latin, the lord bishop of Saintes and a crowd of clerks and layfolk being present." [1] At Clermont he preached in Latin before his inquiry, and later had a sermon delivered to the populace in the vernacular.[2] Bertrand, Archbishop of Bordeaux, later Pope Clement V, had sermons preached at his visitations.[3] We have mention of preaching at visitations of Leominster in 1276 and 1283,[4] and on many of Godfrey Giffard's diocesan visitations between 1282 and 1291.[5] The Worcester register frequently gives the text of the bishop's sermon; at Pershore in 1282 it was " Take away the dross from the silver " (Prov. xxv. 4) ;[6] at Great Malvern, where the prior was evil-living and notorious, " I will come

---

[1] Baluze-Mansi, I. 271b.   [2] Ibid., 279b.

[3] Rabanis, 154-99 passim.   [4] Cantilupe, 116 ; Swinfield, 15.

[5] In the light of a letter giving notice of visitation of Lanthony Priory (probably in Bishop Giffard's time), we cannot be sure that it was always the bishop or his staff who preached. For here the visitor writes : " quia non solum decet sed expedit ut verbi Dei proposicio preambula sit premissis [correccionibus], vos, prior, de succincto ob temporis brevitatem provideatis sermone in vestro capitulo proponendo." If occupied, the prior is to give the task to one of his brethren, otherwise " nobis dumtaxat ipsum predicandi ministerium reservetur." This letter is preserved in a letter-book of Lanthony Priory, Corpus Christi College, Oxon, MS. 154, p. 386.

[6] Giffard, Worc., II. 164, and 233, 234, 235, 236, 244.

and descend upon you." [1]   For nunneries Bishop Giffard's favourite text was from Ecclesiasticus (vii. 26), "Hast thou daughters ? Give heed to their body, and make not thy face cheerful toward them "—the phrase which Abbot Samson quoted with such effect to Jocelin of Brakelond.[2] The bishop of Carlisle preached at Lanercost in 1280 on the text, " Behold, I myself shall require." [3]   In the following year, when he was assaulted at Durham, Archbishop Wickwane preached on what is apparently a modification of 1 Esdras vii. 14, the text taken by Winchelsey at Chichester.[4]

These texts of sermons suggest that the preachers did not depart from the subject of visitation. The discourses that have been preserved complete show the same exclusive attention to the business to follow. A British Museum manuscript has a long homily on the texts " Vide et visita vineam istam " and " Videant et recogitent et intelligant " ; [5] it draws on the prophets and Gratian and the Decretals of Gregory IX, to prove the right of the visitor to visit, his right to fees, the duties of priors and abbots, and the whole *materia* of visitations. Instruction there is, but only such as is strictly relevant to the business which is to follow. The visitands must have proceeded to the bishop's inquiry with a proper sense of the importance of the visitor and of the necessity for the confession of their faults.

Many outsiders might throng the chapter-house to hear the visitation sermon ; but while this was allowable, the building certainly had to be cleared of secular persons before the actual process of inquiry began. We have seen that this happened at Canterbury in 1296 and Chichester in 1299 ; a passage in Graystanes' history of Durham shows

[1] Giffard, *Worc.*, II. 164.
[2] *Ibid.*, II. 234, 244, 246 ; Jocelin, 54.   [3] *Lanercost*, 25.
[4] Guisborough gives the text as " Descendi ut viderem Iudeam et Ierusalem." The editor of Wickwane's register cannot trace this in the Vulgate (Wickwane, ix. note 5).
[5] Royal MS. 8, F. IX. f. 73. The texts are from Psalm lxxix. (A.V. lxxx.) and Isaiah ch. xli. (modified). The first text is also the theme of a sermon in Magdalen Coll., Oxon, MS. 168 (13-14th century).

the same procedure : " mandat Archiepiscopus [Giffard] visitationem suam in capitulo Dunelmensi . . . faciendam ; quo die correctis in capitulo corrigendis, Archiepiscopus cum suis, et omnibus intrare volentibus, capitulum intravit ; finitoque sermone, iniunxit, tam suis, quam omnibus aliis, ut exirent. Remanenteque eo solo, et qui erant de capitulo, dixit se venisse ad visitandum et corrigendum ea quae fuerunt corrigenda." [1] We can quote a passage almost exactly parallel from the register of Rigaud : " Predicavimus inter claustrum et capitulum Sancti Victoris in Caleto, presentibus monachis dicti loci et magna parte parrochianorum ville inibi congregata. Oratione facta, per Dei gratiam, remansimus in capitulo cum conventu, et visitationis officium exercuimus ut decuit, Domino adiuvante." [2] Thus also Simon of Bourges preached in the chapter-house at Clermont : " post sermonem Canonicis tantum in capitulo cum domino remanentibus, visitavit dominus." [3]

The intrusion of outsiders at the inquiry was, however, fairly common. Corbridge thought fit to denounce the custom in his letters of notice to certain monasteries : " We and our clerks propose to spend the day concerned simply with your common good and not with other matters. We therefore firmly order you all, in virtue of obedience and under canonical penalties, that you issue no invitation for that day to strangers and outsiders, who might hinder us in our duty ; such invitations have been given on similar occasions both in our own time and the times of our predecessors with no small expense to the house and impediment to the visitors." [4] At Worcester in 1290 the bishop was actually interrupted, in the midst of his inquiry, by the onset of the prior and others of the house with " Peter de Pinton, Geoffrey de Northwico, Walter de Lodeford, Robert Pet, and many other seculars ".[5] Here the prior was appealing against the

---

[1] Script. Tres, 56.
[2] Rigaud, 617 ; cf. 307-8 (the sermon was delivered in the church).
[3] Baluze-Mansi, I. 279b.   [4] Corbridge, I. 76 ; cf. 112, 145, 261.
[5] Giffard, Worc., II. 380 ; cf. 387.

bishop's visitation, but the manner of the appeal was obviously irregular and the interrupters incurred sentence of excommunication for impeding the visitor.

It is possible that this penalty was regularly proclaimed after the bishop's sermon, as at Worcester in 1284.[1] A form of excommunication issued by Archbishop Pecham is given in his register : " In omnes illos qui visitationem nostram praesentem seu jurisdictionem Cantuariensis ecclesiae in visitatione praesenti impediunt indebite vel perturbant, vel jura nobis seu eidem ecclesiae Cantuariensi debita de consuetudine vel de jure subtrahere moliuntur, aut in damnum vel jacturam nostram seu ecclesiae nostrae Cantuariensis aliqua machinantur, excommunicationis sententiam proferimus in hiis scriptis." [2]

Complaints against the presence of seculars at visitations are made most often by the visitands. Monasteries usually, and the Church authorities always, tried to stop the dissemination of scandal and the leakage of monastery secrets through the *familia* of visiting bishops. Popes and councils were obliged to order not only that the bishop's retinue should be kept within reasonable limits—that was a matter of economy—but also that the bishop should not introduce seculars into the chapter-house during his inquiry.

No general legislation on the matter occurred in the thirteenth century, but papal pronouncements were fairly consistent. Thus Honorius III bade the archbishop of Reims, when visiting the abbey of S.-Remi, take no seculars besides two or three canons of his church, " viris aliis quot expedire viderit religiosis, adiunctis ".[3] As this judgment was inserted in Gregory IX's Decretals,[4] we suppose that it had a general application. Nevertheless, other individual houses secured like mandates for themselves. The abbey of St. Benet Holme obtained from

---

[1] Giffard, *Worc.*, II. 243.

[2] Peckham, I. 161-2 ; cf. I. 147, 200-1 ; Wilkins, II. 47 ; Grégoire IX, 4257 ; Adam de Domerham, ed. Hearne (Oxford, 1727), I. 271 ; F. X. Remling, *Urkundenbuch der Bischöfe zu Speyer* (1852), I. 429 ; and *infra*, 83.

[3] Honorii III, 1796 (Potthast, 5962).   [4] *Decretales*, I. xxxi. 17.

Pope Urban (? IV) that visiting bishops or archbishops should never introduce more seculars than two or three of their canons—" aliis quot expedire viderint religiosis adiunctis ".[1] Honorius IV ordered the archbishop of Canterbury to observe the same limit in visiting the Augustinian nunnery of Canonsleigh (diocese of Exeter).[2] Nicholas IV wrote to the bishop of Coventry after complaint by the priory of " Kemllewich " that he has visited with clerks and other seculars grievous to the house, telling him to take only two or three canons of his church " aliis quot expedire videris religiosis adjunctis." [3] The same pope, however, prohibited the archbishop of Canterbury from introducing seculars into the chapter-house at Worcester,[4] and both Gregory IX and Innocent IV had conceded like privileges to nunneries.[5] But total prohibitions such as these were exceptional.

A peculiar ruling governed the method of visitation at Worcester Priory after 1224. In that year, after a long quarrel between bishop and monks, the archbishop of Canterbury, as arbitrator, decided that the bishop might bring only his clerks into the chapter when he was going to discuss spiritual matters, but might be accompanied by seculars when the temporal affairs of the priory were in question. The pope confirmed this arrangement.[6]

When the monks of Coventry appealed against their bishop's visitation in 1235 one of their complaints was against the introduction of secular and suspect persons.[7] The final agreement of bishop and convent in 1283 settled the matter thus : the bishop should come into the chapter-house attended by two or three of his secular clerks, and two other scribes sworn to him, or else by monks, according to his pleasure.[8] A rather similar ruling

[1] Dugdale, III. 91.   [2] Honorius IV, 632.
[3] Nicolas IV, 2685.   [4] Ibid., 2714.
[5] Grégoire IX, 2393 ; Innocent IV, 642 (two or three religious allowed).
[6] Registrum Prioratus B.M. Wigorniensis (Camden Soc., XCI. 1865), 29a, 37b, cf. 137b. [7] Grégoire IX, 2197, 2902, 2957 (CPR, 141, 150).
[8] Magnum Registrum Album of Lichfield (ed. Wm. Salt Soc., 1926), 305, cf. 143, 224, 343–4, and supra, 34.

was obtained by the abbey of St. Mary's, York, from Pope Urban IV (1262). The abbey had appealed to him against the introduction of secular clerks : " Considering that it is improper for seculars (whose presence may bring laxity in the cloister) to be present when the aforesaid archbishop visits in this monastery, we firmly forbid the archbishop to introduce into the chapter of the aforesaid monastery, on the occasion of future visitations, any seculars beyond two or three canons of his church, suitably attired, together with such regulars as he shall think fit." [1] This judgment recalls the history of the origin of Fountains Abbey. In 1132 Archbishop Thurstan visited St. Mary's, York, and certain monks seceded : on this occasion the abbot withstood the visitation on the pretext that Thurstan was not allowed to introduce seculars. Thurstan, in a letter to the archbishop of Canterbury, states who were in his retinue : the dean, the treasurer, the archdeacon, three other canons, including his chaplain, the prior of Guisborough and Robert, a priest of the hospital.[2] Thurstan declared that he was entitled to have such company, and we know of no contrary order at this early date.

At Durham in 1300 the bishop attempted to visit his chapter " cum multitudine tam laicorum quam clericorum secularium ac regularium alterius ordinis copiosa, tibi [sc. priori] et capitulo memoratis iniuncxit, ut ipsum ad exercendum huiusmodi visitationem admitteretis presentibus clericis et laicis praelibatis." [3] The prior and convent complained that they would not admit the bishop with this crowd, but he might visit them, as was

---

[1] Romeyn, I. 73 ; Corbridge, I. 31 note. This modified the judgment of Honorius III (1226), which allowed the archbishop five or six canons for company (Honorii III, 5850, 6254 ; CPR, 108, 116 ; Gray, 152 ; Romeyn, I. 73). The abbey chronicle (MS. Bodley, 39) and the archbishops' registers show that this limitation was carefully observed.

[2] Memorials of the Abbey of . . . Fountains (Surtees Soc., 1863), I. 8, 24-5.

[3] Boniface VIII, 4296 (CPR, 603) ; Gesta Dunelm., 4 sqq. (the prior's version) ; Guisborough, Chronicle (ed. H. Rothwell, 1957), 346–51 and Records of Antony Bek (ed. C. M. Fraser, 1953).

customary, by himself. The bishop excommunicated the convent, appointed a pseudo-prior, sequestrated the monastery's property and seized its servants. The archbishop of York had intervened without success. Finally, in 1302, the Pope gave a ruling that the bishop should take with him " in visitationis actu, duas vel tres honestas personas, clericali caractere insignatas, quarum una ad minus sit religiosa ordinis supradicti, et unum notarium . . . et non plures." [1] Curiously enough, we see an outcome of this pronouncement in the account of Gainsborough's primary visitation of Worcester (1303) contained in the *Liber Albus*. " His clerks and ours, ' writes the monastic scribe, " discussed a certain new constitution which the pope had recently put forth, respecting the entrance of a bishop for making a visitation. And since it was doubted whether that decretal was common or special, general or local, the Prior made protest that he would admit him on that occasion with two clerks and one notary, always, however, saving our composition if that constitution was not general. ' The Bishop made a like protest ; and the clerks who entered and were with the Bishop in the said visitation were Master Walter of Wotton, Archdeacon of Huntingdon, Master John of Rodborough, and Master John Caleys, notary public." [2]

But these restrictions were not everywhere observed when no protest was made. The passage quoted above from the rolls of Hugh de Welles [3] shows a large number of outsiders present : this was in 1220. A generation later Robert Grosseteste came with a crowd of seculars to Ramsey Abbey, where he made searching examination, but found little amiss.[4] In 1276 Cantilupe visited Leominster Priory " et fuerunt presentes dictis die et loco in visitacione predicta " thirty-three seculars, mentioned by name.[5] Seven years later Bishop Swinfield visited the same house ; besides two officials actually helping him in examination " there were many others

---

[1] Boniface VIII, 4730 (*Extravag. Commun.*, I. vii. 1) ; cf. 3741, 4296 (*CPR*, 589, 597, 603).   [2] *Worcester Liber Albus*, 36.
[3] *Supra*, 59.   [4] Matt. Paris, V. 226-7.   [5] Cantilupe, 117.

present at the said visitation," consisting of the abbot
of Wigmore, thirteen others who were possibly secular
clerks, eight laymen " et quamplures alii." [1] Rigaud's
register rarely throws light on the attendance at his
visitations. When he visited the secular chapter of S.-
Mellon, Pontoise, in 1259, the archbishop took with him
a canon of Rouen, a friar minor and two clerks.[2] When
he secretly admonished the abbot of Jumièges after his
visitation in 1267, it was in the presence of the archdeacon
of Grand-Caux, a canon of Rouen, two friars and a clerk.[3]
At Corneville in the same year the complaints of a monk
against the abbot were witnessed by the archdeacon of
Petit-Caux, a canon of Rouen, the priors of Bourg-
Achard and Pontaudemer, two friars, and four clerks.[4]

Even when the bishop kept within specially prescribed
limits, we see that he was allowed two or three assistants.
For a thorough visitation was a long process. The conscientious visitor examined several monks, if not all, and
put to them a formidable number of questions. Clearly,
the work was too arduous for one man. If a visitor undertook the task alone in a large community he would probably leave it uncompleted. Before his visitation of his
cathedral priory in 1281, Archbishop Pecham wrote to
the convent ordering that (to save time) the depositions
of each monk should be written down beforehand ; then
when he came on visitation they could be read to him in
the chapter-house " so that we may be saved labour, and
your wishes for reforming the house satisfied without
delay." [5] When Archbishop Giffard visited Durham he
conducted the inquiry himself (*remanenteque eo solo, et qui
erant de capitulo*) ; the result was that only five or six
witnesses were examined.[6] At Carlisle, in 1300, all the
canons were not called upon to give evidence. The bishop
inquired as to the state of the house " according to the
depositions of certain canons of the monastery, duly
examined." [7] On the other hand, when Archbishop
Winchelsey visited Worcester Cathedral in 1300 " priorem

---

[1] Swinfield, 15.   [2] Rigaud, 344.   [3] *Ibid.*, 584.   [4] *Ibid.*, 579.
[5] Peckham, I. 226.   [6] *Script. Tres*, 56.   [7] Halton, I. 120.

personaliter et caeteros monachos per suos clericos visitavit." [1]

But the saving of time was not the only reason for bringing seculars into the visitation. In giving judgment in the Durham case mentioned above, Pope Boniface VIII explains his reasons for allowing the bishop to introduce one or more seculars and a notary.[2] He disapproves the contrary custom for three reasons. In the first place, the removal of witnesses " contra communem utilitatem, facultatem probationum, que non est angustanda, restringit." Secondly, it is a slight to the bishop if he is denied those companions who are intended to enhance his dignity. Finally, his dignity is diminished if he is forced " to trust himself alone among persons perchance suspect, as often as he visits them." For the support of his first argument he adduces the need of witnesses and the need (for which the Fourth Lateran Council made provision [3]) of a person to record legal proceedings in writing. Regulars are not allowed by law to appear as witnesses (" propter eorum professionem, que illorum vocem facit funestam, et ipsos arcet a iudiciis et publicis sive civilibus actibus ") ; and they may not do the work of a notary, both because of the contrary enactment and because it is suggested that they would not write down faithfully and truly what they found amiss concerning themselves or the prior and chapter to which they belong. Notaries were not always employed in visitations as a result of this rule : and in their absence their place could be taken, according to the Lateran Council, by " duo viri idonei." Scribes are mentioned in the Coventry agreement.[4]

The bishop's authority ordinarily allowed him to inquire on all topics relating to the temporal wealth of the house and the spiritual welfare of its inmates. The

---

[1] Annales Wigorniae, *Ann. Mon.*, IV. 548.

[2] Boniface VIII, 4730. A notary was present at the visitation of the hospital at Meaux in 1291, and drew up a record of the proceedings (Toussaints Du Plessis, *Histoire de l'église de Meaux* (1731), II. 188).

[3] Article 38. Leclercq-Hefele, V. 1363-4 ; *Decretales*, II. xix. 11.

[4] *Supra*, 67.

substance of his usual inquiry may be found equally well in the comprehensive statutes for the Benedictines which Gregory IX promulgated in 1235 and 1237,[1] in the articles of inquiry for religious houses recorded by the Burton annalist *s.a.* 1259,[2] and in the scattered material which was the outcome of actual inquiries. The close relations of papal statutes, visitors' articles and visitors' injunctions will be easily comprehended when we say that all of the following matters for inquiry find their place not only in the Gregorian statutes and the Burton articles, but also occur repeatedly in the injunctions recorded in Archbishop Rigaud's register.

The visitor asks whether the revenues of the house are properly inscribed and whether accounts are presented to the community ; he asks what pensions or corrodies are granted, and has a balance-sheet set before him. He inquires after the conduct of officials. He inquires whether any monks are stationed alone in priories ; whether alms and hospitality are maintained at a proper standard, and whether the infirm are cared for. The visitor also inquires whether the Church services are performed with due solemnity and regularity. Among the multitude of matters concerning discipline, he asks whether the abbot conforms with the conventual life ; whether the refectory is neglected ; and whether the precincts are closed or whether monks go overmuch abroad. He looks for simoniacal and proprietary monks ; for murmurers and monks ill-famed of incontinence. Finally, he asks whether statutes and injunctions are read at frequent intervals. These are only a small number of the matters out of which a visitor might compose his questionnaire. They suffice to show the comprehensiveness of the inquiry.

The " articles of inquiry in religious houses " which occur in the *Burton Annals* were perhaps used generally by the bishop of Coventry.[3] Some such set of questions

---

[1] Grégoire IX, 3045 ; also in slightly varying forms in Rigaud, 643 *sqq. ;* Matt. Paris, VI. 235.   [2] *Ann. Mon.*, I. 484-6.

[3] There seems no certain proof that they are episcopal articles. Other visitors might inquire on all the same subjects. Nevertheless, the question

would be almost indispensable for the visitor ; we see the actual statutes of Gregory IX take their place in the register of Rigaud. Dr. Rose Graham was the first to call attention to a long series of articles prepared for Archbishop Winchelsey's metropolitical visitations.[1] After a number of questions to be put to diocesans, and further inquiries to be made about the diocesans, come sections concerning secular canons, regular canons, nuns and monks. Comparing these " querenda circa religiosos " with the articles of the Burton annalist we find fairly close correspondence of materials. Eleven of the earlier articles find no parallel in Winchelsey's questionnaire : they deal with proud, selfish and secretive monks, with preaching, manual labour, and conspiracy against the visitor. The later articles include a number of subjects which are hardly touched upon in the Burton record. Winchelsey made inquiry about the observance of injunctions and asked to have them shown. He asked whether monks made profession when they ought to do so, and whether the number of monks was maintained He also asked after vagabonds and fugitives, saw to it that fasts were well observed and the rules against private property. Particularly noticeable are the visitor's persistent inquiries regarding the head of the house. Does he correct misdemeanours sufficiently ? Does he treat the brethren " honeste et mansuete " and refresh the brethren in his chamber ? All his administration is carefully surveyed ; the visitor is to find out whether he guards the monastery's property well, or manumits slaves or destroys woods ; whether the fabric is in repair ; whether the head countenances private trading or holds in his own

" an fecerint conspirationem contra adventum episcopi " suggests that a bishop framed the articles. Moreover, they occur in a chronicle which contains a set of bishop's articles for inquiry in parishes ; if the latter are to be ascribed to Grosseteste, the articles for monasteries may have been his also.

[1] After 1298, for the 13th article refers to the new constitution of Pope Boniface, which only appeared in that year. The articles occur in British Museum MS. *Cotton*, Galba, E. IV, printed in Winchelsey, II. 1289–1303.. Cf. Graham, *Studies*, 333.

hands any of the house's manors or possessions. The list of questions is more comprehensive than that in the *Burton Annals*, and extremely workmanlike.

By great good fortune we are able to compare these articles of Winchelsey's with several sets of injunctions compiled after visitations by the same archbishop. Many are preserved in Winchelsey's register and in the register of Bishop Ralph Baldock of London.[1] Not only do these injunctions cover nearly all the subject-matter of the articles ; but they rarely stray beyond them. Winchelsey found reason to introduce very few new topics : at Gloucester he ordained that only fit persons should be admitted as monks, that chapter secrets should not be revealed, that the abbot should visit dependent cells properly.[2] At Little Malvern he had to revise the bishop's arrangements for the upkeep of the last prior,[3] and at Canterbury made an injunction about anniversaries and the office for the dead.[4] This evidence, joined with the detailed account of the Canterbury visitation, quoted above, shows how systematic was Archbishop Winchelsey's disciplinary work. The general resemblance of the articles to those of earlier visitors and their obvious debt to Gregory IX's Statutes, may make us fairly certain that here we have the usual material upon which visitors worked for the reform of monasteries. Where articles of inquiry were used they were probably in broad outline similar.

Two thirteenth-century sets of articles have been examined. Can we say with reasonable certainty how these were used by the visitors ? Were they sent to the visitands before the visitor arrived, were they read to the visitands as a preliminary to inquiry, or did they serve simply as notes for the visitor's own guidance ? The articles themselves do not help to solve the problem, though the preface to Winchelsey's questionnaire for a

---

[1] Winchelsey, I. 91–3, 98–100, II. 813–77, 1307–9 ; Baldock, 26–9, 31–5, 60–2, 77–9, 84–6.
[2] Winchelsey, II. 857–8.
[3] *Ibid.*, II. 865–6.
[4] *Ibid.*, II. 822.

cathedral chapter reads like a private book of instructions.[1]
Whether or not it was usual for the visitor to send articles
of inquiry to a religious house when he sent notice of
visitation we cannot say. The only thing about the
articles in the *Burton Annals* which suggests that they
were sent to the monastery is their survival in the monastery's chronicle, and this evidence is far from conclusive.[2]
Bishop Frere has said that " articles of inquiry were . . .
sent previous to a visitation in the case of some monasteries : but such were of more local and special interest
[than articles for deaneries] and no one specimen can be
given that would be in any way representative of the class
as a whole." [3] It seems likely, and reasonable to suppose,
that such premonitory articles were only forwarded to
houses publicly defamed. Archbishop Giffard's questionnaire for Bolton dealt with a house where the archbishop expected to find certain faults ; whilst the
inquisition against the prior of Felley " super certis
articulis sibi editis et in scriptis " [4] was obviously exceptional.[5]

As to the method of inquiry, our scraps of evidence
suggest that it resembled the fifteenth-century method
which is fully recorded. While it is unfortunate that of
the few detailed accounts of procedure in the register of
Archbishop Rigaud almost all concern cathedral chapters,
it is improbable that the archbishop used any different
method in monastic houses. We may, therefore, draw
on these accounts for a description supplementary to that
of Winchelsey's methods described above.

[1] " Dicatur sic : Fratres non timeatis veritatem detegere. . . . Et
legatur constitucio " Winchelsey, II. 1290.
[2] Winchelsey's articles for all kinds of visitation occur in the register
of the prior of Canterbury.   [3] Frere, 104.   [4] Giffard, *York*, 319.
[5] An undated document in *Collectanea Anglo-Premonstratensia*
(Camden Soc., 3rd series, vols. VI, X, XII, 1904-6), I. 203, allows for the
publishing of articles by the Order visitor immediately before he com-
mences his inquiry (*Hic legi possunt Inquisitionum Articuli*). In metropolitan visitations it was perhaps more usual for the visitor to send articles
beforehand, at least to the diocesans (cf. Wilkins, II. 83) ; but there is no
sign of the practice in the account of Winchelsey's reception at Chichester.

The archbishop of Rouen visited the chapter of Evreux in 1250,[1] and there he asked whether the canons wished him to make a general inquiry or inquire of each singly. After many words they told him to do as he pleased. Then the archbishop inquired of them all together regarding the church services (which they said were properly celebrated) and learnt that the dean was too infirm to fulfil his duties : " and they replied most courteously and carefully concerning all that we asked of them." Then the visitor, turning to matters of discipline, asked the chapter whether there were any persons in the church of Evreux defamed of incontinence, drunkenness, over-dressing, street-wandering, or trading. They said there were none such, since two clerks had recently been ejected from the choir because of their ill-fame. With this the general inquiry ended.

But the visitor was not content with the evidence of the canons *en bloc*. He passed on to a closer inquiry. " We ordered them to draw to one side and summoned them singly and secretly. First [we called] the precentor, and asked him whether any of the canons were defamed of incontinence, trading, or the like : he said, No. Then we called Peter the archdeacon who, being asked the same question as the precentor, gave the same reply." Two others answered likewise, and one of them was reproved for having an incorrect tonsure ; the archbishop also asked him why he was not yet a subdeacon.

Although Rigaud had given the chapter the choice of two forms of inquiry (*in generali, vel sigillatim*), he in fact used both. And this was probably his regular custom. He used both again at Lisieux at his next visitation in 1254.[2] At the cathedral of Rouen in 1257, having made a general inquiry, the archbishop heard the separate depositions of the chancellor and the succentor, " et postea alios duos insimul," regarding individuals.[3] He also used both forms of investigation there in 1260.[4] It is evident that such was the procedure at the nunnery of Villarceaux

---

[1] Rigaud, 72.　　[2] *Ibid.*, 199.　　[3] *Ibid.*, 285.　　[4] *Ibid.*, 386.

in 1249.[1] The record here gives a fairly coherent account of the nuns' numbers, revenues and debts, how they confess and communicate, how the accounts are kept, how the nuns dress, eat meat, neglect silence, and go out of the cloister ; but following this comes a confused collection, clearly made up of separate testimonies in which the habits of half the nuns are disclosed. Sometimes there was corroboratory evidence : we are told twice that the prioress does not get up for matins. It is a collection of unsifted depositions: in technical language the *detecta*— things revealed to the visitor. The injunctions which follow are written much more neatly than the preceding material, and without corrections.

At Evreux in 1258 Rigaud seems to have held no general inquiry, but proceeded at once to an examination of the dean and treasurer and archdeacon.[2] Rarely, if ever, in the larger houses, can the archbishop have had time to examine all the regular inmates separately. In these cathedral visitations he was content with the examination of a few.[3] The double form of inquiry is indicated by Graystanes in his description of a visitation at Durham, c. 1275 : " prioreque se ad partem trahante, examinavit [archiepiscopus] suppriorem et ex senioribus quatuor aut [quinque] successive, a nullo sacramentum exigens, sed, *quod prius publice, tunc occulte*, requirens ab eis." [4] The *Acta* of Simon of Bourges mentions " multa per multos de monasterio domino relata et revelata, tam palam, quam secreto," at the visitation of Chezal Benoît.[5]

The inquiry which the visitor held was commonly called an *inquisitio*, but differed from the full form of law implied by that word. An inquisition, in its strictest sense, could not be initiated without pre-existing ill-fame. A religious house or its head or other inmates could only be subjected to an inquisition proper when their faults were declared by common report to be scandalous and intolerable. Hostiensis says that inquisition should be

---

[1] Rigaud, 43-4.
[2] *Ibid.*, 305.
[3] *Ibid.*, 72 (four), 220 (one and " quosdam alios,"), 285 (four).
[4] *Script. Tres*, 56.
[5] Baluze-Mansi, I. 278*b*.

made only against a defamed person.[1] Elsewhere he says :
" Si inquisitio fiat contra ipsum : sive sit regularis, sive
secularis, nunquam proceditur, nisi quando fama tanta
est, quod non potest amplius sine scandalo tolerari sive
sine periculo dilapidationis." [2]

Where there was no pre-existing *infamia* the visitor
of a religious house would simply hold a preparatory
inquiry without a complicated legal process. This would
be intended to discover the basis of a formal inquisition,
if such a one should be needed. From the preliminary
examination of the inmates, either separately or together,
the bishop would find whether ill-fame was attached to
any of them.

The first was clearly the most usual procedure. In
the papal registers we certainly find many cases of visitatorial action in defamed houses ; but they were all exceptional cases, and only came to the notice of the Curia
because they were exceptional. The procedure which
prevailed except in flagrant cases is that described by
Durand the Speculator in connection with parochial
visitation.[3] It is irregular, he says, to proceed to an
ordinary inquisition without precedent *infamia ;* yet
when a bishop or archbishop visits, although there be no
precedent *infamia*, he may well make inquiry summarily,
step by step, without turmoil of the courts, concerning
the life and manners of the clergy, to correct them. He
shall inquire of the people how the clergy behave, and if
by chance he find a rector or any other person defamed
or suspected of something, then he may hold inquisition
about it to determine whether truth bears out the ill-
fame ; nor can appeal be made because he inquired without preceding ill-fame. For any ordinary may inquire
regarding the *fama* of his subjects ; and having found
infamia may inquire after the truth of that.

---

[1] *Comment.*, V. (f. 5 *verso*).   [2] *Summa*, V. de Inq. (f. 281 *recto*).
[3] *Speculum*, III. part I. de Inq. § 2, sect. 6 (vol. II. p. 31). A thirteenth-
century formulary contains a similar illustration of the serious character
of formal inquisitions, e.g. " Non debet dari inquisicio, nisi quando
infamatus ammonitus est et incorrigibilis perseueret. Causa inquisicionis
est infamia qua notatur is contra quem datur inquisicio " (Rockinger, 254).

This procedure did not require the exaction of an oath from the visitands. Innocent IV in a passage which found place in the *Sext* ordered archbishops to inquire, in their visitations, " absque coactione et exactione qualibet iuramenti " ; and in a later passage applied the methods of archbishops to bishops also.[1] Dr. Coulton has dealt exhaustively with this subject and shown that the method was usual in practice, " that the oath was no part of *normal* visitation procedure." [2]

The visitand was bound simply by the obligation of canonical obedience to answer truly to his superior. Thus Archbishop Rigaud orders the canons of S.-Lô at Rouen *per obedienciam* to confess if they are blameworthy, and at the nunnery of Montivilliers " precepimus autem eis generaliter, in virtute obedientie, ut nobis de hiis que ab ipsis quereremus dicerent veritatem." [3] Graystanes, in the passage cited above, tells us that the archbishop of York exacted no oath at Durham. Pecham mentions certain canons of Hastings who had concealed the truth, without calling them perjurers.[4]

Only where preceding *infamia* called for a formal inquisition was an oath extracted from the visitands. This *infamia* was not merely idle rumour, and its existence was a serious presumption of guilt in the persons implicated. All kinds of records illustrate this point—we may note illustrations from three episcopal registers. Archbishop Rigaud remarks that at Mortagne " some were ill-famed of incontinence, but the bishop had corrected their excesses, and the ill-fame had somewhat subsided " ; [5] the same archbishop's register has a section devoted to " Diffamationes." Here are many examples of defamed priests who swear to surrender their benefices " if you should again find me defamed and if I cannot purge myself." [6] The same serious interpretation of ill-fame is

---

[1] *Sext*, III. xx. 1, § 4.   [2] *Five Centuries*, II. 481.   [3] Rigaud, 204, 384.
[4] Peckham, II. 608 (quoted Coulton, *Five Centuries*, II. 483).
[5] Rigaud, 372.
[6] *Ibid.*, 649–74. Cf. *Councils & Synods*, II. 175 and n. 1, 264, Grosseteste, *Epist.*, 147, *Ann. Mon.*, I. 308, Giffard, Worc., f. 67v, Gandavo, I. 548.

to be found in the register of Archbishop Pecham, where the visitor declares that canons defamed with women, if they converse with them or have access to their homes, " unless they can declare their innocence by definite indications or testimonies, shall be reckoned as convicted and shall be punished." [1] About the same time Bishop Cantilupe of Hereford ordained : " regarding those who are defamed we order the prior to make due correction within a short time." [2] The force of *diffamatio* was obviously very strong in these cases. That this was the general rule is so clear [3] that we should not trouble to labour the point had not certain writers unreasonably depreciated the importance of charges based on common report.

In a house against which this *infamia* was directed, the community was in the position of an individual condemned by the common report of his neighbours and obliged to purge himself. The community had to swear its innocence or confess its faults ; and the essence of the inquisition to which it submitted (less formal than the practice of the courts) [4] was an oath. This was exacted from each individual or from one as a representative of all ; they swore to tell the whole truth regarding what they knew or believed to need correction in their church.[5] If they were guilty they were thus bound to confess or perjure themselves.

Consequently, we find on examination that examples of oath-taking at visitations are all of them in exceptional circumstances. In 1240 the bishop of Poitiers had serious dispute with the abbey of Luçon. The bishop declared the abbot to be gravely defamed and the house depraved, and when he wished to put the inmates on oath they refused. On the part of the abbey it was maintained that there was no preceding ill-fame.[6] A similar case is found

<hr/>

[1] Peckham, I. 164.　　　　[2] Cantilupe, 148 ; cf. Rigaud, 31.
[3] See Coulton, *Medieval Studies*, 1st series (2nd edition, 1915), 122 ; *Five Centuries*, II. 237-8, 470-1 ; *Linc. Visit.*, I. 234.
[4] Fournier, 278 ; cf. Innocent IV, 408.　　[5] *Decretales*, V. i. 17.
[6] Grégoire IX, 5152 (Potthast, 10871).

in the register of Pope Innocent IV : the bishop of Angers stated that when he went to visit the house of S.-Florent Saumur, the abbot and convent refused to swear an oath " de veritate dicenda *super hiis de quibus ad aures eiusdem episcopi insinuatio clamosa pervenerat.*" [1] Archbishop Rigaud held a visitation at S.-Martin of Pontoise in 1258 " et quia quidam ex eis erant de incontinencia infamati, et erat domus in malo statu, nos ibidem dimisimus fratrem Adam Rigaudi et magistrum Ricardum de Sappo, pro inquirendo de statu domus." [2] This reads more like the formal *inquisitio* than like the usual procedure.

About the same time in England, Grosseteste stated that the business of visitation cannot be duly accomplished without most careful inquisitions, in which is often required the oath of those who are to be interrogated.[3] But we cannot infer from this that inquisition was the normal process. Indeed, Grosseteste's exaction of oaths on certain occasions (*nos visitans extorsit a singulis iuramentum*) was regarded as an unwelcome innovation, on account of which Walter de Gledelle, canon of Dunstable, fled from the house to become a monk of Woburn,[4] and the abbey of Ramsey obtained a papal privilege, " de juramento non faciendo in visitatione." [5] The report of a visitation by Archbishop Ludham at Newburgh Priory shows the prior " iuramentum exhibens corporale quod omnia quae erant in monasterio corrigenda . . . revelaret." [6] The context strongly suggests that the prior or convent were defamed beforehand. Such was the case at Bolton in 1275 ; on this occasion each witness was " iuratus et examinatus." [7]

When Archbishop Pecham examined certain sworn witnesses at Rochester Cathedral in 1283, he was holding his inquiry in response to a special request, and was careful to state beforehand that he had come, not as metropolitan,

---

[1] Innocent IV, 794.   [2] Rigaud, 312.
[3] Burton Annals, *Ann. Mon.*, I. 423 ; cf. Wilkins, I. 751 (Council of Lambeth, 1261).   [4] Dunstable Annals, *Ann. Mon.*, III. 152.
[5] *Ramsey Cart.*, II. 153.   [6] Giffard, *York*, 216.
[7] *Ibid.*, 321-2 ; cf. 304.

but as patron of the church.[1] One of the few cases of
oath-taking where *infamia* is not mentioned comes from
the church of Fermo, in central Italy. Here the bishop,
delegated by Innocent III, had reformed his canons :
" fecit autem in primis iurare Canonicos ipsius ecclesie ut
super reformatione eorum et Firm. ecclesie daretur ei
fidele consilium." [2] The fact of a papal order to visit
suggests that the church was notorious ; so this example
cannot be said to contradict the foregoing evidence. The
circumstances in which the bishop of Meaux took an oath
from the inmates of the hospital there (in 1291) were also
exceptional. After celebrating Mass there, he had called
upon the Minister of the house to prepare for visitation.
There was some opposition, and certain sisters absented
themselves when the bishop called them before him in
the refectory. Even those who did appear were loth to
answer the bishop's questions. Then he threatened excommunication on those who should keep him waiting
any longer, and with that the opposition broke down :
" Prius iuramento ab eis praestito, eidem de statu dictae
domus . . . secundum quod eosdem interrogare voluit,
responderunt." It is not surprising that in the face
of such unwillingness the visitor should have thought it
necessary to take an extreme measure.[3]

These examples cannot be said to invalidate the argument that use of the oath was rare. They have been
given at some length merely to allow an estimate of the
extent of exceptional practice.

Nothing could make the matter clearer than a passage
in Archbishop Romeyn's register. After giving the form
of notice sent to religious houses to say that he is coming
" visitacionis et inquisicionis officium apud vos paternis
affectibus exercere," the archbishop makes the following

---

[1] Edmund of Hadenham, *Annales Ecclesiae Roffensis*, in Wharton's
Anglia Sacra (London, 1691), I. 353.
[2] M. Catalani, *De Ecclesia Firmana* . . . *Commentarius* (Fermo,
1783), 360. Half a century later the bishop of Fermo was himself defamed,
and gave his oath to the visitors sent to inquire against him (Urbain IV,
ordinaire 743).   [3] Du Plessis, *Église de Meaux*, II. 186-7.

note : " Memorandum quod consimilis littera emanavit eodem die ad visitandum priorem et conventum de . . . sine verbo inquisicionis, quia illud verbum non debet poni nisi ob magnam causam, videlicet, si domus fuerit diffamata, vel alias, de domo diffamata." [1] Seldom can a medieval clerk so perfectly have anticipated and laid to rest the uncertainties of the modern historian.

We should, however, note a proceeding which came near to the exaction of an oath. Certain monks confessed to Archbishop Corbridge that they had omitted to tell the truth at his last visitation, " sicque sentenciam excommunicacionis majoris in tales per nos latam dampnabiliter incurrerunt." [2] Apparently the visitor had included in his excommunication of obstructors the condemnation of those deponents who concealed the truth. This is parallel to the action of the franciscan Wigmund the German, considered exceptionally strict by Eccleston, who " had received from the minister-general so strict and minute a form of visitation, and especially in that all should be excommunicate, *de facto*, who should in any wise conceal any matters from him . . . that there was such trouble among the brethren as had never been in the Order." [3] Though deponents were bound to tell the truth freely in virtue of canonical obedience, they were not generally forced to speak by fear of the penalties of perjury. Probably the authorities realized that the imposition of an oath caused more deadly sin than it prevented. For a good deal of misdoing went undiscovered.

The system of inquiry had several obvious defects. If the examination of each individual was thoroughly secret and searching the bishop would probably hear much fiction with the facts. On the other hand, if there was any publicity, if testimony leaked out, so that the convent knew what an individual had deposed, there was danger of retaliation. Finally, there was always the chance of a conspiracy of silence among the visitands.

[1] Romeyn, I. 51. [2] Corbridge, I. 106.
[3] Quoted Coulton, *Five Centuries*, II. 482-3, from *Monumenta Franciscana* (Rolls series, 1858), I. 29-30.

Archbishop Rigaud, visiting les-Deux-Amants in 1262, found a number of matters requiring correction, but " all the other [complaints] were put forward in a spirit of contentiousness (as was at once apparent) by a certain brother called Babot, so they were accounted frivolous." [1] At Eu, two years later, the visitor was told a lot of things about the abbot which he did not believe; two years later, having again listened to the same charges, this time " with diligent investigation and deliberation ", he concluded that they proceeded from rancour and hatred and originated with evil-disposed persons. [2] At Eu, on an earlier visit, the archbishop had mentioned one William de Archis, who " irreverenter et tumide in capitulo loquebatur et effrene, quod nobis plurimum displicuit." [3] He found a similar grumbler at Jumièges in 1258; [4] and at S.-Victor complained that Robert of S.-Amand was a murmurer and a liar (*murmurator est et inventor mendaciorum*). [5] The papal registers yield a few further examples of charges preferred " contenciose " by malevolent persons. [6]

The temptation to pay off a grudge favoured false witness, which neither involved the accuser in perjury nor discovered him to the accused. Doubtless the temptation was too great for some regulars. The visitor must sometimes have been faced, not with a clean sheet, but with a crowded bill of petty charges—personal lapses of which many were not worth recording while some never existed. The monastic life, with all its self-contained intimacy, was

---

[1] Rigaud, 444; cf. 484. [2] *Ibid.*, 496, 542.
[3] *Ibid.*, 408. [4] *Ibid.*, 324. [5] *Ibid.*, 47.
[6] Grégoire IX, 980, 1185, 1604; Innocent IV, 7244, 7473, 7630; Alexandre IV, 1190. A case of false defamation at parochial visitation occurs in the Hereford records of 1397. It would be a mistake to draw any extensive deduction from an injunction at Norwich in 1492. The *Comperta* at visitation showed that there was no scholar sent to Oxford, and Bishop Goldwell accordingly made a long, reproving injunction (*Norwich Visitations*, ed. A. Jessopp, Camden Soc., 1888, 4, 7). But the obedientiary rolls show that from the beginning of the century until that very year there had constantly been a scholar sent to Oxford. This is the only year in the fifteenth century when such a complaint could have been made (H. W. Saunders, *An Introduction to the Rolls of Norwich Cathedral Priory*, Norwich, 1930, 185).

favourable to malicious fabrication when monks were in dispute. The practice of mutual proclamation of faults in chapter [1] was designed for a community near its ideal, living harmoniously, imbued with Christian charity and humility ; it too easily degenerated into tale-bearing in its worst form. Archbishop Wickwane desired that faults should be charitably remarked " et non ex fervore vindicte." [2]

But we must not exaggerate the importance of this factor in visitations. Those historians who discount the personal charges revealed to visitors, as being unsubstantiated and made through malice, must think very ill of the monks' charity. We have no right to believe that frivolous accusations seriously misled a visitor, except where a conspiracy had been formed to damn an individual's character. Such conspiracy must have been rare : where it occurred it usually concerned an unpopular head and a bishop would not take action against a head without mature consideration and close inquiry. Overstatement of offences would therefore be reduced by further inquiry, and those cases of ungrounded charges which we meet in Rigaud's register probably come near to the total of such cases in the archbishop's visitations.

Retaliation on accusers was a far more serious hindrance to discipline. When the truth had been spoken and the penalty of guilt imposed, the visitor went away, the abbot resumed his supreme authority, the informer and the object of his accusation lived together cheek by jowl. Revenge was not only possible ; it was to be generally expected. Thus Archbishop Pecham enjoined that the prior of Mottesfont should not punish any for their statements at the visitation in 1284. At Wherwell Abbey he ordered none to inquire of accusations made at the

---

[1] " Unus non clamat alium " and " Unus clamet alium " are common phrases in visitation literature (see *infra*, 158-9).

[2] Wickwane, 133 ; cf. Winchelsey, 99. The Order visitor for the Benedictines of the province of Canterbury (1219) is told to be cautious in accepting evidence : " Qui tamen non credat omni spiritui ; set que audierit, diligenter discutiat," etc. (*Chapters of the English Black Monks*, ed. W. A. Pantin, Camden Soc., 1931, I. 13).

visitation, and repeated the injunction for Romsey Abbey.[1] Winchelsey ordered that none should reveal what was asked in visitation or find out what others said to the visitor or prevent due correction in any way. None were to be molested for what they had said under pain of the greater excommunication.[2] Corbridge ordered his commissaries : " injungatis ne quis monachorum ipsorum ab alio querere seu alii respondere presumat, quis, quid, seu de quo vel quibus dixerit clam vel palam." [3] Dr. Coulton has collected a large number of references to the practice of revenge,[4] and the papal registers of the thirteenth century yield additional examples. Honorius III tells an abbot not to hinder the process of inquisition against him by excommunicating, suspending or transferring his priors and monks.[5] Nicholas IV has to make the same sort of injunction regarding the abbots of S.-Denis and Mont S.-Michel.[6] The abbot of S.-Savin in Poitou had excommunicated and ejected a monk who opposed him, and disobeyed Innocent III's order to reinstate.[7] Honorius III accorded protection to the abbess and nuns of Sta. Margarita, Bologna, against Martha, lately their abbess, removed by the diocesan.[8] In the register of Nicholas IV is a lurid story of the abbot of Gaillac, who was defamed of many vices, and who feared that they would come to the ears of the authorities. He succeeded in inducing the greater number of his monks to swear that they would not speak against him, but he terribly afflicted those who refused to conceal the truth.[9] The letters of Boniface VIII contain two cases of similar violence on the part of wicked abbots against monks who wished to expose them.[10]

By fear of revenge, therefore, visitands could be induced to suppress the truth ; and it was very difficult for

---

[1] Peckham, II. 647, 655, 661.

[2] Winchelsey, *Articles*, 2 and 3 (f. 61).   [3] Corbridge, I. 107.

[4] *Five Centuries*, II. 278, 487-8. The abbot's resumption of power after the bishop's visitation is admirably illustrated in *Visitations of . . . Norwich* (Camden Soc., 1888), 114 *et sqq.*   [5] Honorii III, 1429.

[6] Nicolas IV, 1096, 5777.   [7] Honorii III, 86, 860 (Potthast, 5614).

[8] *Ibid.*, 1610.   [9] Nicolas IV, 6586 ; cf. Boniface VIII, 2600.

[10] Boniface VIII, 3610, 4291.

a bishop to dispel this fear, since he had little control over a monastery between the times of visitation. But besides the numerous cases of coercion, complete or attempted, we must take into account the occasions when matters were hushed up by common consent ; a conspiracy of silence was too often to the advantage of a whole convent for coercion to be always necessary. The border-line between conspiracy and intimidation is very faint. The authority of the abbot ordering silence might coincide perfectly with the will of his monks. The abbot of Gaillac, as was seen above, induced the *major pars* of his convent to connive at his very serious offences. Dr. Coulton has assembled a valuable collection of instances of conspiracy and collusion, many of them belonging to the thirteenth century.[1] In the nature of things we cannot expect the evidence to be complete, but there is sufficient to show that precautions against conspiracy were taken and were needed. Among the articles of inquiry in the *Burton Annals* occurs the question, " an fecerint conspirationem contra adventum episcopi ? " Archbishop Winchelsey inquired at the visitation of his suffragans, " an episcopus decanus vel quivis alius de capitulo aliquas inhibiciones fecerit vel sentencias protulerit iuramenta vel promissiones extorserit vel penas adiecerit ne quis veritate detegat de inquirendis super statu personarum aut rerum ecclesie." [2] The archbishop began his inquiries by reading to the chapter that constitution of Boniface VIII which declared all such commands and oaths and promises to be invalid.[3] At Newburgh Priory Archbishop Ludham found that the prior, an evil liver, had " extracted from the brethren an abominable oath that they would not reveal to the visitor what was worthy of correction in the monastery, forbidding them, under pain of excommunication, to reveal the same, yet in the archbishop's presence swearing a corporal oath that he would reveal everything worthy of correction in the monastery, in its head and in

---

[1] *Five Centuries*, II. 272 *sqq.*, 486-7.
[2] Winchelsey, *Articles*, 59 (f. 62).   [3] *Ibid.*, 3 (f. 61); *Sext*, I. xvi. 4.

its members, except occult crimes."[1]   Archbishop
Giffard found that the prior of Bolton (who had been
suspended) " ordered his canons in virtue of obedience to
agree in all things at our visitation." [2]

Pope Alexander IV addressed a letter to the diocesan
bishops of France in 1256.   In this letter he says that he
has heard how certain abbots and other heads of religious
houses in France forbid their subjects to reveal, to their
hurt, the state of the monastery, its inmates and its property, when the bishop visits them, excommunicating
them if they do reveal it.   Whence it happens that when
the bishops visit these houses they cannot discover their
condition.   And thus many matters requiring correction
in their head or members are allowed to go unreformed.
Diocesans are therefore empowered to revoke such sen-
tences directed by regular prelates against their subjects.[3]
Pope Gregory X instructed the visitors of Corbie to begin
their inquiry by nullifying all oaths sworn, all confederations or conspiracies open or secret made, by persons of
the monastery, even if such confederations have been
strengthened by oath-taking.[4]

This was a matter discussed by the Quodlibetists :
" Whether monks are bound to obey an abbot who is a
dilapidator and not exempt, if he forbids them to reveal
the truth to a visiting bishop ? " [5]   Pierre de S.-Omer
asks, " may a prelate coerce a subject whom he knows is
bound by oath to some one not to reveal a secret, the
revelation of which would be very useful ? " [6]   Other
doctors repeated the question.[7]

The very fact that this question could be argued in
the schools illustrates an important point.   The visitation
of bishops, even while it was completely accepted as a

---

[1] Giffard, *York*, 216.   [2] *Ibid.*, 304.
[3] Alexandre IV, 1324 (*Autun Cart.*, 1) ;   cf. Innocent III, I. 67
(Potthast, 73).   [4] Grégoire X, 418.
[5] Gérard d'Abbeville, quodl. XVII quaestio 8 (Glorieux, 125).
[6] Glorieux, 234-5.
[7] Eustache de Grandcourt and (?) Richard de Middleton (Glorieux,
235, 273).

part of the normal machinery of administration and as an instrument of monastic reform, did not appeal to the average monk's sense of justice. It was not moral influence, but mere business efficiency which gave the system such value as it had. The question of conspiracy of silence was therefore one which could be discussed as a purely legal problem, and if the visitor could be legally evaded no one thought worse of the evader. Despite the preambles of popes and bishops giving mandates to their delegates, the visitor was not normally received with charity nor his visitation regarded as a blessing. In the eyes of the regulars the episcopal visitor remained always an outsider to be outwitted, whose intrusion should be curtailed as much as possible. No special malignity, but a common habit of mind, might account for this attitude. It was also partly due to the visitors' constant insistence on their legal rights. For them, Professor Claude Jenkins says: " A visitation was not only an obligation of pastoral care : it was a vindication of jurisdiction and a very definite exercise of its functions. It began with the suspension of all subordinate jurisdictions and its legal aspect was brought out by every document connected with it as well as by the inevitable exaction of fees, or at least the attempt to exact them." [1]

Jocelin of Brakelond records the misleading statements about the condition of St. Edmunds which the prior made to the archbishop-legate at his visitation, and confesses that he himself was somewhat shocked at the hoodwinking.[2] The Tewkesbury annalist tells with evident satisfaction how the bishop of Worcester (armed, as he said, with papal letters) forced the monks in his diocese to live according to his statutes : " Qui in ecclesia nostra fecit maximum scrutinium per subpriorem Wygorniae et tertium priorem Gloucestriae ; sed ars arte deluditur, nihil invenientes nisi ordinatum et honestum, juxta ordinis

---

[1] *Episcopacy Ancient and Modern*, ed. C. Jenkins and K. D. Mackenzie (London, 1930), 80.

[2] Jocelin, 5-6 ; cf. *Evesham Chron.*, 107, and Matt. Paris, V. 259 (abbots inducing their monks to secrecy by hollow promises).

observantiam [1251]." [1]   These passages, meant for the
edification or delectation of monastic readers, show very
clearly the spirit of passive resistance which defeated so
many attempted reforms from without.

An even more instructive history is that of Evesham's
battle for exemption. We have an account of the whole
unsavoury proceedings from the mouth of one of the
principal actors—a monk of the abbey, who finally dis-
placed its wicked abbot.[2]   A rascally man, Roger Norris,
had been raised to the abbacy in 1191. Seven years later,
in response to the monks' complaints, the archbishop
came, much agitated, to Evesham. He made diligent
inquiry, but the abbot gave presents, corrupted monks,
and bought his safety.[3]   The monks, it seems, were ready
to complain against him, but equally ready to withhold
their complaints in return for favours. In 1202 Abbot
Roger was a public scandal, and Bishop Mauger of Worcester intervened.

Mainly in order to correct Evesham, he had armed
himself with papal letters bidding him visit the churches
subject to him by diocesan law, regardless of appeals.[4]
Thomas of Marlborough, the chronicler, tells us that the
bishop was a just, God-fearing man, " zelo bono ductus " ;
nevertheless, Thomas was the first to oppose the bishop's
visitation.[5]   The bishop's visit was said to be unprece-
dented though, in fact, Bishop John of Coutances seems
to have visited the monastery and legislated for it.
Bishop Mauger was not admitted, and therefore excommunicated the monks.[6]   The dispute lasted long, with
complications which need not be mentioned here.
Thomas of Marlborough took the monks' case to Rome,
played his cards with great skill and, after an interim
judgment in favour of the bishop (April, 1205),[7] won his

---

[1] *Ann. Mon.*, I. 146. Cf. *Disticha Catonis:* " Sic ars deluditur
arte."

[2] Cf. Cheney, *Pope Innocent III and England*, 194–9.

[3] *Evesham Chron.*, 107.

[4] Innocent III, V. 24 (Potthast, 1664).   [5] *Evesham Chron.*, 109-10.
[6] *Ibid.*, 116-18.   [7] *Ibid.*, 131.

point and obtained exemption for the abbey in December, 1205.[1]

The important features of this case, for our present purpose, are two. The monks, much as they hated Abbot Roger's rapacity and dissolute life, would rather suffer him than submit to the bishop's authority. This is made evident by the fact that on three occasions they all made their peace with the abbot when his deposition was imminent, and one of these times (when the bishop had been temporarily awarded full powers) " would tell the bishop nothing, though he commanded this under pain of excommunication." [2] Thomas of Marlborough himself also saved the abbot, whom he had little cause to love, when the bishop's representative in Rome was about to produce new evidence against him.[3] Only when the abbey's exemption was finally assured did the brethren speak out against their vicious head and secure his removal in 1213. The other notable feature in Marlborough's narrative is the writer's apparent honesty. He was convinced throughout that he was working for the abbey's welfare and believed that submission to the bishop would be the worst of fates.[4]

The habitual hostility to bishop visitors which cropped up in the Evesham dispute may be illustrated equally well from a piece of monastic legislation and a moral tale of

---

[1] *Evesham Chron.*, 169-70, 179-83 (Potthast, 2660 ; *Decretales*, V. xxxiii. 17). [2] *Ibid.*, 121 ; Coulton, *Five Centuries*, II. 358.

[3] *Evesham Chron.*, 199 ; Coulton, *Five Centuries*, II. 363-4.

[4] Marlborough implies that he thought exemption meant no slackening of discipline ; for " papal legates scrutinize and correct the transgressions of exempt more than of non-exempt houses " (*Evesham Chron.*, 201 ; transl. Coulton, *Five Centuries*, II. 364). This is hardly in agreement with St. Bernard's views on exemption or with Innocent III's statement in 1203, that exempt houses were in a worse state than those under diocesan control (Innocent III, V. 159), and what are we to think of the purity of Marlborough's motives when we find the following record in the Annals of Dunstable, s.a. 1233 ? "When the Order visitor wished to visit the monastery of Evesham the abbot took exception because his monastery was only exempt from the church of Worcester and was therefore subject to Canterbury. And this the abbot and convent proved by letters patent, and the visitors went away " (*Ann. Mon.*, III. 133).

the thirteenth century. The General Chapters of the Benedictines held at York in 1221 and 1256 stated that many monks (" subdoli et spiritu maligno ducti ") hid matters deserving correction from their chapters and from their Order visitors, and saved them to reveal to the bishop's clerks at the episcopal visitation, " maliciose, non zelo ordinis set ulciscende causa pravitatis." [1] The idea underlying this statement was familiar : the idea that scandal must be prevented, that the world must not know of the monastery's faults ; [2] it followed naturally that the bishop must only be the corrector in the last resort.

In a franciscan *Liber Exemplorum* one of the suggestions for a preacher's moralization is the story of an abbess who conceived of a certain clerk. Her nuns perceived her plight and, taking delight in it, revealed the situation to the bishop. He appointed a day for visitation and promised trouble to the abbess if he found anything wrong. Then the abbess prayed to Our Lady and asked for mercy. Mary heard her prayer, miraculously took the child from her womb, sent it by an angel to a hermit to be fostered, " et eam a confusione procurata et promissa liberavit." [3] The story was designed to show the mercy of Our Lady, but in doing so it seemed to encourage the idea that the discipline of a bishop visitor might be evaded in every possible way.

Sometimes special privileges interfered with the bishop's investigations in religious houses, and there were besides certain constant, recognized limitations to his power of learning all the truth. The abbey of Bec-Hellouin obtained from Pope Innocent III the privilege that the diocesan should not of his own authority proceed to inquisition against persons of the monastery unless any

---

[1] *Benedictine Chapters*, I. 239–40, 244 ; *Augustinian Chapters*, xliii, 35.

[2] See Coulton, *Five Centuries*, II. 261–2, 479.

[3] *Liber Exemplorum* (British Society Franciscan Studies, 1908), 32–3. According to the version of the story by Étienne de Bourbon and others, the child eventually succeeded the visitor as bishop (*Anecdotes Historiques*, ed. Lecoy de la Marche (1877), 114 and 115, n. 1).

were gravely defamed—not by evil-disposed, but by good and honest people.[1] At all times the vexed question of occult sins and the right to reveal them practically made a complete testimony optional. Thus the obstacle to inquiry specifically defined and allowed at Bec, virtually existed (in a lesser degree) where no such privilege had been given.

St. Benedict's Rule ordered the monk to confess secret sins, not to the community, but " to the abbot or to his spiritual seniors who know how to heal their own wounds and not to disclose and make public those of others." [2] In the life of Lanfranc occurs the story of a mad monk who in chapter threatened to expose to the archbishop the secret faults of his brethren. While Eadmer admits that the conduct of the monks needed reform and says that this served as a lesson to them, the threat of the madman is obviously given as an evidence of diabolical possession.[3]

The canon law confirmed this idea that the occult crimes of the religious are not to be published. Gratian cites Nicholas II, who invokes the example of Noah's sons to show that offences ought to be covered up.[4] To harmonize this with the passage of the *Decretum*, which says that " he who ceaseth from opposing a manifest transgression is not free from the stain of secret fellowship therein " (I. 83, 3), the glossator remarks that the former is understood of occult crimes, for we are forced to make accusation of manifest crimes after admonition.[5] Hostiensis says that the business of the ordinary is not to make public secret offences : " occultos peccatores celet, non publicet." [6] Again he says : " occulta enim omnino relinquentur soli Deo," and " cum occultus sit solum Deum habet ultorem." [7] In a letter embodied in the

---

[1] Innocent III, suppl. 235 (Potthast, 4158). This prevented the *inquisitoria preparatoria* of which Durand speaks (see *supra*, 78).

[2] *The Rule of St. Benedict* (transl. Gasquet, 1909), 83 (c. XLVI.).

[3] A. J. Macdonald, *Lanfranc* (1926), 172-4. [4] *Decretum*, I. XCVI. 8.

[5] Gloss of *Decretum*, I. XCVI. 8, quoted Coulton, *Five Centuries*, II. 262. [6] *Summa*, I. de Off. Ord., 7 (f. 64 *verso*).

[7] *Comment.*, I. de Off. Ord., XIII. 4 and I. de Temp. Ord., XVIII. 5 (f. 164 *verso*, 103 *verso*).

Decretals Innocent III declares that even where there was such definite ill-fame as to call for a formal inquisition with the exaction of an oath, that oath did not include occult crimes among the crimes to be revealed.[1] We have seen that Archbishop Giffard made the same proviso when he took an oath from the prior of Newburgh (*supra*, page 81). Archbishop Winchelsey ordered bishops, deans, and chapters to reveal all that ought to be revealed " iuxta scientiam aut credulitatem suam vel secundum quod fama est . . . nichil de occultis vel prius correctis aliqualiter detegendo." [2] All this bears out the words of Trithemius, who wrote at the end of the fifteenth century : " de occultis non est nimis curiose inquirendum." [3]

Various reasons have been given in the foregoing pages for supposing that the visitor did not learn all the truth in his inquiries. In his attempts to do so, his authority was thwarted not only by deliberate falsehood, but by that suppression of facts which resulted from the hostile frame of mind of those examined. He had, moreover, to arrive at a mean between the scandal of the gossipmongers and the silence of more complacent brethren. In later records, where there is fuller detail, we often see conflicting evidence placed before the bishop. As Professor Claude Jenkins says, " allowance has to be made for a tendency natural to certain temperaments to return too readily the answer ' Omnia bene.' " [4]

No doubt the bishop might learn a great deal from personal observation in the monastery. Defects of fabric could not be concealed from his eye so easily as defects of morals. But while we can be sure that an alert visitor noticed *corrigenda* himself, we have little evidence of his going in search for it. On one occasion the bishop of Meaux made the tour of a hospital, visiting personally the sisters' dormitory, the infirmary, the brethren's dormitory,

---

[1] *Decretales*, V. i. 17, cf. V. i. 18 ; Durand, *Speculum*, I., part IV. § 7, no. 38 (properly 30) (vol. I, p. 329), quoted by Coulton, *Five Centuries*, II. 268.   [2] Winchelsey, *Articles*, I. (f. 61).

[3] De Visit. Monach., c. V, *Opera Pia* (1604), 983.

[4] *Episcopacy Ancient and Modern*, 81.

and the minister's room; but we know of no similar record.[1]

Having learnt all he could from his inquiries, the bishop sifted and classified the *detecta* (laid bare by the deponents); the result was a collection of *comperta* (discovered by the bishop). These matters the visitor would present to the convent as being worthy of correction. Sometimes there was nothing evil to report;[2] but usually the visitor had to comment on some *comperta*.

In a full chapter the bishop called upon particular offenders to confess or find compurgators, and sometimes saw penances performed on the spot. Seldom have the records of these processes survived; the visitation of Canterbury Cathedral quoted above (page 61) gives by far the best account in this period. The process of purgation was commonly employed. Rigaud of Rouen often demanded it.[3] In 1248, when Grosseteste visited Dunstable,[4] one Henry de Bilenda, being defamed before the bishop, could not purge himself, and to escape the reformer's severity slipped secretly away at dawn and joined the Cistercian community of Merevale. We find Romeyn prescribing penance for certain canons who failed in their purgation at his last visitation of Drax,[5] and restoring to his good fame the prior of Thurgarton who (being not lightly defamed of incontinence) produced enough compurgators.[6] Purgation might be held over till after the visitation: an example of this occurs in Corbridge's register.[7]

The publication of the *comperta* was frequently, if not always, accompanied by some oral injunctions from the visitor. The register of Archbishop Giffard furnishes the best example in the thirteenth century. This visitor often had *comperta* transcribed, and the record of his

[1] Du Plessis, *Église de Meaux*, II. 87.
[2] *Ann. Mon.*, I. 146; Rigaud, 3, 4, 8, 15, 54, etc.; Wickwane, 137 note; Corbridge, I. 153, 287; Giffard, *Worc.*, II. 234, 243; Baluze-Mansi, I. 280b, 284b; *Chron. Petroburgense* (Camden Soc., vol. 47, 1849), 25.   [3] Rigaud, 13, 163.   [4] *Ann. Mon.*, III. 178.
[5] Romeyn, I. 154.   [6] *Ibid.*, I. 245.   [7] Corbridge, I. 198.

visitation of Newburgh Priory in 1275 is a series of *comperta* each followed by its appropriate injunction.[1] Wickwane, in the priory of Monk Bretton, expounded orally to the convent, " medicinaliter," those things which needed correction " tam in spiritualibus quam in temporalibus."[2] Corbridge's register notes " quod dominus in propria persona fecit correcciones apud Appelton."[3] The prioress and convent of Polslo were visited by Bishop Bronescombe of Exeter, who " statuit quedam sine scriptis."[4] Cantilupe of Hereford, writing to Leominster priory, says: " modum vero correccionis in aliquibus premissorum vobis meminimus viva voce plenius expressisse."[5] When Pecham visited St. Benet Holme in 1280, he corrected all that needed correction publicly, in chapter, in the presence of all the clerks and the monks.[6] Next year at Coxford he reproved individuals personally in the priory chapter.[7] At Meaux (Seine-et-Marne) in 1291, the brethren of the hospital, sitting in the cloister, received the bishop's corrections, injunctions and precepts.[8]

Even when the bishop uttered corrections on the spot, he often prepared written injunctions, or at least reserved the right to make such injunctions if necessary.[9] These were formal documents and sometimes, as in Pecham's register, elaborate literary exercises, rich in metaphor and Biblical allusions. The form of these final injunctions was determined by the fact that they were meant to be permanent and canonically binding. We must not sup-

---

[1] Giffard, *York*, 328-30 ; cf. 146.

[2] Wickwane, 140. The reader must ignore the memories of the terms " Spiritualia " and " Temporalia " as they occur in fiscal documents, for there their significance is quite different. Generally speaking, when the words occur in visitation records, unless specifically concerned with the differentiation of revenues, they refer to matters of spiritual or temporal welfare—not to the spiritual income derived from certain ecclesiastical sources and the temporal income comparable to any layman's revenue.

[3] Corbridge, I. 52 ; cf. I. 210.   [4] Bronescombe, 280.   [5] Cantilupe, 48.

[6] Barth. Cotton, *Hist. Anglicana* (Rolls series, 1859), 161.

[7] Peckham, I. 165 ; cf. II. 654, 669.

[8] Du Plessis, *Église de Meaux*, II. 188.   [9] Cantilupe, 48.

pose that the usual phrases were strung together without regard for the houses to which they were despatched. Professor Hamilton Thompson warns us to remember " the medieval habit, so often disregarded by modern writers, of using common forms as a groundwork for special variations and expansions with the utmost elasticity and freedom." [1] They were formal but not formalities. Where they were vague they were meant to be comprehensive ; and if they lacked specific denunciations it was that they might outlive the occasional offender. For this reason the particular was generalized and changes of administration omitted. On an occasion when Pecham had to be more explicit he enjoined a number of things upon the prior of Mottesfont and then turned to general legislation : " quae autem sequuntur, tam per te quam per successores tuos perpetuo volumus observari." [2]

Injunctions were usually issued with the visitor's seal attached,[3] and coupled with a special order that they should be observed. Archbishop Giffard, in one instance, gave a time limit : " Haec autem omnia supradicta precipimus in virtute obedientiae corrigi infra mensem." [4] Pecham on one occasion ordered the injunctions to be read at all visitations so that it might be known how they were observed.[5] This practice was not infrequent. When the bishop of Ely visited his cathedral in 1300 " he scrutinized all the statutes and injunctions of previous bishops and archbishops, and . . . issued a fresh compilation, containing those which were useful and necessary, but shortening some, omitting others which were superfluous, and adding others to prevent the recurrence of dissensions and scandals." [6] Pecham, stern though he was, was not always inexorable ; at the end of his injunctions for Reading Abbey (1281) he says : " siquid autem

---

[1] Gravesend, xxx.   [2] Peckham, II. 647.
[3] *Ann. Mon.*, III. 132 ; Bronescombe, 281 ; Giffard, *York*, 212 ; Swinfield, 168 ; *Cartulaire de Louviers*, ed. Th. Bonnin (1870-7), I. 213.
[4] Giffard, *York*, 317.   [5] Peckham, I. 265.
[6] Dr. Rose Graham, *Trans. Royal Hist. Soc.*, 4th series, XII. (1929), 66 ; cf. Peckham, I. 82, 223.

7

in hac ordinatione nostra durum forte vel importabile majori aut saniori [parti] capituli videatur, temperamentum libenter curabimus impendere quatenus nobis de prudentum virorum consilio secundum Deum videbitur expedire." [1]

Any injunctions made for a monastery were unalterable and unescapable by its inmates. The earliest set known, sent by St. Hugh or Hugh de Welles of Lincoln to the priory of Nun Coton, ends with the threat of anathema on them who break the statutes ; [2] Matthew Paris, commenting with horror on Grosseteste's visitations of 1251, says that the bishop called down horrible Mosaic curses on transgressors of his statutes ; [3] and excommunication, if we may judge from later records, always remained the extreme punishment for breach of injunctions. There are frequent orders for injunctions to be read in chapter. Sometimes they were to be read weekly [4] or more often monthly,[5] sometimes quarterly,[6] or thrice, twice or once yearly.[7] The visitation articles in the *Burton Annals* made it the business of the visitor to inquire " whether the statutes of the Council of Oxford concerning Religious, and those of Chapters General and of Episcopal Visitors, be read more than once a year in Chapter." [8]

Injunctions were usually despatched to the monastery after the visitor had left, and his officials had been allowed

---

[1] Peckham, I. 226 ; cf. *ibid.*, I. 346, and Pontissara, I. 644.

[2] Dugdale, V. 677 ; cf. III. 46 ; Winchelsey, II. 851.

[3] Matt. Paris, V. 226-7.   [4] Wickwane, 133.

[5] Peckham, II. 649 ; Pontissara, I. 121, 127 ; Wickwane, 141, 143, 144, 150 ; Giffard, *York*, 206.

[6] Romeyn, I. 154 ; Winchelsey, II. 851, 877, *Reg. H. Woodlock* (CYS 1940–1) I. 316, 509, 511.

[7] Romeyn, I. 265 ; Giffard, *York*, 213, and Winchelsey, II. 866 ; Romeyn.   [8] Trans. Coulton, *Five Centuries*, II. 469 ; *Ann. Mon.*, I. 485.

time to arrange the *comperta* into the usual formulæ.[1] But this practice was not invariable. Pecham most often sent his injunctions after;[2] on at least two occasions, however, he presented them to the monastery himself at the time of visitation.[3] This was also the usual custom of Archbishop Wickwane.[4] In Pecham's register we have a document which is apparently unique : the archbishop's commission to an official to deliver his injunctions at the priory of Holy Sepulchre, Canterbury—" discretioni tuae committimus et mandamus quatenus personaliter accedens ad monasterium Sancti Sepulcri, Cantuariae, cum ordinatione nostra, quam priorissae et monialibus loci eiusdem transmittimus, eandem eis diligenter exponas, faciens ipsam in omnibus observari." The commissary is also to see some administrative changes effected.[5]

Bishop Frere says, " injunctions . . . properly speaking are orders given for the enforcement of what is already enforceable." [6] And when we find that injunctions rarely if ever stray beyond the bounds of conciliar legislation and the judgments of popes, we may be encouraged to think that they were formal and of small importance. Nevertheless, the injunctions of visitors alone gave these wider pronouncements some disciplinary value ; without them we may doubt whether these laws would have been known in the cloister. As it is, one must remark that Gregory IX's statutes for the Black Monks are very seldom mentioned in English monastic records of the following half-century, and very rarely appear in the catalogues of medieval libraries. In contemporary Normandy houses often possessed copies of them, as demanded, but injunctions for the reading of them frequently had to be made.

The episcopal visitor had obstacles to overcome besides those arising out of the system of inquiry. Impunity was

---

[1] Giffard, *Worc.*, II. 87, 100, 104, 242 ; Pontissara, I. 125, 126; Cantilupe, 48, 144, 148 ; Giffard, *York*, 248 ; Romeyn, I. 131 ; Winchelsey, 98.

[2] Peckham, I. 81, 162, 259 ; II. 622, 625, 661, 666, 706, 717 ; III. 782, 798, 800, 805, 843.   [3] *Ibid.*, III. 800, 823.

[4] Wickwane, 55, 87, 88, 130, 131, 134, 140, 144, 141, 143, 145, 148, 150; cf. Giffard, *York*, 313 ; *Ann. Mon.*, III. 264 ; Bronescombe, 280, 281.

[5] Peckham, II. 708 ; cf. Giffard, *Worc.*, II. 83.   [6] Frere, 111.

gained by opposition to the bishop's visitation, or by an appeal instituted after the visitor had been admitted. A very considerable number of thirteenth-century cases of this sort might be cited. Archbishop Rigaud came to the priory of Sigy in 1258 and summoned the prior to attend his visitation—"which the said prior did not wish to do, but wished to appeal in writing ; and we found the gates of the priory closed and he would in no wise let us enter." When the archbishop reached the mother house of S.-Ouen, some three months later, he complained about the Sigy affair to the convent "which, however, gave no definite reply on the subject." [1] There was no visitation of the priory for the next three years.

Rigaud visited the priory of S.-Martin at Gisors in 1248, but in the next year he could not enter because the occupants shut the door on him. He summoned them to appear before him and make amends, but they treated the request with contumacy, and only in 1252 did one of the monks make his appearance. The following year the archbishop instructed the dean of Gisors and others to signify to the prior of Gisors that he must appear and declare if he wished to admit the archbishop to make an inquisition in his house. This was to inquire regarding the observance of Gregory IX's statutes, and the demand therefore had the weight of Innocent IV's special mandate of 1253. Nothing more is recorded for seventeen months. Then the archbishop personally and orally called upon the prior of Gisors to receive him " ad visitacionem et pro-curacionem." The prior for no reason asked for a delay until the following Tuesday. Apparently the result of this delay was unsatisfactory ; more than two years later we find the late prior of Gisors (now prior of Vesly) absolved from the sentence of excommunication incurred for non-observance of the Gregorian statutes and for non-payment of procurations at Gisors. The next year (1258) the archbishop came and took procuration from a new prior at Gisors.[2] Thus the archbishop had been evaded for ten years, and the man who had opposed him

---

[1] Rigaud, 318, 327.   [2] Ibid., 13, 51, 141, 168, 205, 281, 311.

was given the headship of another house. Incidentally we may note that this is the prior of Gisors, who in 1249 was said to be frequenting the nunnery of Villarceaux for the sake of Sister Idonia (who was defamed with another man).[1]

Even power to punish at a visitation did not necessarily mean power to improve. Deposition was an extreme measure, not favoured by visitors, since the delinquent had to be maintained and a suitable successor found for his office.[2] When this penalty was attempted it was very difficult to effect the removal of an unworthy abbot or prior: if he was the dependent of another monastery the mother house interfered; if he was independent he could appeal and protract proceedings, sometimes even persuading the Curia of his innocence when the local authorities were convinced of his guilt.[3] In the Gisors case cited above the archbishop could excommunicate a contumacious prior, guilty of irregularities against the Gregorian statutes and suspected with a nun, but could not prevent him from being promoted (while excommunicate) to another priory, presumably by the abbot of Marmoutier.

In England in the thirteenth century there were several notorious cases of abbots deserving deposition, yet holding to their office despite the complaints of visitors. At Evesham, at Great Malvern and at Bardney the diocesans found themselves powerless, although the abbots' faults were flagrant. In the first case a shady claim to exemption, in the second case the rights of the mother house, and in the third case an appeal to the metropolitan, hindered condemnations which were undoubtedly deserved.[4]

[1] Rigaud, 43.
[2] At the Cluniac visitation of Castle Acre Priory (1279), it was reported that " the prior is too extravagant. He would resign gladly enough if he could, but the difficulty is to find someone willing to replace him, and take over the house " (G. F. Duckett, *Visitations of English Cluniac Foundations* (London, 1890), 34). [3] Honorii III, 5075.
[4] It would be necessary to deal far more exhaustively with this important aspect of visitors' difficulties, had it not received much treatment from Dr. Coulton in various parts of *Five Centuries*, volume II.

Bishops found it extremely difficult to deal with defects in priories whose mother house lay beyond the sea. Among the collected letters of Grosseteste are three letters to the abbot of Fleury, in which the bishop asks that a suitable prior be appointed to the abbey's cell of Minting, and complains of the evil life of the monks in this priory. The bishop has himself dealt with some of the inmates and threatens further proceedings if need be.[1] As regards Archbishop Romeyn's troubles with Blyth Priory (dependent on Holy Trinity, Rouen) the editor of his register may be quoted : " With the view of giving the priory some kind of independent status the archbishop intimated to the abbot of the Holy Trinity that he would allow no prior of Blyth to be removed without his sanction. The foreign nationality of the monks gave rise to another difficulty. As was natural, they were constantly longing to go back to their native land. Losing hope of return they became slack in their devotions and bore the yoke imposed upon them by the observance of their rule very reluctantly. The archbishop proposed as a remedy that their sojourn in the English house should not exceed four or five years at most. Whatever the cause, the character of nearly all the monks about whom we have any information was very unsatisfactory. It looks as if the mother house drafted her most objectionable members into her English dependency." [2] Romeyn's contemporary at Canterbury, Pecham, wrote a strong letter to the abbot of Séez, who had placed a prior at Arundel, but allowed him no authority and claimed that he, the abbot, held all disciplinary power.[3]

Comparable difficulties arose when bishops dealt with mother houses in other dioceses. Bishop Swinfield of

---

[1] Grosseteste, *Epistolæ*, 166-9, 318-21.

[2] Romeyn, I. xiii.-xiv. A happier relationship is revealed by the letter of the bishop of Chichester (*c.* 1204-7) to the abbey of Lessay in Normandy. The bishop has visited and corrected the abbey's cell of Boxgrave and sends a report (*Calendar of Docts. preserved in France*, vol. I, ed. J. H. Round, 1899, 332).

[3] Peckham, II. 561 ; cf. III. 786 (a letter about the prior of Pembroke, dismissed to Séez by the archbishop).

Hereford had to write to the abbot of Reading in order that certain matters should be corrected at Leominster ; he stated that unless the abbot made correction he would be in duty bound to treat these things more severely himself.[1] In 1298 Bishop Sutton of Lincoln wrote an urgent letter to the prior of Kenilworth, saying that reforms must be made in the cell of Brooke. Kenilworth cast doubts on the need for action and asked for delay. When next year the prior of Brooke resigned into the hands of his superior, the bishop held that he alone could receive the resignation ; finally he deposed the prior for contumacy.[2]

These hindrances to bishops' operations, together with the internal defects of the visitatorial system, go far to show why even the best and most patient of reformers fell short of complete success.

[1] Swinfield, 149.
[2] *The Rolls and Register of Bishop Oliver Sutton*, ed. R. M. T. Hill, II (Lincoln Record Soc. 1950), 145–8, 157–9.

CHAPTER IV.

EXPENSES OF VISITATION.

THE process of visitation has been examined, from the despatch of notice to the despatch of injunctions. One important matter has been omitted as requiring separate treatment. The most permanent feature of the visitation system and the most fruitful cause of corruption and dispute was the procuration fee. The word " *procuratio* " was used to denote the hospitality which a house owed to a visitor, or the fee which it paid in lieu of entertainment. Procuration was indeed exacted in certain circumstances when no visitation had been made. But this sort of payment has nothing to do with the present subject and will not be considered here. Even an economical bishop had to spend a large amount on the upkeep of his establishment of clerks and servants during visitation. He was entitled, therefore, to exact a fee from each religious house, as well as from the parishes, which he visited : " quia qui seminat spiritualia metere debet carnalia." [1] Innocent IV, commenting on his own constitutions, wisely remarks that the law that procurations shall be paid is of public utility, for if none were paid, visitation would be neglected ; and a custom which hinders visitation is not to be tolerated.[2]

Generally speaking, the procuration fee was indissolubly linked with the visitation. Innocent III stated that procuration fees are so bound up with visitation that they cannot be remitted.[3] They may have been refused

[1] Hostiensis, *Summa*, IiI. de Cens. 14 (f. 223 *verso*) ; cf. *ibid.*, I. (f. 65 *verso*). The phrase is adapted from I *Corinth.* ix. 11, which is quoted by Innocent III (*Decretales*, III. xxxix. 17).

[2] Innocent IV, *Comment.*, f. 185 *verso*.   [3] *Decretales*, III. xxxix. 21.

because they were not paid to the visitor's predecessor ; but just as visitation cannot be prescribed by custom, neither can procuration.[1] The pope instructs diocesans. to enforce payment of procurations by religious who have refused them ;[2] writes directly to the prelates who owe, exhorting them to pay ;[3] and supports the diocesan's excommunication of prelates who refuse to pay.[4] On the other hand, the diocesan is sternly prohibited from exacting procurations from unvisited priories and granges.[5] Innocent III forbade this in the Lateran Council,[6] and replied likewise to several prelates who wrote to him about the matter.[7] Later popes confirmed this rule,[8] although exceptional privileges were occasionally granted to visitors.[9]

The constant correspondence with the papacy dealing with procurations shows how anxious the bishop was to maintain his rights and how burdensome the monastery considered this tax. The Third Lateran Council fixed the maximum retinue allowed to visitors of various ranks. Archbishops were to be content with forty or fifty horses ; bishops were not to exceed twenty or thirty. They were not to travel with dogs for the chase, or birds, " sed ita procedant, ut non quae sunt sua, sed quae Jesu Christi, quaerere videantur."[10] Orders to keep within the prescribed limits occurred in Celestine III's time, and they repeated in the Council of Westminster, 1200.[11]

[1] Innocent III, XV. 87, supplement 65 (Potthast, 4499, 1875) ; Potthast, 5022 ; Grégoire IX, 951.

[2] Innocent III, I. 464, 476 (Potthast, 452, 471) ; Grégoire IX, 1021-2.

[3] Honorii III, 2752, 5600 (Potthast, 6383, 7463) ; Grégoire IX, 654 ; Potthast, 4056.   [4] Grégoire IX, 1158.

[5] Hostiensis, *Summa*, III. de Cens. (fol. 224 recto).

[6] Leclercq-Hefele, V. 1360 (*Decretales*, III. xxxix. 23) ; cf. Wilkins, *Concilia*, II. 9 ; Winchelsey *Articles*, 14.

[7] Innocent III, XVI. 26, supplement 222 (Potthast, 4722, 5084).

[8] Honorii III, 1857, 5155, 5858, 6251 (Potthast, 7668) ; Grégoire IX, 196, 1258, 1424, 1770, 4754 ; Martin IV, 146.

[9] Innocent IV, 4204-5 (Potthast, 13069-70) ; Boniface VIII, 763.

[10] Leclercq-Hefele, V. 1091 (canon 4). *Decretales*, III. xxxix. 6.

[11] Wilkins, *Concilia*, I. 505 ; cf. Winchelsey, *Articles*, 69.

Finally the chapter was copied into Gregory IX's decretals.

Thereafter many exhortations are made to bishops to be moderate in their charges and to keep within the prescribed limit. Houses are told that they need not pay more than the Lateran Council required,[1] and visitors are told to be less expensive.[2] But for many years we find no legislation to fix a scale of charges. Grosseteste, addressing the pope in 1250, had spoken of procuration of monasteries as being " customary, and by long custom approved and found tolerable ";[3] yet there had been complaints against English visitors before this. In Normandy Archbishop Rigaud was remitting procuration fees in whole or in part at many visitations;[4] Innocent IV granted remission to the abbess of Prato for five years on account of poverty;[5] Gregory IX had given a similar indulgence twenty years earlier.[6] The local variation was so great that no fixed charge could be enforced. Simon of Bourges noted on one visitation that prices had risen nine-fold above the normal, and thus explained his enormous procuration fees.[7] The length of journey involved must also have been an appreciable factor. When the visitor lived quite close at hand, his rights to procuration were sometimes reduced. Honorius III, effecting a compromise, admitted the archbishop of York to visitation of St. Mary's Abbey, York, but declared the abbey to be free from the payment of fees providing it

---

[1] Innocent III, I. 140, 286, X. 88, XIV. 54, 56 (Potthast, 185, 313, 3136, 4250, 4246); Honorii III, 5146, 5837 (Potthast, 7536), 6009; Innocent IV, 709, 733, 7634; Alexandre IV, 1720, 1851 (Potthast, 16750), 2408; Urbain IV, 365; Nicolas III, 457, 468 (Potthast, 21516); Boniface VIII, 3696 (Potthast, 24964); Dugdale, VI. 288 (after oppression by the archdeacon of Richmond, *temp.* Innoc. III); *Cartulary of St. Frideswide's,* ed. S. R. Wigram (Oxford Historical Society, 1895-6), I. 40 (a.d. 1193), 59 (a.d. 1258).

[2] Grégoire IX, 1110 (Potthast, 9089), 3243, 4368 (Potthast, 10601), 7556; Innocent IV, 7314 (Potthast, 15259), 7583; Hartzheim, III. 633, 803 (Legatine pronouncements at Vienna and Magdeburg, 1267 and 1266.)

[3] Wharton, *Anglia Sacra* (1691), II. 347.

[4] Rigaud, 84, 117, 189, 219, 236, 241, 245, 251, 252, 260, 280, etc.

[5] Innocent IV, 6454.   [6] Grégoire IX, 966.   [7] Baluze-Mansi, I. 289a.

gave lodging to the archbishop when he visited after his consecration.[1] Gregory IX allowed the diocesan to visit the nunnery of St. Mary of Capua, but he was to receive no procuration for the visitation, " cum propter hoc ipsum, ob vicinitatem loci, non oporteat sumptus facere speciales." [2] Perhaps on the same principle the bishop of Autun was allowed no procurations when he visited the abbey of S.-Martin, Autun.[3] At Bayeux (1269) the bishop acknowledged that he might only take procurations from S.-Vigor-le-Grand on account of his first visit (though he might make visitation " cum expediens fuerit ").[4]

At the middle of the thirteenth century an important change was attempted. This was the restriction of procuration fees to payments in kind. It was ordered by a papal judgment of 1246 (often numbered among the decrees of the Council of Lyons), and given universal force in the same year.[5] Then, in 1250, Archbishop Boniface of Canterbury encountered opposition in the visitation of his province.[6] The matter was referred to Rome, and Innocent IV pronounced eventually in favour of the archbishop's right in 1252.[7] Eleven weeks later the pope wrote to the bishops of Lincoln, London and Wells to fix the maximum procuration to be exacted in future by any prelate.[8] This letter, preserved by the Burton annalist, declared that procurations " in victualibus et necessariis " should not exceed " summam vel valentiam quatuor marcarum argenti," according to the common price of

[1] Honorii III, 5850 (*CPR*, 108 ; Gray, 152 ; Romeyn, I. 73).

[2] Grégoire IX, 2393 ; Hostiensis does not agree with this ruling : *Summa*, III. de Cens. 14 (f. 223 *verso*).   [3] *Autun Cart.*, 147.

[4] *Antiq. Cartularius Ecc. Baiocensis* (1902-3), I. 210.

[5] See *infra*, 135-7. As will be seen, the rule was at the best of times interpreted loosely to admit payment in money for provisions bought on the spot by the visitor. Gregory IX had forbidden his legate to take money procurations from the English Cistercians in 1240 (Matt. Paris, IV. 81-2).

[6] Matt. Paris, V. 186-8 ; *Ann. Mon.*, I. 300 ; *Abingdon Chron.*, 7-8.

[7] Innocent IV, 5670-2.

[8] *Ann. Mon.*, I. 300-1 ; although a bishop's maximum allowance of followers was much smaller than that of an archbishop, this rule made no difference between their respective fees.

things in each place. On 28th February, 1254, the pope
repeated the order, apparently giving it a universal force.[1]
Neither of these rules was perfectly obeyed.[2] In
England a certain amount of evidence remains to show
that money was paid to visitors, and paid in excess of the
four-mark limit. After Archbishop Boniface's metropolitan visitation of 1250 the suffragans of Canterbury
expended large sums at the Curia in an•effort to limit the
incidence and amount of the procurations.[3] However,
he made another metropolitan visitation in 1253, and took
procurations at the rate of four marks ; [4] again, at Worcester and Bristol in 1260, he exacted only the just
amount ; [5] nor did his successor take money at Worcester
in 1273 when " cum clericis suis [a] conventu procuratus
fuit in refectorio." [6] But three years later Archbishop
Kilwardby came to Osney : his procuration charges, all
told, came to more than twenty-four marks, and the
chronicler points out that Boniface, "bonae memoriae,"
used to receive only four marks, apart from gifts.[7] In
1284, Pecham did not take procuration at Osney in food
and drink as was then usual, but asked to be paid in
money according to the ancient custom.[8] At Peterborough, in the same year, he had for his procuration

---

[1] Innocent IV, 7314 (Potthast, 15259, with a reference to Lokeren,
Abbaye de S.-Bavon, I. 213 ; Matt. Paris, VI. 289-90). The identical
letter contained in the *Regesta Innocentii III*, suppl. 121-2, from the
archives of Reims (Potthast, 3312) is almost certainly misplaced. The date
and pontifical year are those of Innocent IV's letter in the Vatican
register. Vendeuvre had not noted the confusion, and therefore ante-dates
the order by forty-six years (Vendeuvre, 163).

[2] Shortly afterwards the abbey of Marmoutier was told specially that
in accordance with this rule it need pay to no visiting prelate above the
sum of four marks (Innocent IV, 7556).

[3] Matt. Paris, V. 348.   [4] *Ann. Mon.*, III. 190.

[5] *Ibid.*, IV. 446, for Worcester ; and for the agreement with St.
James's Bristol, a sixteenth-century Canterbury cartulary, Bodleian MS.
Tanner 223, f. 97.   [6] *Ann. Mon.*, IV. 465.

[7] *Ibid.*, IV. 270-1 ; " in denariis secundum concilium generale,"
says the chronicler, quite wrongly. The statement shows what uncertainty
prevailed on these crucial points of law. Incidentally, all gifts were illegal.

[8] *Ibid.*, IV. 297.

four marks.[1] His successor presumably adhered to the stricter practice, since his visitation articles included the question (to be asked of a suffragan) : " an procurationem ratione visitacionis ante constituciones nouellas domini Bonefacii pape in pecunia numerata vel aliquid munus receperit vel a suis recipi permiserit a visitatis ? "[2]

In 1290 Godfrey Giffard, bishop of Worcester, visited the prior of Bekeford by his commissaries and had procuration in money.[3] Two years later, at the Cistercian abbey of Hayles, he had four marks for procuration.[4] In 1293 he apparently did not visit Stanley Monachorum, but received procuration from the prior in money.[5] In 1301 it was the complaint of the convent of Worcester that the bishop once charged thirty marks at Tewkesbury, and even more at Pershore : but the bishop said that he only charged the customary procuration and said that at Pershore it was in food and drink.[6] Rather earlier (in 1283) the bishop of Coventry made a composition with his monastic chapter. For all procuration charges he was to receive ten marks from the prior and convent, on condition that no demand for food or drink was made against their wish. The prior was also to contribute 200 marks for the renovation of the bishop's house, where he could lodge his *familia*. Here he was to entertain his retinue at his own cost during visitations, with the help of the ten marks paid for procuration.[7] This was a far more generous allowance than the law permitted, and directly contradicted the law which enjoined payment in kind. It was in spite of the fact that Gregory X, in the Council of Lyons (1274), had renewed (" exigit perversorum audacia ") the constitution of Innocent IV against prelates receiving procuration in money, with the penalty of double reimbursement.[8]

---

[1] *Chronicon Petroburgense* (Camden Soc., vol. 47, 1849), 100.
[2] Winchelsey, *Articles*, 13 ; cf. *ibid.*, 68.   [3] Giffard, *Worc.*, II. 379.
[4] *Ibid.*, II. 426 ; cf. 428.   [5] *Ibid.*, II. 434.   [6] *Ibid.*, II. 551.
[7] *Magnum Registrum Album* of Lichfield (ed. Wm. Salt Soc., 1924), 305 (f. 255).
[8] *Sext*, III, xx. 2 ; Grégoire X, 576 ; Mansi, XXIV. 97-8 ; Potthast, 20950 ; Leclercq-Hefele, VI. 202-3.

On the continent houses sometimes obtained special protection against the exaction of procurations in money.[1] More prominent in the papal registers than these cases are the records of privileges given to prelates enabling them to take pecuniary fees. In 1256 the archbishop of Reims is told that he may receive money from the less important places of his province if they wish to pay procurations thus.[2] Urban IV grants the same privilege by special favour to the bishop of Limoges in 1264 without mentioning the preference of the visitands.[3] Nicholas IV and Boniface VIII allow the archbishop of Lyons to take money in the visitation of his province.[4] The archdeacon of Bar (who was a cardinal's chaplain) was given the privilege in 1296, which was also granted sometimes to legate-visitors.[5]

Where prelates were given permission to visit by deputy the grant often included the right to pecuniary procurations. The bishop of Beauvais was allowed to take money in 1253 while he was absent from his diocese.[6] The bishop of Poitiers was allowed to visit by deputy and take money in 1290.[7] Stephen de Maulay, archdeacon of Cleveland, in 1291 gained the same privilege, to last until he returned from the Holy Land.[8]

In the pontificate of Boniface VIII there is a marked increase in the number of privileges up to the year 1298.[9] In that year Boniface modified the previous legislation regarding procurations by a chapter in his addition to the *Corpus Iuris*. Experience had shown, the pope said, that the prohibition of money payments often caused inconvenience both to visitors and visitands. As early as 1295 he had allowed a bishop to take procurations in money, since the customary hospitality caused a great and

---

[1] Alexandre IV, 533, 554 ; Clément IV, 1778.
[2] Alexandre IV, 1174.   [3] Urbain IV, 2759.
[4] Nicolas IV, 6927 ; Boniface VIII, 2551, 4021.
[5] *Ibid.*, 1103 ; Clément IV, 1778 ; Nicolas IV, 1358.
[6] Innocent IV, 7119 ; cf. Boniface VIII, 2666, 3162.
[7] Nicolas IV, 2592 ; cf. 5766.   [8] *Ibid.*, 6016.
[9] Boniface VIII, 298, 2677, 1149, 1406, 1667, 1796, 2460.

burdensome concourse of nobles.[1] Now, in 1298, he ordained that in future money might be taken if the visitands wished " pro sumptibus modicis faciendis in viatico." [2] The decision was a part of the canon law at last, but it had been acted upon before it was enunciated. For the remainder of Boniface's pontificate the pope usually granted right to exact money procurations when he granted right to delegate the duty of visitation.[3] In 1298 he gave the bishop of Clermont the power to absolve archdeacons and archpriests guilty of exacting pecuniary procurations.[4] These frequent privileges had no regard for the preferences of the visitands, and a number of them were granted to non-resident archdeacons, whose only wish was to secure a revenue. Occasionally visitors were released from the limits imposed by the Lateran Council and Innocent IV ; [5] but the papal registers show no case of this privilege being granted to an episcopal visitor.

Thus, after an attempt at reorganisation, the law of procurations was practically in its old condition at the end of the thirteenth century. The tax remained a constant source of disagreement between visitor and visitand. At the best of times the visitand found the expense of hospitality very burdensome, and tried by all ways to evade it ; while a rapacious prelate would try to make as much profit as possible from his visitation circuits.

The English records rarely tell us what procuration was paid to visitors unless it was considered excessive.[6] We are, however, fortunate in possessing very full evidence for the fees in thirteenth-century Normandy. After the first few years of his visitations, Archbishop Rigaud usually recorded the cost of his visits.[7] It was no doubt useful

---

[1] Boniface VIII, 1059 ; cf. Corbridge's complaint, *supra*, 65.
[2] *Sext*, III, xx. 3 (Swinfield, 349).
[3] Boniface VIII, 2686, 3462, 3662, 3742, 3746, 3822, 3933, 3940, 4148, 4154, 4200, 4209, 4223, 4264, 4657, 4918, 4922, 4962, 5192.
[4] *Ibid.*, 2708.
[5] Clément IV, 104 (Potthast, 19199) ; Boniface VIII, 764.
[6] *Supra*, 106.
[7] This evidence has been examined by Vendeuvre, 163-8.

for the visitor to refer in later years to this certain proof of reception in a religious house; it was useful for the visitand to set on record the amount which was due from him, so that he might check extravagance or seek remission in the future.

Rigaud's record of procuration usually takes the form of a note, " Ipsa die, procurati fuimus ibidem. Summa— libre—solidi—denarii." [1] The *Summa* seems to be the total estimated cost of the hospitality which the archbishop enjoyed. Its entry neither implies that he paid the account which was presented to him, nor suggests that he received payment in money. The archbishop was careful of his privileges, but he was not an unscrupulous man. It is unlikely that he would regularly act in contradiction to the orders of Innocent IV against money fees. There were occasions, however, when he seems to have taken a fixed amount of money instead of hospitality. In 1256, at S.-Martin of Hez " habuimus pro procuracione XL solidos parisienses." [2] This can hardly be construed as hospitality which cost the house forty shillings. The same applies to the entry for S.-Mellon of Pontoise in 1251; " and they paid us one hundred shillings of Paris *nomine procuracionis*, and straw and beds, and hay for the horses, and wood." [3] The charge was the same in 1253, but then there was dispute about the hay. [4] The special arrangement between the archbishop and this chapter was apparently not modified in deference to the pope's ordinance of 1254. S.-Mellon paid pecuniary fees to the end of Archbishop Rigaud's days. [5] At Liaucourt the archbishop noted: " debent nobis, pro procuracione nostra, IIII libras parisienses tantum." [6] In later years the agreement changed or was more carefully recorded: " habuimus quatuor libras parisienses, pro procuracione nostra, et domos, et utensilia, secundum quod continetur in compromissione." [7] The priory of Serans-

---

[1] Rigaud, 225 ; cf. *passim*.   [2] *Ibid.*, 254.
[3] *Ibid.*, 132.   [4] *Ibid.*, 166.
[5] *Ibid.*, 240, 278, 316, 345, 391, 448, 478, 504, 535, 570.
[6] Rigaud, 41, 193.   [7] *Ibid.*, 254, 282, 319, 393, 489.

le-Bouteiller paid a sum of money annually and provided
" utensilia domus, forraginem pro equis, et stramina pro
familia et equis, et ligna." [1] In 1257 the house did not want
to pay for the fodder which had been bought outside the
town, and produced an agreement made with Archbishop
Theobald in 1227 to prove its claim.[2] Rigaud copied the
agreement into his register and noted the terms at later
visitations. The archbishop seems to have obeyed the law
in general, but disobeyed it where contrary custom existed.

We can supplement our Norman records of procurations with the evidence of Simon of Bourges' visitations.
The archbishop travelled, on one journey at least, with
more than thirty horsemen ; for a prior grumbled at his
retinue, saying he was only liable to procuration for thirty
horses, and could not, nor ought to, spend above four
pounds.[3] At Angles the visitor was well feasted by the
abbot, and accounts were presented to show how much
the hospitality had cost. Everything was included except
the fodder for the horses, on which the abbot would set
no price ; and the diocesan's representative and the archbishop's servant wrote down the reckoning in their
records.[4] When the archbishop was about to leave
Mortemer the chapter complained about the presentation
of accounts by the visitor's household. They said that his
servants " expensas factas non ita rigide computaverant,
ut debuissent, et prout ipsi computaverant, secundum
ipsorum assertionem ; et ita gravabantur, ut in grossis
carnibus, et pollatura, et palea, et in feno." [5] At Angles
and at Mortemer there was obviously no definite fee for
visitation. Elsewhere on Simon's journeys we find the
same practice. Hospitality was the obligation and not
the payment of money.

[1] Rigaud, 167, 192, 255, 282, 320, 393, 490, 529, 567.
[2] Ibid., 282, 776 ; cf. 79.
[3] Baluze-Mansi, I. 279b. (Nevertheless, he paid all the archbishop's expenses, amounting to £10 5s.)
[4] Baluze-Mansi, I. 268a. Dr. Coulton says that Simon paid for all this good cheer (Five Centuries, II. 230). But this is not proved by the presentation of accounts. [5] Baluze-Mansi, I. 269a.

Vendeuvre estimates that Rigaud's procuration cost from four to twelve pounds, and normally between six and nine pounds.[1] " Les sommes portées par l'archevêque [Simon] dépassent de beaucoup celles indiquées par Eudes Rigaud : les prieurés pauvres ne paient pas moins de 7 à 9 livres, et la procuration entière est en moyenne de 13 à 15 livres ; elle atteint même 17, 18, 19 et 20 livres." [2]

To this extensive evidence for two provinces, we can add isolated records from various French dioceses—records of special agreements in which the cost of procuration is mentioned. According to an agreement made in 1194, the bishop of Orléans was entitled to 45 shillings *parisis* in a priory dependent on Saint-Père de Chartres.[3] The bishop of Poitiers, when he obtained recognition of his rights over the abbey of Maillezais in 1200, recorded the procurations which were annually due to him from the cells of this monastery. In one his expenses might amount to 70/-, in two more the charge was 65/-, in one 60/-, and in two 40/- ; from each of two priories he took 35/-, and from each of six 30/- ; in one he was only entitled to 20/-. In these totals of expenses the priors were not to reckon straw and other unimportant things, such as pots and pans and mattresses and bed-clothes. A little later the same bishop was denied procurations when he visited a cell of Vendôme : it was eventually decided that procurations had been paid in the past, and should be paid in the future at the rate of 60/- per annum.[4]

Towards the middle of the century we find similar variety of practice, with a rather higher average of cost in terms of money. Thus the bishop of Autun was allowed (1249) to take 60/- annually from a priory of S.-Bénigne, Dijon ; [5] at another priory he might take (1252) 50/- of money of Dijon, "et hoc propter paupertatem dicti prioratus." [6] 60/- of Paris was the amount allowed to the

---

[1] Vendeuvre, 167. The livre tournois (= ·4 marks, approx.) is here meant.   [2] *Ibid.*, 170.   [3] *IAD, Eure-et-Loir*, H. 529.
[4] *Poitiers Cart.*, 6, 10.   [5] *Autun Cart.*, 138.   [6] *Ibid.*, 266.

bishop of Chartres (1225) in one priory of Bec, and £4 in another, but the bishop might only take procurations from one of the two in any one year. Elsewhere the same bishop took 100/- from a priory; and twenty-six years later, at S.-Georges de Vendôme poverty was the excuse for a payment of the same amount.[1] The bishop of Meaux (1246) received 100/- of Provins annually from the abbey of S.-Faron in his city.[2] Half a century later the bishop of Cambrai consented (1302) to accept £12 a year in lieu of hospitality at S.-Martin de Tournai.[3]

In the diocese of Evreux we find a peculiar method of compromise. In 1239 the bishop had a rent (worth £4 *tournois* per annum) assigned to him instead of the procuration which he used to take from S.-Taurin for the manor of Louviers. Thirty years later a successor renounced all rights to procuration from the abbey of S.-Taurin in return for the payment of £200 *tournois* in the form of a rent of £20 per annum. In 1290, after the bishop and the abbey had been in dispute on the subject of visitation, the archbishop of Rouen ordained that while the bishop might visit S.-Taurin annually, and more often if necessary, he had no right to ask for procuration more than once a year.[4]

It will be observed that for the most part these figures are considerably below those found in the Rouen register and the *Acta* of Bourges, and certainly come well within the four-mark limit; we should remember, however, that they are records of special rights or privileges of monasteries, or concessions to bishops, and therefore probably fall short of the usual rate in the dioceses concerned.

[1] *Cartulaire de N.-D. de Chartres,* ed. Lépinois et Merlet (1862-5), II. 110, 116, 151.

[2] Toussaints Du Plessis, *Histoire de l'ég. de Meaux* (1731), II. 146.

[3] Berlière, *Inventaire des* Libri Obligationum, *etc.* (Rome, 1904), xxiv, note 5. In 1246 the pope confirmed the agreement of the bishop of Cambrai with the abbey of Saint-Sepulchre limiting procuration to £6 *parisis* (Innnocent IV, 2121).

[4] Grand Cartulaire de Saint-Taurin, ff. 263, 53 *sqq.* (*IAD, Eure,* H. 794).

In the agreement with Maillezais the varying resources of the priories seems to have been considered. But generally we find little trace of proportioning the procurations to the revenues of the visitands. No general law could allow for these variations, and it must have been difficult to apply even a local scale. Archbishop Simon of Bourges travelled with considerable pomp, whereas Rigaud, whose retinue cannot be estimated, certainly rested content with a modest *familia*. But Rigaud's procurations were not proportionate to the capacity of the houses visited. Neufmarché and Eu paid almost equal amounts in procuration in 1259, but the income of one was £200 and of the other £900.[1] As a consequence of the heavy burden on small, poor houses the visitor often remitted his procuration in whole or in part. Occasionally Rigaud paid all expenses himself, and sometimes repaid a house for part of the cost of hospitality. The canons of Gaillonnet paid him one hundred and ten shillings in 1254 for procuration : they ought to have paid all his expenses for the day had he demanded it, for they owed an entire procuration fee ; however, because they were poor and the archbishop had many folk with him at the time, he remitted the rest.[2] At the nunnery of Almenèches in 1260 he lunched with the bishop of Séez at the abbey's expense : it owed him an entire fee, but because of its poverty he rested content with the lunch and passed on.[3] On other occasions he remitted three pounds out of expenses amounting to £6 2s. od., three pounds out of £12, five pounds out of £8 10s. od.[4] Simon of Bourges showed similar indulgence to poor houses in his province.[5] At S.-André, a Premonstratensian house, he visited with little ceremony or expense, " condescendens loci ipsius sive compatiens paupertati." [6] About the same time Bishop

---

[1] Rigaud, 360-1.   [2] *Ibid.*, 189.   [3] *Ibid.*, 374.
[4] *Ibid.*, 219, 307, 427 ; cf. 241, 280, 306, 625.
[5] Baluze-Mansi, I. 282*b*, 288*a*, 289*a*, 289*b*, 292*b*, 292*b*, 293*a*, 293*b*, 294*a*, 296*a*, 301*a*, 308*b*.
[6] *Ibid.*, I. 279*b*. Bertrand de Got twice remitted the procurations due to him (Rabanis, 166, 178).

John of Winchester was asking the papal legate to spare
the nuns of Wintney to whom, on account of their
poverty, he had remitted his own procuration.[1] Even
more notable examples of the clemency of prelates are the
promise of the archbishop of Mainz (1294), that, in view
of the many burdens of the churches, he will exact no
procuration on account of visitation during the next
four years,[2] and the letter of Archbishop Pecham rescind-
ing his order for the exaction of procurations due from
the diocese of Chichester.[3]

Apart from the many occasions when the visitor's
right to procurations was uncertain or contested,[4] the
visitor usually safeguarded his rights if he granted remission temporarily. Rigaud found when he visited
S.-Martin of Chaumont in 1254 that although the priory
owed procuration he had remitted it for the last five
years because of the poverty of the house ; " but lest we
should lose our right, we bade the prior pay forty shillings
of Paris to our clerk for our expenses."[5] Several documents were copied into the archbishop's register to
record the fact that the visitor had not diminished his
rights by his clemency.[6] The archbishop of Dublin, in
1257, extracted a similar declaration from the bishop and
clergy of Leighlin.[7]

Visitors found another method of relieving poor houses.
Hostiensis remarks that if houses are too poor to pay
separately, they may be joined for purposes of procuration.[8]
Various popes gave instructions to this effect [9] to their

[1] Pontissara, I. 299 ; cf. Giffard, *Worc.*, II. 6.
[2] *Hessische Urkunden*, ed. L. Baur (1862), II. 489 ; it would be
interesting to know whether the archbishop visited during the following
four years.   [3] Peckham, II. 572.
[4] Rigaud, 51, 79, 82, 83, 234, 249, 252, 302, 327, 345, 353, 530,
554-5, 557 ; Baluze-Mansi, I. 280a.
[5] Rigaud, 193.   [6] *Ibid.*, 84, 117, 236, 556-7, 625, 781-2.
[7] *Calendar of the* Liber Niger Alani (Journal of the Royal Society of
Antiquaries of Ireland, 1897, XXVII, 171), 674.
[8] *Summa*, III. de Cens. 18 (f. 224 *recto*).
[9] Clément IV, 296 ; Martin IV, 472w ; Honorius IV, 803 ; Boniface
VIII, 1610.

legates, and episcopal visitors sometimes spread their expenses over several houses.[1] Rigaud took one procuration from two priories in 1266 for another reason—"quia vocati fuimus a domino rege Francie, visitationis nostre exercicium accelerare studuimus."[2]

The economic side of the visitation system cannot be praised. When the payment of fees was unorganized there was too much opportunity for extortion ; but the rules demanding procuration in kind were often impracticable or tiresome. Finally, no satisfactory division of the burden was devised. Great houses could afford more than they paid, but small houses could not bear the cost of hospitality. Although bishops were often to blame for travelling with superfluous followers, even Rigaud, who was probably exceptionally careful, was a heavy burden for some poor priories. It is easy to explain the constant efforts of monasteries to obtain exemption. The episcopal visit might, according to strict regulars, be contrary to the spirit of monasticism, but this was not the reason for opposition. Visitation was a mark of authority, procuration was a tax : these facts made bishop and regular antagonistic.

[1] Baluze-Mansi, I. 272b, 278a, 286a, 288b.   [2] Rigaud, 556-7.

CHAPTER V.

THE DURATION AND FREQUENCY OF VISITATIONS.

THE length of a visitation naturally concerned the visitands very deeply if they had to entertain the visitor's company at their own expense While there appears to have been no general ruling on the length of time a bishop might occupy in the visitation of a single house, it seems to have been usual for hospitality to be extended to him for one day and one night. Thus the bishop of Worcester in 1290 visited Worcester Priory : " cum septies viginti equis venit, et per tres dies visitavit cum magna multitudine, procuratus primo die tantum." [1] There is the suggestion of an established rule to this effect (which may have been merely local) in the letter of Innocent IV to the archbishop of Reims, allowing him on visitation " ex justa causa in una ecclesia aliquot morari diebus, constitutione aliqua non obstante." [2]

If a visitor was supposed to pay for his keep after the first day of visitation, we should expect to find proceedings hurried as much as possible. Sometimes the business at one house was too much for one day. On several occasions Archbishop Rigaud continued his investigations on the morrow,[3] and once interrupted his visitation of Bourg Achard, holding inquiries there on the 5th and the 11th of September, 1248.[4] Archbishop Pecham arrived on visitation at St. Benet Holme on 6th December, 1280,

---

[1] *Ann. Mon.*, IV. 503-4 ; cf. *ibid.*, III. 276. Similarly, Archbishop Bertrand de Got stayed at the abbey of Clairac in 1304 : " deux nuits la premiere aux despens dud : abbe et la second aux siens " (Rabanis, 154; cf. 165, 198).   [2] Innocent IV, 3738.
[3] Rigaud, 386, 609.   [4] *Ibid.*, 8.

and did not utter his corrections in the chapter there until
8th December.[1] In his letter of notice to Canterbury,
Archbishop Winchelsey reserved the right to continue the
visitation if (as happened) he could not complete it in
one day.[2] But such was not the usual practice. Visitors
rarely stayed two nights in the same place. In 1271 the
bishop of Winchester conducted his visitation—in the
cathedral church " feria secunda, et apud Hydam feria
tertia, et in abbatia de Sancta Maria feria quarta, et
postea per episcopatum." [3] Entries in English registers
regarding the sending of notice show that the visitor
sometimes planned to visit a number of houses on successive days.[4] The records of Rigaud and Simon of
Bourges confirm this custom. A careful examination of
bishops' itineraries would probably lead to the same
conclusion.

When a visitor stayed for more than one day and night
in one place it was sometimes to allow him to visit other
houses the more conveniently. Archbishop Rigaud often
used this method of visiting small priories : procurations
were then paid to the place where the visitor lodged.
In 1282 the bishop of Worcester " visited St. Augustine's
of Bristol and remained there for three days, the first
day at the cost of the said house, and on the other two
days . . . he visited the houses of St. James and St.
Mark." [5]

Where small priories lay close together they could be
dealt with more quickly. Rigaud of Rouen and Simon of
Bourges sometimes visited two or more in one day. But
eventually the law provided against visitors making profit
out of this hurried work. Boniface VIII enacted that
" non liceat visitanti nisi unam procurationem recipere
una die sive unum locum visitaverit, sive plura." [6]

[1] Bart. Cotton, *Hist. Anglic.* (Rolls series, 1859), 161.
[2] Winchelsey, 69 ; cf. Rabanis, 165 (a two days' visitation).
[3] *Ann. Mon.*, II. 110.
[4] Wickwane, 22, 54 ; Romeyn, I. 51, 71 ; Corbridge, I. 43, 76, 123,
210 ; *Vetus Liber Archidiaconi Eliensis* (Cambridge Antiq. Soc., 1917), 19.
[5] Giffard, *Worc.*, II. 146 ; cf. 244, 340. Bertrand de Got adopted the
same practice (Rabanis, 194).   [6] *Sext*, III. xx. 3.

Visits were generally so brief that the visitor must
frequently have failed to carry out a thorough examination. This avenging angel, whose descent upon a house
was announced beforehand, had disappeared again before
he could possibly have learned the daily habits of its
inmates and their obscurer faults. Only a series of such
visits could acquaint the visitor with the true life of the
monastery.

" La residence des Evesques et des Metropolitains dans
leurs Dioceses et dans leurs Provinces, aussi bien que celle
des astres dans le Ciel, est dans une course et une agitation
continuelle. . . . Ils courent d'une extrémité à l'autre et
portent par tout la lumiere et les flammes de la charité." [1]
The business of his diocese left the medieval bishop
very little time for residence in one place. Annual
visitation of the whole diocese was considered desirable in
early times, as is shown by Gratian's canons from Tarra-
gona (614) and Toledo (633) ; [2] though at the Council of
Lugo (569) it was found that dioceses were too large to
admit of so frequent circuits.[3]   In these passages no
mention of monasteries will be found, and nowhere does
the canon law lay down a definite rule as to regularity in
the amount of monastic visitation.

The *Decretum* sets down two early pronouncements on
the subject : [4] " Visitandi exhortandique gratia ad monasterium, quotiens placuerit, ab antistite civitatis accedatur ;
sed sic karitatis offitium illic inpleat episcopus, ut grava-
men aliquod monasterium non incurrat."

" Non semel, sed sepius in anno episcopi visitent
monasteria monachorum, et si quid corrigendum fuerit,

---

[1] Thomassin, Pt. I. bk. 2, c. 43.   This may be compared with a medieval simile, taken from a thirteenth-century sermon addressed to prelates
(Bibliothèque Nationale, MS. *Latin* 10455, f. 42a).   " Prelatus esse debet
sicut Mardocheus, de quo dicitur in figura boni prelati (Hest'. [Esther
ii. 11]) ; enim deambulabat cotidie ante vestibulum domus in qua electe
virgines servabantur, curam agens salutis Hester."

[2] *Decretum*, II. X. i. §§ 10-11.   [3] Thomassin, Pt. II. bk. 2, c. 66.

[4] *Decretum*, II. XVIII. ii. §§ 28-29 (Gregory I and the C. of Orleans,
645, a.d.).

corrigatur." The vagueness of the *Decretum* continued in practice. There was no consistent legislation from the Curia, no established custom. The most common custom was that which applied the rule of annual visitation which ruled diocesan visits ; but the lapse of this in practice and occasional contrary decisions destroy all uniformity. Innocent III on one occasion enjoined annual visitation of French monasteries,[1] but at another time ordered " quod idem episcopus, quum ad ipsam ecclesiam causa correctionis accesserit, moderatam ab ea procurationem recipiat bis in anno." [2] Honorius III in 1226 declared that the archbishop of York might visit St. Mary's, York, once a year, or twice if urgent necessity required it.[3] Gregory IX allowed the archbishop of Capua to visit St. Mary's, Capua, annually.[4]

In 1237 the Legate Otto ordered the English prelates to go round their dioceses to correct and reform " temporibus opportunis." [5] This was the practice of the bishop of Bayeux (to visit religious houses " cum expediens fuerit "), as we learn from an agreement made in 1269 with the priory of S.-Vigor-le-Grand.[6]

The Saxon author of a formulary in the first half of the century states that every archbishop and bishop is obliged to visit his diocese once a year.[7] Hostiensis gave, as one opinion on the subject, " Dicunt quidam quod singulis annis semel potest episcopus visitare, si causa subest (*Decretum* II. X. iii. 9 and 7) sed si necessitas non subest, tunc de triennio in triennium." [8] At the Legatine Council of Würzburg (1287) the Legate bade bishops and archbishops visit diligently their dioceses once a year, or at least biennially.[9] One may infer from a remark of John Pecham that he aimed at annual visitation in his diocese.[10] The abbot of Glastonbury complained

[1] Innocent III, suppl. 144 (Potthast, 3976).
[2] Potthast, 2146 ; *Decretales*, III. xxxix. 21.
[3] Honorii III, 5850, 6254 (*CPR*, 108-9) ; Gray, 152 ; Romeyn, I. 73.
[4] Grégoire IX, 2393.   [5] Wilkins, I. 654.
[6] *Antiquus Cartularius Eccl. Baiocensis*, ed. V. Bourienne (1902-3), I. 210.   [7] Rockinger, 251.   [8] *Summa*, III. de Censib., 19 (f. 224 *recto*).
[9] Hartzheim, III. 731.   [10] *Supra*, 51.

when the bishop of Bath visited for the second time within a year, as though this were irregular. The bishop apparently did not claim the right to visit whenever he wished, but pointed out that the second visitation was at the request of the monks.[1]

A special arrangement between the bishop of Autun and the convent of S.-Martin, which received the approval of the pope in 1257, only allowed the bishop to visit once during the rule of each abbot. His rights were very stringently regulated and no procurations were due to him ; his old rights in the cells of the abbey were, however, maintained intact.[2]   At Battle Abbey there was only triennial visitation on behalf of the diocesan.[3]   At S.-Taurin of Evreux the monks were obliged to pay a procuration once a year to the bishop, as diocesan ; if the prelate desired to make the visitation of the monastery more often he could do so at his own expense.[4]

This variety of custom is reflected in the practice of the times, and where no special arrangement was made between a religious house and its diocesan we may assume that no regularity existed. There was probably not so much regional variation or variation in different periods as irregular incidence within each circuit. One of the best features of the visitatorial system of bishops was this fact that the visitor might descend upon notorious houses as often as he chose ; while those whose government and morals were above reproach could be relieved from the burden of unnecessary visits. But the elasticity of the system, theoretically favourable to its efficiency, does not seem to have always had the desired result. Too often it meant that bishops neglected their duty and monasteries went unreformed. The evidence unfortunately is seldom clear : we hear more of parochial than of monastic visitation.

Summing up the evidence for a slightly later period, Miss E. K. Lyle says : " Most bishops attempted to make

---

[1] *VCH Somerset*, II. 90.   [2] *Autun Cart.*, 146-8.
[3] *Supra*, 41-2.   [4] *Supra*, 115.

a general tour through their dioceses soon after installation, but thereafter all depended upon circumstances. Judging from the evidence obtainable, two complete personal visitations might be considered a high average for an episcopate." [1] Professor Hamilton Thompson says of Richard Gravesend, bishop of Lincoln from 1258 to 1279, " it may be inferred from the dates relating to Lincoln and Northampton that he aimed at accomplishing a triennial round of the whole diocese and, allowing for absence and illness, did what he could." [2] In another place the same authority writes regarding Thomas of Corbridge, archbishop of York (1300-4) : " There are few examples of consistent diligence in the episcopal office more conspicuous than that which is disclosed to us by the itinerary of Corbridge ; and it is doubtful whether any other English prelate in the middle ages managed, in the short space of four years and a half, to come within measurable distance of completing two visitations, and those exceptionally thorough, of his diocese." [3] This is borne out by the Exeter registers of the thirteenth century. " Bishop Bronescombe (1257-80) began his first visitation in August, 1259, and it lasted until February, 1260. Still he did not visit all the diocese, North Devon being left out. The following year he went over much the same ground as before. He did not again make a general visitation of the diocese, and did not visit North Devon thoroughly until 1272. Bishop Quivil's (1280-91) itinerary does not give evidence of any general visitation." [4]

Although English bishops certainly combined parochial and monastic visitations in one circuit,[5] as was Archbishop Rigaud's custom in Normandy, it is possible that they " were on the whole more zealous and punctual in visiting their convents than their dioceses." [6] This conclusion of

[1] Lyle, *English Bishop*, 36.   [2] Gravesend, xvii.
[3] Corbridge, II. xx.   [4] Lyle, *English Bishop*, 35.
[5] Cf. *Ann. Mon.*, III. 147 ; *Vetus Liber Arch. Eli.*, 19 ; Bart. Cotton, *Hist. Angl.*, 159 ; *Household Expenses of Richard de Swinfield* (Camden Soc., LIX, 1854), I. 84, 86.   [6] Frere, 81.

Bishop Frere's might be inferred from the fact that
visitation of regulars, unlike visitation of deaneries, was
rarely the archdeacon's duty: so that the absence of
the other disciplinary authority made the bishop's visit
particularly important. Nevertheless, we must not estimate zeal and punctuality by regularity in this work.
Bishops did not often visit all the religious houses in their
jurisdiction on one circuit ; more often they only visited
a house when it was peculiarly necessary for the inmates
or convenient for themselves. Bishop Halton of Carlisle,
who came to the diocese in 1292, did not make his primary
visitation of the cathedral until 1300.[1] Parallels are not
lacking from other regions. We may add to our certainty
by examining the details of two registers. We have fairly
full evidence from which to judge the frequency of
monastic visitation in York under Romeyn (1286-1296)
and in Worcester under Godfrey Giffard (1268-1302).
This consists of notices of forthcoming visits (except
where these were expressly cancelled) and of notes regarding visitations accomplished. We cannot be sure
that the material is complete, but both registers are
comprehensive documents in which omissions of this sort
are unlikely.

John le Romeyn occupied the see of York for ten and
a half years. In the whole period he visited thirty-two
religious houses (in person or by deputy) fifty-five times.
In the first two years he visited twenty-four houses (one
of them twice) and five houses. He visited (in person or
by deputy) one house four times ; six houses three times
each ; eight houses twice each ; seventeen houses only
once each.

Godfrey Giffard ruled over Worcester diocese for
nearly thirty-three and a half years. In this time he made
ninety-seven visitations (in person or by deputy) of
twenty-seven houses. He visited nine regular houses in
1268, four others in 1269. He visited (in person or by
deputy) three houses six times each ; seven houses five
times each ; six houses four times each ; three houses

[1] Halton, I. xxxii.

three times each ; three houses twice each ; five houses once each.[1]

Neither of these records is comparable with that of Archbishop Rigaud of Rouen who, in his diocese alone, visited forty-nine houses 682 times in all in twenty-one years. Romeyn's register shows just a quarter the frequency ; Giffard's shows much less. Yet these prelates were not unbusinesslike nor outrageously lax. It is not unfair to suppose that the evidence for other episcopates, if it were as complete as it is for these two, would yield much the same result. England and Normandy comprised three of the best ordered provinces of the Latin Church in the thirteenth century.

The upheavals of war, the badness of roads and frequent infirmities prevented bishops and metropolitans from carrying out their visitations with sufficient regularity. In 1248 the archbishop of Auch was allowed to exact procurations without visiting his diocese " durante persecutione vicecomitis Lomanie." [2] In 1255 Boniface, archbishop of Canterbury, confessed that he could not visit the four Welsh dioceses in his province " propter guerrarum discrimina, penuriam victualium et plura impedimenta alia." [3] The archbishop of Mainz also sought indulgence in case he had to stop his visitation because of war.[4] Others received the same indulgence,[5] and the outbreak of war interrupted Archbishop Winchelsey's visitation in 1296 (supra, page 61). John Pecham wrote to the bishop of Exeter in 1282 to postpone his visitations : " aeris intemperie et viarum inexperta difficultate multipliciter impediti [sumus]." [6] About the same time Archbishop Simon of Bourges refrained from going to visit Aurillac at the advice of his companions " since they said that the roads were impassable because of the wintry

---

[1] The figures for Giffard's visitations are not compiled from the table given by Mr. Willis Bund (Giffard, *Worc.*, I. xciii.). The figures in that table are not only frequently inaccurate, but misleading even when they are accurate, since they include occasions when procurations were paid without a visitation taking place.

[2] Innocent IV, 4204 (Potthast, 13069).   [3] Alexandre IV, 407.
[4] Nicolas IV, 1250.   [5] *Ibid.*, 2372, 2394.   [6] Peckham, I. 304.

weather." He took procuration from the prior of S.-Gervais without going to the priory, for the prior warned him that " the mountains were infested with robbers who waylaid the passers-by." [1] After a later visitation of Simon's there is a list of six houses " which my lord omitted in the visitation of Albi diocese, both because of their distance and because of the summer heat." [2] Rigaud of Rouen was on several occasions unable to visit owing to his chronic rheumatism.[3] At another time he failed to visit certain priories in the diocese of Rouen " propter eorum paupertatem," [4] and once had two priors come to him for examination, as he could not visit them.[5] When Rigaud held no visitation, he exacted no procuration. Not so Raymond, bishop of Périgueux, who was allowed by Honorius III to pocket the fees, although he was too ill to visit.[6] A considerable number of other prelates made similar excuses to the Curia, but undertook to find delegates to visit in their place.

" Licet Episcopi sint Christi vicarii non tamen possunt ubique esse," said Hostiensis.[7] It became an established principle of canon law (arising out of practical difficulties observed in the Fourth Lateran Council) that a bishop might have delegates who could take his place on almost all occasions.[8] The other business of the diocese, or affairs of state, might, it has been seen, prevent a bishop from visiting personally as often as he saw that religious houses needed correction. The enormous size of many medieval dioceses was in itself sufficient excuse for a prelate not visiting every church in person. In England, for instance, the diocese of Lincoln extended over nine

---

[1] Baluze-Mansi, I. 299*b*, 293*a* ; cf. Nicolas IV, 247.

[2] Baluze-Mansi, I. 303*a*. In 1410 the bishop of Grenoble " propter gravitatem persone sue non potuit accedere ad loca de Villario Reculato . . ." So he had the *confirmandi* come to him, and sent a chaplain to visit (*Grenoble Visit.*, 112).

[3] Rigaud, 219, 466 ; cf. 113, 334, 355, 635.

[4] *Ibid.*, 251-2.   [5] *Ibid.*, 92.   [6] Honorii III, 4485.

[7] *Comment.*, I. xxxi. 15, § 4 (f. 166 *recto*, vol. I.).

[8] Leclercq-Hefele, V. 1340 ; *Decretales*, I. xxxi. 15.

counties, and the same trouble was as keenly felt in thirteen-century Germany.[1]

Fournier and Schmalz have shown that by the twelfth century the archdeacon had ceased to be practically the bishop's deputy, and that he was not so much a help as a hindrance to the bishop's authority.[2] In his place the bishop created his " officialis." The official had a quasiordinary jurisdiction,[3] but his general commission did not give him the powers " inquirendi, corrigendi, aut puniendi aliquorum excessus, seu aliquos a suis beneficiis, officiis, vel administrationibus amovendi " : these powers could only be given him by special commission.[4] This was a pronouncement of Boniface VIII, taken (so the gloss says) from an *extravagans* of Alexander IV. Presumably the law had been indefinite on the subject until after the middle of the thirteenth century, so we may suppose that no serious contestation of authority had hitherto occurred. An example of a special commission occurs in the register of Archbishop Corbridge who, it has been seen, was very active in visiting—at least by proxy. The terms of the archbishop's general commission to John de Nassington, appointing him to the officiality of York, include the special power : " necnon ad inquirendum de excessibus subditorum nostrorum et canonice corrigendum eosdem cum potestate cohercionis canonice, vices nostras, quousque eas duxerimus revocandas." [5]

Traces of visitation by delegates occur early in the thirteenth century. Hugh II of Lincoln visited by deputy at Peterborough ;[6] and his official visited Dunstable in 1233 and left his sealed injunctions behind.[7] There was a commission appointed for the visitation of Cartmel in 1248,[8] and in 1251 two monks of Worcester and Gloucester took the bishop's place in the visitation of Tewkesbury.[9] When Archbishop Kilwardby visited the diocese of Ely in 1277 he planned to visit three religious houses in person,

[1] Hauck, *Kirchengeschichte Deutschlands*, V. 182-3.
[2] Fournier, xxviii. *sqq.* ; Schmalz, 41.   [3] *Ibid.*, 51.
[4] *Sext*, I. xiii. 2.   [5] Corbridge, I. 1.   [6] *Supra*, 14.
[7] *Ann. Mon.*, III. 132.   [8] *VCH Lancs.*, II. 145.   [9] *Ann. Mon.*, I. 146.

and two more "per clericos." Unfortunately, the commission for these deputies is not recorded with the itinerary.[1]

For the later thirteenth century we need not rely on the brief notices of chroniclers ; the episcopal registers yield fuller information about delegates. From this evidence we see that a special commission was required in practice as in law before the official or any other person could conduct a visitation. Moreover, this delegate was not always empowered to correct ; he might only be told to inquire. Such was the mandate of Godfrey Giffard to his official of Worcester in 1277.[2] In the next year the official was ordered both to visit and to correct.[3] When the bishop dealt with his priory of Worcester he had to act circumspectly. In 1300, according to the *Annales Wigorniae*, he sent delegates to visit the priory, but the chapter complained ; he then armed the delegates with a formal commission, which was as follows : " Vobis committimus vices nostras, hoc modo videlicet, ut vos, sacrista, quatenus contingit spiritualia, soli visitetis, defectus et excessus quos inveneritis corrigatis ; quoad temporalia vos, officialis et sacrista praedicti, simul hujusmodi visitationis et correctionis officium et ea qualitercunque contingentia sub forma debita impleatis." [4] According to Giffard's register there were two separate commissions granted to the visitors : one to inquire and one to correct.[5] In other dioceses we find the same special commissions, sometimes limiting the powers of the visitor,[6] sometimes putting the whole process in his hands.[7]

Frequently in the pontificate of Corbridge, the archbishop followed up his personal visitation by appointing a commission to correct *comperta*.[8] Archbishop Romeyn

---

[1] *Vetus Liber Arch. Eli.*, 19.
[2] Giffard, *Worc.*, II. 92 ; cf. 201, 495, 531.   [3] *Ibid.*, II. 100 ; cf. 123.
[4] *Ann. Mon.*, IV. 546-7.   [5] Giffard, *Worc.*, II. 528.
[6] Giffard, *York*, 54 ; Romeyn, I. 55 ; Corbridge, I. 124, 126.
[7] Wickwane, 46, 175 ; Romeyn, I. 203 ; Pecham, 31 ; Swinfield, 362-3.
[8] Corbridge, I. 109, 147, 177, 186.

occasionally entrusted such correction by special mandate to the head of the house concerned.[1] Archbishop Rigaud left the correction of the chapter of Bayeux to the bishop, " vice nostra ", and delegated the power to the official of Bayeux at Ste.-Trinité, Caen. The diocesan was told to inquire after the archbishop's visitation at the nunnery of Almenèches. The dean of Bray was to see that injunctions were obeyed at S.-Aubin ; and the archbishop left a canon of Rouen at Corneville in 1267 to investigate a dispute which had been raised at the visitation.[2] Pecham, after a metropolitical visitation, handed over the punishment of certain comperta in Hereford diocese to the dean of Hereford—" quae etiam correctioni vestrae relinquenda duximus, ex gratia speciali." [3] Early in the next century Bishop Wodelok of Winchester appointed a commission to see whether his recent injunctions at Tanbridge Priory had been obeyed.[4] In the northern registers we sometimes find letters of recommendation sent to monasteries telling them to receive the archbishop's delegate as their visitor.[5]

Various reasons for delegation of this business occur, though more often none is stated. The prelates are " variis arduis occupacionibus implicati " [6] or " nonnullis prepediti negociis." [7] Bodily infirmity accounted for some mandates ; Godfrey Giffard had to postpone visitations because of his " accustomed gout," [8] like Rigaud of Rouen, who sent his officials to visit when rheumatism overtook him.[9] Sheer senility was the excuse of Hugh d'Arcy, bishop of Autun, when he obtained leave to visit and take procurations by deputy, in 1290.[10] War and

---

[1] Romeyn, I. 72, 226.   [2] Rigaud, 93, 94, 374, 361, 579.

[3] Peckham, II. 503 ; ibid., III. 1060 (Commission for St. Asaph's).

[4] Surrey Archæolog. Collections, IX. (1888), 125-6.

[5] Wickwane, 151, 152, 312 ; Romeyn, I. 55 ; Corbridge, I. 199, 282.

[6] Wickwane, 175 ; cf. Grégoire IX, 3709 (Potthast, 10365).

[7] Romeyn, I. 55 ; cf. Alexandre IV, 792 ; Nicolas IV, 1070 ; Honorius IV, 644, 974.   [8] Giffard, Worc., II. 165.

[9] Rigaud, 474 ; cf. Gravesend, xviii. ; Nicolas IV, 538, 2083 ; Boniface VIII, 1149, 3742, 4922, 4959.   [10] Autun Cart., 328.

civil unrest prevented prelates from visiting.[1] The bishop of Clonfert in 1296 actually obtained an indult from the pope " during four years, to visit by deputy places in his diocese to which he cannot go with safety to himself." [2] The bishop of Poitiers was allowed to visit by deputy while he was in dispute with the French king, since he had been molested by royal officials and bailiffs and dared not visit his diocese.[3] The bishop of Cahors had actually been kidnapped by Gaillard de Roche and other sons of iniquity, so he was allowed to visit by deputy for a year and take procurations meantime.[4] An archdeacon of Rouen, in 1235, was unable to visit personally on account of the enormous animosity he had aroused (not by his own fault).[5] While the bishop of Beauvais went crusading the prior of S.-Victor and a Templar chaplain were appointed to be his visitors.[6] The absence of bishops on business at the Roman court also called for the appointment of delegates.[7]

Delegates had their difficulties. The archbishop of Salzburg sent his archdeacon to a house where the unfortunate man was set upon and ejected.[8] " It was not always safe to be the bearer of the Bishop's orders for corrections," says Mr. Willis Bund ; the delegate to St. Sepulchre's, Warwick—a canon of the house—was imprisoned and deprived of his belongings till the bishop's clerk intervened.[9] But hardships as great were occasionally suffered by even more important dignitaries in their visitations.[10] Boniface VIII in 1302 gave among the

---

[1] Boniface VIII, 3746, 4962, 5192.
[2] *CPR*, 565 (Boniface VIII, 1170).
[3] Nicolas IV, 2592 ; cf. *ibid*., 3211 ; Boniface VIII, 2460.
[4] Urbain IV, 1792.
[5] Grégoire IX, 2818 ; cf. Innocent IV, 3660.   [6] Honorii III, 2815.
[7] Boniface VIII, 2666, 5295, and *ibid*., 3162, completed by documents in the archives of Agde (Devic et Vaissete, *Hist. Gén. de Languedoc*, ed. Privat, 1875, V. 1359).   [8] Honorii III, 3745 (Potthast, 6767).
[9] Giffard, *Worc.*, I. xcvii, II. 126. The delegates of the archbishop of Bordeaux were resisted at Montignac and elsewhere in 1304 ; the reason is not recorded (Rabanis, 167).
[10] Innocent III, XV. 105, a papal visitor ; XV. 144, an abbot of Cluny (Potthast, 4513, 4551).

reasons for allowing the bishop to introduce attendants into the chapter at his visitation, the fact that it were no small diminution of the bishop's dignity if he were made to trust himself alone (*seque solum . . . committere compellatur*) among persons perchance suspect.[1] In 1225 the bishop of Glandèves had actually been killed during the visitation of his diocese,[2] and though such an occurrence as this was quite exceptional, lesser acts of violence happened more often.

It will be observed that the foregoing evidence of visitation by deputy comes mainly from the last quarter of the thirteenth century. While this may not unreasonably be taken to indicate some slackness on the part of diocesans, it does also point to a fuller recognition than before of the duty of regular visitation and, be it added, the right to regular procuration.

[1] Boniface VIII, 4730.
[2] Honorii III, 5394; cf. references in Coulton, *Five Centuries of Religion*, II. 489.

CHAPTER VI.

METROPOLITAN VISITATION IN THE THIRTEENTH CENTURY.

THE right of metropolitans to visit was established in very early times,[1] and monks were held to be especially under their care.[2] In the ninth century Hincmar of Reims vigorously vindicated the right of the archbishop to enter the dioceses of his suffragans and correct in them.[3] But while the theory is clear there is little trace of the early practice of visitation: " le métropolitain n'intervient que quand les règles sont violées." [4] Before the thirteenth century the practice is rare ; and consequently at the beginning of the century the details of the law have not been worked out. Only at the very end of the period was a fairly complete set of regulations embodied in the *Corpus Iuris*.[5] As might be expected, the way to definition led through disputes, reproaches and appeals ; and we know most about metropolitan visitation in the thirteenth century, because archbishops were sometimes negligent or over-zealous, and required stimulus or support from the papacy.

Innocent III's programme of reform included regular visitations, not only by diocesans, but also by metropolitans. He wrote to this effect to the archbishops of Reims, Sens and Lund in 1205 ;[6] and told the archbishop of Compostella to follow the practice of neighbouring provinces in the visitation of his own.[7] On behalf of

[1] Con. Turin (397 a.d.) canon 2 (Mansi, III. 861); Thomassin, Pt. I. bk. 2, c. 43.
[2] E. Lesne, *La Hiérarchie Épiscopale* (Paris, 1905), 140, note 1.
[3] *Ibid.*, 141-2.   [4] *Ibid.*, 142 ; cf. 7, note 4.   [5] *Sext*, III. xx. 1.
[6] Innocent III, VIII. 12, 52, 194 (Potthast, 2436, 2495, 2662).
[7] *Ibid.*, X. 76 (Potthast, 3124 ; *Decretales*, III. xxxix. 22).

the archbishop of Bourges, he denied that procurations are not due because they were not paid to the
archbishop's predecessor.[1] Honorius III maintained the
same vigilance. He told the suffragans of Trondhjem to
receive the archbishop on visitation, receive his statutes
and admonitions and pay procurations. He made a
similar injunction for the province of Salzburg a year
later.[2] The same pope bade the archbishop of Amalfi
visit his province ("secundum constitutiones canonicas")
whenever it should be necessary, exact procurations and
correct whatever he ought to correct.[3] In 1222 Honorius
III is found, strange to relate, reproving Stephen Langton
because he has neglected to visit his province of Canterbury.[4] Fifteen years later another archbishop of Canterbury was resisted at his visitation, and secured the
authority of Honorius' successor to visit, *non obstante* the
opposition of certain bishops and regulars.[5] In 1239
the English bishops again resisted the primate. They
appealed to Rome, demanding " utrum metropolitanus
visitare possit monasteria suffraganeorum, ubi episcopi non
sunt negligentes ? "[6] This point was not settled at once,
and was raised eleven years later.

Gregory IX also legislated for the provinces of Bordeaux and Arles. The archbishop of Bourges might visit
the former (as primate of Aquitaine) once every seven
years, for fifty days.[7] The archbishop of Arles, on the

[1] Innocent III, XV. 87 (Potthast, 4499).
[2] Honorii III, 3056, 3709 (Potthast, 6539, 6760).
[3] *Ibid.*, 531.   [4] *Ibid.*, 3891.
[5] Grégoire IX, 3646 (*CPR*, 162). We ought probably to connect
with this two letters regarding the visitation of Worcester, copied on to the
fly-leaf of St. Gregory's Dialogues, in a manuscript in Clare College,
Cambridge. Here the bishop of Worcester (probably Walter de Cantilupe)
asks Archbishop Edmund of Canterbury to refrain from visiting the
cathedral priory, which is not liable to metropolitical visitation and was
not visited in the past by Archbishops Stephen and Richard. The
archbishop, in reply, acquiesces. (See M. R. James, *The Manuscripts of
Clare College, Cambridge*, no. 30.)   [6] *Ann. Mon.*, III. 151.
[7] Grégoire IX, 4936 ; confirmed in 1255 by Alexander IV (Alexandre
IV., 405) ; mentioned in 1284 by Archbishop Simon of Bourges (Baluze-
Mansi, I. 267*b*).

other hand, was allowed to visit his province annually,[1] and to take moderate procuration for fifteen persons and horses. Early in the pontificate of Innocent IV we find orders of the same sort : the archbishops of Rouen and of Reims are told to enforce their right despite opposition.[2]

With pope Innocent IV some of the prevalent doubts regarding the metropolitan's powers are cleared away ; not universally, indeed, for we shall find in some quarters an amazing ignorance of the law still causing disputes, but dispelled in the main by a series of papal declarations which after another half century become part of the *Corpus Iuris* in Boniface VIII's sixth book of Decretals.

The pronouncements of Innocent IV relative to visitation which appear in the *Sext* are commonly attributed to the Council of Lyons (1245).[3] It is, however, certain that they were first pronounced in a curial judgment for the archbishop of Reims in the following year. Shortly afterwards they were sent to the University of Paris with the request that they might be used as binding laws, supplementary to the Gregorian decretals. They were later sent with other constitutions of Innocent IV (including the decrees of Lyons) to Paris and Bologna.[4]

---

[1] Grégoire IX, 5081 ; this was in exceptional circumstances and had a definite object—" pro dissolvendis impietatis colligationibus et profliganda heretica pravitate."

[2] Innocent IV, 471, 472 (Potthast, 11260), 1293.

[3] Mansi, XXIII. 667 *sqq.* ; Graham, *Studies*, 330 ; Frere, 82.

[4] The judgment of Innocent IV comprises the whole of the important constitution " Romana ecclesia, que . . .," split into ten parts in the *Sext*. The part relating to visitation (" Statuimus, ut quilibet . . .") comes at the end. The dating of the evidence is as follows :—

    I. *Sentence of Innocent IV delivered at Lyons xvi. Kal. Apr.* 1246. Reg. Innocent IV, 1831 ; G. Marlot, *Metropolis Remensis Historia* (Reims, 1679), II. 538-9. Marlot only gives the passage on visitation extracted from a longer letter addressed to the archbishop of Reims.

    II. *The same, contracted and divided into chapters xi. Kal. Mai,* 1246. Varin, *Arch. Administ. de la Ville de Reims,* I. 2e ptie. (Docs. Inédits hist. France, 1839), 670 ; Denifle et Chatelain, *Chartularium Univ. Paris.* (Paris, 1889), I. 188 (n. 152) ; Potthast, 12062. Varin used Bib. Nationale MS. *Latin* 5210 for the long

Thus the confusion of ascription has arisen, but thus also is explained the very startling number of disputes which occur on the same topics in the following years. The rules were published, it is true, but they probably did not have the same publicity as the acts of the Council of Lyons.

The judgment of Innocent IV was designed to settle a number of separate points of law, but it is framed in such a way as to give, in brief, a sketch of the process of visitation. An archbishop must visit all the churches of his diocese before he visits his suffragans. In the circuit of his province he must neither omit to visit a diocese nor go back on his steps. At every place he visits he is to open proceedings by setting forth the Word of God. His inquiries may apparently include all topics, but he himself only deals with cases of notorious guilt ; the examination of defamed persons he hands over to the diocesans " ut super his solenniter inquirant." And if the bishop will not make the inquiry, says Innocent in his Commentaries, let the archbishop inquire " quia eius curam habet, et ad eius pertinet officium, et propter negligentiam episcopi." [1]

preamble directed to the archbishop of Reims, but for the latter part of the letter he goes to MS. *Latin* 4295 as the other copy is not complete. MS. 5210 has no date and MS. 4295 is dated *xi. Kal. Mayi anno tertio* (f. 208 *recto* a). Varin inexplicably gives the date as *x. Kal. Mai anno X*, but indexes the letter and refers to it as though it belonged to 1246. Denifle takes his letter from Bib. Nationale MS. *Latin* 4295. It has the preamble to the University of Paris. Potthast gives references to the places of these constitutions in the Decretals.

III. *Letter of Innocent IV enclosing the judgment in its second form together with his other constitutions* [of later date]. Denifle et Chatelain, *op. cit.*, I. 188 (n. 153). Cf. Boehmer, *Corpus Iuris Canonici* (1747), II. xxxi. n. 103 ; Friedberg, *Corpus*, II. col. 971 (note *a* to Tit. VIII cap. 1) ; Leclercq-Hefele, V. 1661-2.

The constitution is mentioned by the Legate at Reims in the next year (Innocent IV, 3737 ; cf. 3738). It may be noted that Archbishop Rigaud refers in his later synods to the ruling of the Council of Lyons on procurations (Rigaud, 287, 357, 387, 482) ; he must have mistaken the occasion of the promulgating of this constitution.

[1] Innocent IV, *Comment.*, f. 186a. "Alii dicunt" that by the bishop's negligence the hearing of such cases does not devolve on the superior, but this is not defined by the canons (*ibid.*).

The visitor must proceed " absque coactione et exactione qualibet iuramenti, ad ipsorum emendationem per salubria monita, nunc levia nunc aspera, iuxta datam sibi a Deo prudentiam diligenter intendens." In all this the metropolitan is to seek the advice of his suffragans, but he is not bound to act according to their counsels. For procurations he is to receive fees in kind, not in money ; neither he nor his household may accept gifts.[1]

The disputes between metropolitans and visitands after 1246 are not only as acrimonious as in the days before the legislation, but frequently concern those questions which had apparently been settled. Thus in the register of Honorius III appears a case between the bishop of Le Mans and the archbishop of Tours. The bishop complained that the archbishop, in his visitation, took cognizance of all cases which were sent to him " per simplicem querimoniam " (and even committed the hearing of them to other persons) ; the archbishop maintained that such was the ancient custom of his own and of the neighbouring provinces.[2] A similar complaint against the archbishop of Rouen in 1237 had resulted in a decision that the archbishop had cognizance of such cases but could not carry on the processes outside the diocese of their origin.[3] Not content with this pronouncement the suffragans had appealed to the pope in 1252 : the affair dragged on for two years and Archbishop Rigaud went to Rome to win his case.[4] It will be noted that this is six years after the decretal *Romana Ecclesia*. Still later (in 1282) the suffragans of John Pecham stated that the archbishop punished offences in their dioceses beyond his metropolitical power—" videlicet in non notoriis et occultis." But the archbishop, in response, claimed that he had the legal right to punish such offences as these, and further appealed to custom.[5]

---

[1] *Sext*, III. xx. 1. Matthew Paris put these constitutions into his additamenta, in connection with the claim of Archbishop Boniface (Matthew Paris, VI. 188 ; cf. V. 127).

[2] Honorii III, 2248. [3] Pommeraye, *Concilia*, 247 (Rigaud, 127-9).

[4] Rigaud, 129-31, 162-3, 172, 176, 184, 749-54 ; Innocent IV, 7823 (Potthast, 15454). [5] Peckham, I. 328, 332 (Wilkins, II. 75-6).

The chief disturbance of the province of Canterbury occurred in the pontificate of Innocent IV (after the publication of the constitution *Romana Ecclesia*), and left as its fruits some important papal rulings, preserved by Matthew Paris and the Burton annalist. This was in the days of Archbishop Boniface of Savoy, a prelate much maligned by contemporaries. In 1249 Boniface returned to England from the Curia, and commenced to visit his province, armed with papal authority though not, as Bartholomew Cotton states, privileged to visit exempt monasteries. His action raised opposition on all sides. The Black Monks preferred to be visited by their fellows rather than by an outsider, and held a Chapter at Bermondsey to discuss and initiate reforms of their own.[1] In 1251, a conference of suffragans, led, it seems, by Grosseteste, agreed to withstand the archbishop's visitation and taxed their clergy for the cost of the appeal.[2] It seems that Boniface had begun the circuit of his province, had extorted more than thirty marks from the poor cathedral priory of Rochester, and later treated with enormous violence those London churches which attempted to resist him. In fact he disabled for life the subprior of Saint Bartholomew's, so rude was his handling of the innocent old man. This is Matthew Paris' version of the affair.[3] The exempt monk of St. Albans represents the opposition as laudable resistance to an extortionate foreigner " who was deficient both in morals and learning and desired to visit, not to make religion flourish or to reform morals, but for the sake of a low cupidity which had with him degenerated into habit." [4]   All

---

[1] Barth. Cotton, *Hist. Angl.* (Rolls series, 1859), 127 ; Matt. Paris, V. 81, VI. 175-85 ; *Benedictine Chapters*, ed. Pantin, I. 31-46.

[2] *Ann. Mon.*, III. 181 ; Matt. Paris, V. 186. The bishops discussed the threatened visitation at Winchcombe on the day after the dedication of Hayles Abbey, and appointed a representative at the Curia on Nov. 6, 1251 (HMCR, Wells, II. 563).   [3] Matt. Paris, V. 120-3.

[4] *Ibid.*, 187. The attachment of Adam Marsh to Archbishop Boniface somewhat lessens the force of Paris's condemnation. The friar accompanied Boniface on this celebrated circuit, and also in a later visitation. *Monumenta Franciscana* (Rolls series, 1858), I. 162, 328.

Matthew Paris' hatred of secular prelates and foreigners is concentrated in execration of Boniface. But the suffragans could give no adequate reason for their conduct when the case was carried to the Curia. The pope, indeed, released the London clergy from the archbishop's excommunication, but the primate won his chief battle —for the general right of visitation and procuration throughout the province.[1] One grievance of the bishops was the interference of the archbishop where a diocesan had not been proved to be negligent ; but the archbishop's right was vindicated, and this was confirmed by Boniface VIII in the *Sext*.[2] This same dispute produced a new, more definite settlement of the procuration difficulty, by laying down a limit of four marks : the rule was applied to other provinces,[3] but not included in the *Corpus Iuris*. One of the pope's letters in the *Burton Annals* also determined that the metropolitan should visit his suffragans and their chapters before he proceeded to the visitation of their dioceses. This rule was only applied in England.

One matter had been left entirely undetermined by the general legislation of Innocent IV. The frequency of metropolitans' visitations was not fixed. The result was many appeals to custom and many separate judgments in the Curia. The suffragans of Rouen made it a grievance that Archbishop Rigaud claimed to visit the province whenever he wished.[4] They said that this was contrary to the custom of triennial visitation. But custom did not avail them : the archbishop rejected the force of custom, and judgment was given in his favour.[5]

In the next year (1255) Pope Alexander IV provided that the archbishop of Armagh (primate of all Ireland) should visit the province of Tuam every five years and continue twenty-seven days in visitation, instead of the earlier practice of septennial visits of unlimited duration.

---

[1] *Supra*, 107.   [2] *Sext*, III. xx. 5.
[3] See p. 108 *supra*, and notes thereon.   [4] Rigaud, 129-31.
[5] Pommeraye, *Concilia*, 265 (Innocent IV, 7823 ; Potthast, 15454 ; *Sext*, V. ii. 7).

This privilege was published in a provincial synod of Drogheda in 1262.[1] A little later the primate was opposed by the bishop of Meath, who claimed exemption for himself and his clergy. The matter was finally settled in 1265 in favour of the archbishop of Armagh. He was allowed to visit every fourth year " as he and his predecessors have been wont to do, and receive due procurations, in victuals or else four marks only "—according to the choice of the visitands.[2]

In the province of York, the metropolitan never established completely the right of visitation in the diocese of Durham. One archbishop after another tried to visit the cathedral, in person or by deputy. While a bishop was alive no metropolitan ever entered the cathedral. During vacancies of the diocese in 1274 and 1311 there were visitations, but no permanent arrangement was made. The bishops of Durham resisted with armed force and claimed their rights as lords palatine. By dint of calling in the civil power and forging bulls, they were able to maintain their independence for centuries : the Reformation came and still the matter remained in dispute.[3]

Our chief information on the law of visitation by metropolitans is found, not unnaturally, in the history of disputes. But we possess besides some commonplace records in registers and chronicles which tell us a little of the ordinary working of the system.

From the papal registers we learn that the archbishop of Rouen was permitted by Innocent IV to proceed to provincial visitation when he had visited only the *loca famosa* of his diocese ;[4] and that the same pope allowed

---

[1] Alexandre IV, 882 (*CPR*, 324 ; Potthast, 16056 ; Theiner, *Vetera Monumenta Hib. et Scot.*, 1864, 68, n. 180). Cf. Wm. Reeve, *Visitation Acts of Archbishop Colton*, 1850, vi.

[2] *Register of St. Thomas, Dublin* (Rolls series, 1889), 71-3. Cf., for confirmation in 1289, Nicolas IV, 1735 (Potthast, 23123). Metropolitan visitations in Ireland were somewhat irregular, it would seem ; c. 1318, the archbishop of Dublin visited the diocese of Ossory for the first time in forty years (Cotton, *Fasti Ecclesiæ Hibern.*, II. 273).

[3] Graystanes, c. xv-xxi and appendices ; summarized by Frere, 84-7.

[4] Innocent IV, 7550 (Potthast, 15374) ; Rigaud, 743.

metropolitans sometimes to interrupt their visitation and return to it [1] in spite of the pope's constitution.[2] Urban IV gave the archbishop of Cologne leave to visit, and told the archbishop of Tarentaise to reform decayed houses of his province.[3] Before the well-known visitations of Simon of Bourges, his predecessors had visited the province of Bordeaux in 1247 and 1265, and the province of Bourges on at least six occasions since the beginning of the century. A testimony to good feeling between visitor and visitands, not the less pleasing because unusual, appears among these records. Archbishop Simon de Sully visited the monastery of S.-Antonin de Rouergue in 1230. The monks testified that he had been a " good pastor, thinking not of his own gain, but of the things that are God's. He has acted moderately and decently. We have no reason for complaint, and on the contrary, rejoice in his visit and his presence, which were thoroughly necessary to us and our church." A generation later the monks of the same priory shut their doors on the visitor and yielded only to strong measures.[4]

The archbishops of Reims, whose disputes had been the occasion of Innocent IV's legislation, made use of the powers accorded to them: in the register of Pope Honorius IV we learn incidentally that the archbishop of Reims is frequently absent from his cathedral on the visitation of his province.[5] The same prelate, along with others, is allowed to pass in the course of visitation through dioceses which he does not visit.[6] In 1300 the archbishop of Mainz follows up his metropolitan visitation by issuing injunctions for the diocese of Speyer.[7] In 1302 the

---

[1] Innocent IV, 3322, 3739, 7242. Also Urbain IV, 353 (caméral) ; Jean XXI, 38 ; Honorius IV, 884 (Potthast, 22354) ; Nicolas IV, 1250, 2372, 2394 ; Boniface VIII, 297, 484, 5161, 5162 ; Rigaud, 742.

[2] *Sext*, III. xx. 1, § 2.   [3] Urbain IV, 184, 2557.

[4] Labbe, *Nova Bibliotheca* (1657), II. 116, 118 ; Lacger, *RHE*, 297-301 ; cf. the comment of Godfrey Giffard's registrar on Pecham's visitation of Worcester diocese, " De cujus visitatione tam clerus quam populus dictum archiepiscopum laudabiliter commendarunt " (Peckham, II. 749).   [5] Honorius IV, 662.

[6] Innocent IV, 4947 ; Alexandre IV, 852, 984.

[7] F. X. Remling, *Urkundenbuch der Bischöfe zu Speyer* (1852), I. 428-30.

archbishop of Benevento, having tried to visit a diocese by
deputy and exact pecuniary procurations, is opposed on
the grounds that he has no privilege to do so.[1] Urban IV
granted a special indulgence to a diocesan that he need
not admit the patriarch of Antioch's metropolitan visitation unless the patriarch visited in person.[2] It is clear
that normally a metropolitan might commission deputies
to take his place ; the practice was common in England.
Hostiensis says that he sees no reason against the archbishop sending another in his place, although some maintain that only bishops have this privilege.[3]

In the province of Canterbury in this period, scattered
notices of visitations suggest that each archbishop at least
tried to carry out the circuit of his province once. After
the dispute of 1252 Boniface of Savoy set out on his
visitation again in 1253, and proceeded through the
dioceses of Canterbury, Rochester, London, Norwich, Ely
and Lincoln.[4] This time even Matthew Paris grudgingly
admitted his conduct to be unexceptionable : " et propter
moderationem admissus est benigne. Et haec caute fecit,
ut scilicet sic visitandi haberet ingressum et possessionem."[5]
In 1257 he came to Abingdon and, having made no complaint on the spot, wrote afterwards to the abbot and
diocesan, asking for the removal of two monks.[6] Three
years later Boniface was at Worcester.[7] In the last ten
years of his life, he does not appear to have made any
visitation in his province. In 1273 Kilwardby went to
Worcester,[8] and the next year made a visitation of Winchester diocese.[9] He was at Osney, where he took excessive procurations, in 1276.[10] A year later he visited
more of Lincoln diocese, including Peterborough Abbey
and the priory of Dunstable.[11] In November we find him

[1] Boniface VIII, 4609.   [2] Urbain IV, 1489 (Potthast, 18845).
[3] Hostiensis, *Comment.*, VI. III. de Censib. 1 (vol. 2, f. 25 *verso*).
[4] *Ann. Mon.*, I. 313-14, III. 190.   [5] Matt. Paris, V. 382.
[6] *Abingdon Chron.*, 9.   [7] *Ann. Mon.*, IV. 446.   [8] *Ibid.*, IV. 465.
[9] *Ibid.*, II. 118.   [10] *Ibid.*, IV. 270. See *supra*, page 108.
[11] *Chronicon Petroburgense* (Camden Society, 1849), 25 ; *Ann. Mon.*,
III. 276 ; Madox, *Formulare Anglicanum* (1702), 8.

warning the archdeacon of Ely of his coming visitation.[1] Early in 1278 he visited at Salisbury,[2] and resigned his archbishopric in June of the same year. Of Pecham's visitations we have many records in the register of his letters. Other references are scattered in monastic chronicles, and a cartulary at Chichester[3] contains the following verses :—

" In senis annis cursus fuit ista [*sic*] Johannis :
Cantia,[4] Londonia,[5] Lichefeud,[6] Norfolchia,[7] Bada,[8]
Cornub.,[9] Herforda,[10] Wygorn.,[11] Cicestria,[12] Rofa,[13]
Winto,[14] Seynt Aseph,[15] Bangor,[16] Menevia,[17] Landaph.,[18]
Lincol. pregrandis,[19] brevis Ely,[20] Sar mediocris.[21]
Cursu finito {Idem currendo redito
{Meritis sibi Christe finito."

[1] *Vetus Liber Archidiaconi Eliensis* (Cambridge Antiq. Soc., octavo publications, 1917), 18.

[2] *Ann. Mon.*, IV. 473 ; HMCR, Various Collections, VII. 30-1.

[3] *Ibid.*, I. 189.

[4] Peckham, I. 61, **1279** ; I. 226, 245, III. 1066, **1281** ; I. 339, II. 397, **1282** ; II. 706, **1284** ; III. 924, **1286** ; III. 947, **1287** ; III. 970, **1289**.

[5] *Ibid.*, I. 81, 93, III. 1020, **1279**.

[6] *Ibid.*, I. 91, 111, 130, 154, III. 1064 ; *Ann. Mon.*, III. 282 ; *Annal. Cestrienses* (Lancs. and Chesh. Record Soc., 1887), 106, 134, **1279-80**.

[7] Peckham, I. 162 ; *Ann. Mon.*, IV. 284 ; Barth. Cotton, 161 ; Joh. de Oxenedes, 257, **1280-1**.

[8] Peckham, I. 200, 259, 1004 ; HMCR, Wells (1907), I. 149, **1281**.

[9] Peckham, I. 269, 304, III. 1073, **1282**.

[10] *Ibid.*, II. 421, 430, 478, 503, 526, III. 1072, **1282-3**.

[11] *Ibid.*, II. 496, 512, 596 ; Giffard, *Worc.*, II. 170, **1282-3** ; *Ann. Mon.*, IV. 491 ; Bodleian MS. *Tanner* 223, f. 129 *verso*, **1285**.

[12] Peckham, II. 531, 552, 561, 572, 608, 613, **1283**.

[13] *Ibid.*, II. 621 ; Wharton, *Anglia Sacra*, I. 353, **1283**.

[14] Peckham, I. 161, 292, **1281** ; *ibid.*, II. 640, 645, 650, 658, 666, 717, **1284**.

[15] *Ibid.*, II. 675, III. 1060 ; Haddan and Stubbs, *Councils*, etc., I. 571 ; *Annal. Cestrienses*, 114, **1284**.   [16] Peckham, III. 782, **1284**.

[17] *Ibid.*, III. 779, 782, 786, 794, 800, 810 ; HMCR, VIII. Appendix, 320a ; Bodleian MS. *Tanner* 240, f. 130 (Haddan and Stubbs, *Councils*, etc., I. 576), **1284**.   [18] Peckham, III. 778, 794, 798, 805, **1284**.

[19] *Ibid.*, III. 788, 823, 843, 854 ; *Ann. Mon.*, III. 315, IV. 297 ; *Chron. Petroburg.* (Camden Soc. 1849), 100 ; Joh. de Oxenedes, 264, **1284**.

[20] *Ibid.*, 264, **1285**.

[21] Peckham, III. 908, 916 ; Swinfield, 168 ; *Abingdon Chron.*, 30, **1285**.

Archbishop Winchelsey, like his predecessor, left several highly important visitation records in his register, as well as the valuable articles of inquiry preserved in a register of the prior of Canterbury.[1] Dr. Graham has drawn attention to the mass of evidence for Winchelsey's visitation of 1301 in her important essay on "the metropolitical visitation of the diocese of Worcester."[2]

* These references, though not exhaustive, are perhaps sufficient to show that metropolitan visitation was known and practised in many parts of Europe in the thirteenth century ; we recall that this sort of visitation accounts for much of Archbishop Rigaud's famous register, and of the *Acta* of Simon of Bourges.

While some metropolitans sent injunctions to particular monasteries in the dioceses of their suffragans, it is unlikely that this practice was universal. The rapidity of the archbishop's visitation and the legal restrictions of his jurisdiction would tend to make the framing of particular injunctions difficult. Thomassin says, "Le fruit de ces visites consiste principalement à faire assembler, aussitôt après, le concile provincial, et y faire des ordonnances conformes aux besoins qu'il y a remarqués."[3] This is certainly borne out by the German records of councils, and by the relation of Rigaud's synods to his visitations. Moreover, we find that more than once Pecham adopted the plan of issuing injunctions for general observance in a diocese.[4]

Where an archbishop visited as primate, and not as metropolitan, his power of direct action was still more narrowly limited. Summarizing the rules (1232) which governed the visitations of Bordeaux by the archbishop of Bourges, M. de Lacger says, "S'il découvre quelque excès notable, il en donne avis au diocésain, ensuite à l'archevêque, finalement au Saint-Siège, auxquels il appartient d'apporter le remède selon l'exigence des cas.

[1] *Supra*, 73.
[2] Graham, *Studies*, 330-59 (Trans. Royal Hist. Soc., 4th series, vol. 2, 1919).   [3] Quoted, Lacger, *RHE*, 296, note 1.
[4] Peckham, II. 737, III. 794, 797.

Sa fonction ordinaire est toute d'inspection, non, à proprement parler, de réforme et correction des abus." [1]

A topic which concerns almost every contemporary mention of these visitations remains to be discussed ; it is the relation of the archbishop's work to the work of the diocesan. Though the law decided that the archbishop might visit although his suffragans were not negligent, there could clearly be little use in the metropolitan visitation unless the archbishop had some faults to find. All his other business in monasteries was the exaction of procurations and the confirming of episcopal injunctions. It must be admitted that none of these duties were likely to make his visit welcome to a suffragan, except where a particularly rebellious religious house was concerned.

The Rouen register shows a considerable amount of interaction between the two visitations, and some cooperation between the two authorities, metropolitan and diocesan. When Rigaud visited the nunnery of Almenèches in 1255 he found that the bishop of Séez had there made " a certain good ordinance, which we caused to be read to us, and which they had not observed because of their poverty ; and we ordered them to observe it at least in such matters—regarding dogs, for instance—as could not be excused by poverty." [2] At Bival he ordered that the archdeacon's precepts should be firmly observed.[3] At Ivry, having found that a monk went alone to celebrate Mass at the castle, Rigaud made a note to speak about it to the diocesan. A little later, at a priory in the same diocese, he had to speak " de Johanne Chicaut amovendo."[4] In 1255 he proposed to speak to the bishop of Lisieux about a retired abbot of ill repute, and to the bishop of Evreux about a priory loaded with debt.[5] The bishop of Séez was with him at a visitation in this year and promised that he would properly correct the *comperta* at Mortagne.[6] His successor was with Rigaud five years later at Almenèches and received orders from the archbishop for the reorganisation of the house, because the latter could

---

[1] Lacger, *RHE*, 56. [2] Rigaud, 236. [3] *Ibid.*, 268.
[4] *Ibid.*, 70, 71. [5] *Ibid.*, 198, 221. [6] *Ibid.*, 233.

not spare any time himself.[1]   Rigaud also admonished the
bishop of Séez to make up the numbers in monasteries to
their proper level.[2]

When in 1267 the archbishop of Reims visited the
cathedral of Laon, the bishop in full chapter complained
of the conduct of his canons.   He confessed himself in-
capable of coping with the disorders of his church, and
at his request the archbishop drew up a long set of rules
for the reform of the chapter.[3]

Simon of Bourges, visiting the diocese of Clermont,
confirmed some episcopal injunctions at the bishop's
request ; [4] at other times we find him writing to the
diocesan on behalf of some injured monks, and promising
to confer with him about the condition of a dilapidated
house.[5]

The bishop of Aosta was present in 1263 at the
metropolitan visitation of the priory of San Orso, Aosta,
by the archbishop of Tarentaise.   In 1286 his successor
made statutes for his canons, acting in conjunction with
the archbishop.[6]

Archbishop Pecham knew when to annul, as well as
when to confirm, the acts of his subordinates.   He contradicted the diocesan's orders when he visited Leominster
Priory, and had a door replaced where Thomas de Cantilupe, bishop of Hereford, had repeatedly forbidden it.[7]
In 1281 he wrote to the bishop of London complaining
that his arrangements at Walden Abbey had been put
aside by the diocesan.[8]   On the other hand, he added the
weight of his authority to injunctions made for Reading
Abbey by the bishop of Salisbury,[9] and those of the bishop
of London for the nuns of Barking, and offered suggestions
to the bishop of St. Davids for the reform of the religious
of his diocese.[10]   In one case he shows great consideration

[1] Rigaud, 374.   [2] Ibid., 236.
[3] Actes de la Prov. eccl. de Reims, ed. Th. Gousset (Reims, 1843),
II. 402-6.   [4] Baluze-Mansi, I. 298b.   [5] Ibid., I. 303b, 279b.
[6] F. Savio, Gli Antichi Vescovi d'Italia, I. Piemonte (1899), 105, 108.
[7] Peckham, II. 505-7 ; Cantilupe, 88, 95.   [8] Peckham, I. 212.
[9] Swinfield, 168.   [10] Peckham, I. 82, III. 796.

for the rights of his suffragan. In 1283 he ordered the coadjutresses of the abbess of Romsey to communicate with the bishop of Winchester or his official if the archiepiscopal injunctions were not observed. Only if the bishop was negligent were they to appeal to the archbishop.[1] In the same year, after visiting Rochester, he ordered the bishop to enforce certain injunctions in the cathedral priory and at Lesnes.[2] His successor Winchelsey (who never showed much faith in the old bishop of Worcester) bade the retired prior of Little Malvern enter into the convent life and forgo his pension and his separate household " non obstante quacumque ordinacione loci dyocesani seu alterius in contrarium facta." [3] From Winchelsey's questionnaire for a metropolitan visitation we see that the archbishop counted on making direct inquiries concerning the visitation of the suffragan, so that he might better supplement the latter's deficiencies. The archbishop asked (among other things) whether the bishop had taken procuration in money, whether he had made diligent inquiry and imposed fit punishment, whether he had allowed the sale of corrodies, and " an sollicite inquisiuerit de monachis et aliis religiosis vacabundis incontinentibus carnibus abutentibus in obedientibus suis prelatis et alias contra ordinem suum delinquentibus." [4] In 1299 he approved and added to the injunctions of the bishop of Rochester for Malling Abbey.[5]

Sometimes the archbishop's visit was a work of supererogation. If the diocesan did his duty the provincial visitor might not be needed. Rigaud found in one house that certain of the canons had been defamed of incontinence " sed episcopus eorum excessus correxerat, et infamia aliquantulum cessabat." [6] At Dunstable, in 1284, Pecham found " omnia prospere "—for the bishop of Lincoln had lately visited the house.[7] Cases such as these

[1] Peckham, II. 661.   [2] Ibid., II. 624, 626.
[3] Winchelsey, f. 80 ; cf. Peckham, I. 101, III. 843, 854.
[4] Winchelsey, Articles, f. 61.
[5] VCH Kent, II. 147 (quoting Winchelsey, f. 70).
[6] Rigaud, 372.   [7] Ann. Mon., III. 315.

must have helped to make the metropolitan visit unpopular among both bishops and monks. The archbishop's display of authority and demand for procuration
may well have produced irritation among his subjects, even
when they had not to fear punishment for offences.

It should not be forgotten that in archbishops', as in
bishops', visitations business was often transacted which
was not concerned with discipline. Thus when Pecham
visited Norwich Cathedral in 1281, the monks asked him
to inspect and confirm the charters belonging to the
church.[1] Probably every visitation by the archbishcps of
Canterbury in this period could be similarly traced by
confirmations and exemplifications in monastic cartularies.

Metropolitan visitation was a recognized process in
the thirteenth century and was fairly commonly practised.
But what has been said regarding the insufficient frequency
of the bishop's visitation applies with even greater force
to the archbishop's visitation. The visitor was too remote
from the ordinary monastic life of his province, and too
seldom visited the monasteries, for his circuits to be of
regular assistance in maintaining discipline. Furthermore,
he had to contend, not only with the natural distrust of
the religious, but also with the hostility of suffragans,
jealous for their independence.

---

[1] British Museum, Cotton Charter, II. 21 ; *Mon. Ang.*, IV. 19–20 ;
C. R. Cheney, *Notaries public in England* (Oxford, 1972), 161–3, 34–5.

CHAPTER VII.

THE EFFICACY OF ARCHBISHOP RIGAUD'S VISITATIONS OF THE RELIGIOUS HOUSES IN THE DIOCESE OF ROUEN: 1248-1269.

THE incompleteness of existing visitation records has been insisted on in earlier pages. The documents which would be of most value to the modern historian are precisely those memoranda which a clerk would discard as useless when a visitation was completed ; and in their place usually remain only a few injunctions or warnings of visitations to come. As a result of these conditions, historians have been driven to use the records simply as an index to the vicious ways of monks and the maladministration of monasteries. Their work has certainly been valuable, especially when an age of romantic " medievalism " had succeeded to an age of malicious scandal-seeking. It has demonstrated the fact, now indisputable though perhaps not always recognized, that at least as early as the thirteenth century monachism had to contend with disorders which were everywhere recurring. On the other hand, this has tended to an exaggeration of the evils. While our records show what were the most common, they do not show how common these defects were. We have not a complete measure of the evil and no measure at all of the good. In the absence of records for each religious house, it is dangerous to generalize from a few, especially as we deal mainly with the Benedictine Order. For in the *particularisme* of Benedictine houses, which Dom Berlière stresses, lay their hope of regeneration as well as a cause of decay : it enabled monastic discipline to survive in a disordered age and provides exceptions to every seeming rule of decadence.

(149)

The journal of Archbishop Rigaud of Rouen is the one thirteenth-century document which has the appearance of completeness. Yet historians have not been sufficiently attracted to it. They have usually been content to use the register as they use other episcopal registers—to find examples of evils, not to estimate their extent. Nevertheless, some analysis of the evidence for nunneries has been made by Dr. Eileen Power ;[1] Mr. Snape draws up tables of income and debt in the Norman monasteries as an appendix to *English Monastic Finances*; Professor Jenkins gives a detailed summary of the evidence for monastic learning and literacy and some other statistics in an article in the *Church Quarterly Review*; while Dr. Coulton gives some interesting figures in his very valuable chapters on Rigaud in *Five Centuries of Religion*. These studies throw a fairly clear light on some aspects of Norman monastic life in the period of Rigaud's journal, and probably do so without much distortion. Their value naturally depends upon the completeness of the register, or at least on our power of estimating its omissions.

But leaving on one side for the moment the question of completeness, we see that the material can be used for a purpose where incompleteness is not a serious disadvantage. Whatever its omissions, the journal is unique in the *amount* of evidence it provides : the detailed survey of a broad field. It provides sufficient, as no other register can, for us to estimate the efficacy of a prelate's work over a large area in the task of monastic visitation. This aspect of the journal is well worth some observation. Archbishop Rigaud was a great man, of saintly character and marked practical ability. An ordinary well-kept episcopal register, as Professor Tout observes, " tells us nothing as to either the intellectual or moral character of the prelate by whose orders it was kept, but rather of the good organization of his household or diocese." [2] But the journal of Rigaud differs from the ordinary register in revealing the archbishop as a man who felt deeply his

[1] Power, 634 *sqq.*   [2] Halton, I. xliii.

responsibility in regard to his diocese and province of Rouen : it is a monument to personal paternal care, not to bureaucratic efficiency. Rigaud was continually moving among his flock to minister to their wants. His visitations of monasteries, both metropolitan and diocesan, were singularly regular and well conducted.

For our purpose the provincial visitations, outside the diocese of Rouen, are not sufficiently complete. Moreover, the action of the archbishop in these instances must have been profoundly modified by the work of suffragans. The evidence for the diocese of Rouen is therefore all that concerns us. All calculations, quotations and references are derived from Rigaud's diocesan visits.

In the diocese of Rouen the archbishop visited no less than forty-nine houses of regulars, each six times or more in the space of twenty-one years. Forty-five of these houses were visited more than ten times each.[1]

These figures testify to the archbishop's industry ; his method as well as his industriousness help the historian. For Rigaud was very methodical. The statutes of Pope Gregory IX, *super reformatione monachorum ordinis Sancti Benedicti*, which are placed in the midst of his register,[2] were his complete guide. His inquiries can almost always be connected with these statutes, and the regularity of the entries suggests that he usually inquired into all the more important matters about which the pope had legislated.

Rigaud may therefore be considered an exemplary prelate, above the ordinary in character and capacity. And at the same time his diocese was a well-ordered one. It seems probable that the Norman regular clergy, like their neighbours in England, were a little above the average of continental monachism. This being so, an inquiry into the efficacy of Rigaud's visitations becomes an inquiry into the possible success of the visitatorial system when worked under favourable conditions. It is an inquiry of some importance, since episcopal visitation came in the next two centuries to be generally regarded as the best, if not the only, method of monastic reform.

[1] See Appendix I.   [2] Rigaud, 643 (f. 121 *verso*).

It will be seen that in pursuing this inquiry we are not concerned directly with the moral and financial state of the Norman monasteries, but only in so far as this appreciably alters in the twenty-one years from 1248 to 1269. For this reason the incompleteness of the journal is of less importance than it would be were we seeking a complete survey of Norman monachism. The disadvantage of its omissions seems small when compared with the systematic arrangement of its contents. Nevertheless, the occurrence of these omissions is in itself instructive. The matter resolves itself into two problems : How much of the proceedings were left unrecorded ? How much was the archbishop unable to discover ?

To take the first question : have we here a complete record of proceedings ? For the compiling of injunctions it was not necessary to record every offence discovered : some matters a bishop would deal with on the spot. The vagaries of a particular monk would never need to be mentioned except where they formed grounds for general injunctions.[1] A note of Archbishop Pecham illustrates this point. In his injunctions to Coxford Priory in 1281 he wrote, "Haec pauca pro multis vobis scribimus, ceteris nihilominus quae specialibus personis in capitulo injunximus in suo robore duraturis."[2]

But, it may be argued, Rigaud's register contains far more than was needed for injunctions ; witness the large number of proper names, the exact allocation of offences. This is true. Nevertheless, Rigaud's record always had a future purpose, and its scope was thereby limited. Administrative changes made on the spot need not be mentioned in the account of a monastery's visitation, for they will have no sequel : there need be no inquiry next time. This certainly accounts for the failure to record in their proper place numerous injunctions which crop up later in the register because they have not been obeyed.

At Villarceaux in 1249 we have an admirable example of the way in which injunctions were compiled from

---

[1] Cf. *supra*, 96.   [2] Peckham, I. 165 ; cf. *ibid.*, II. 654, 669.

detecta and *comperta*.[1] It illustrates, moreover, the fact that Rigaud ordinarily wrote down more than was needed for the compiling of injunctions. But both the injunctions and the preceding notes leave unrecorded a fact which comes to light in an entry two years later. In 1251 the archbishop notes that two nuns have been removed, as he ordered at the last visitation.[2] For all we know there may have been an order of equal importance concealed by the summary entry of II. Kal. Sept. 1261 : "Visitavimus duos monachos de Pratellis commorantes apud Sanctam Ragdegundim iuxta Novum Castrum. Paucos habebant redditus et pernoctavimus apud Bellum Beccum." [3] At Bourg Achard in 1248 the archbishop remarked, "alia sunt ordinanda " : [4] they find no place in the register. At Jumièges the archbishop took counsel in chapter regarding priories in 1256, but only next year did he record [5] what had been the result of this deliberation. There is a considerable number of other occasions when the archbishop had to renew injunctions or continue proceedings, of which we find no previous mention.[6]

One feature of the manuscript which is not reproduced in the printed text is the gap between consecutive entries which is found most often in the early part of the register. Where the bare notices, "Ibidem visitavimus," "Visitavimus ibidem," are written on folios 2 *verso* and 3 *recto*,[7] gaps occur each about 1½ inches in depth. Something must have emerged from these visitations of S.-Victor and Auffay, and the scribe had left room for the record : but the space was never filled, and we are told nothing, good or bad. Rigaud did not, therefore, have every *compertum* written down. We can check this from the register in the cases cited above, but there may well be many more which never needed later comment, and which consequently cannot be traced.

Another consideration must affect our view of the

[1] See *supra*, 95. [2] Rigaud, 43, 117.
[3] *Ibid.*, 407. [4] *Ibid.*, 8. [5] *Ibid.*, 265, 292.
[6] *Ibid.*, 247, 265, 339, 430, 571, 636 (Regulars) ; 194, 334, 385, 397, 434, 488, 520, 532, 559 (Seculars). [7] *Ibid.*, p. 5.

register. The question occurs which was mentioned above : How much was the archbishop unable to discover ? Rigaud suffered from the same disadvantages as other episcopal visitors. Forty-seven times in monasteries of monks he remarks that " unus non clamat alium " ; forty-seven times he says the same of regular canons.[1] The complaint refers to the ordinary procedure in chapter, but if the monks did not proclaim against each other then they would scarcely do so to the archbishop. Although in the nunneries of the diocese Rigaud found occasion to make the complaint only once, he mentions five occasions when serious offences had been concealed from him. Sometimes offences were discovered long after they were committed. For the diocese of Rouen alone, counting only the visitations of regular houses, there are fourteen examples recorded.[2]

These are usually the worst cases, where constant repetition at last prevented *infamia* from being stifled. It is hardly possible to avoid the inference that many of the less scandalous offenders went scot-free. Dr. Coulton rightly objects to the statement that " little seems to have escaped his inquiry." [3] The archbishop never, so far as we know, demanded whether there was conspiracy or collusion to defeat his inquiries, but we know of cases where it would have been pertinent to do so. In one place he ordered the sisters to be punished " pro eo quod turpitudinem et scelus dicte Ysabelle celaverant." [4] On another occasion he accepted the assurance of the nuns of S.-Saëns that there was no truth in a rumour " dicebatur communiter in villa " ; but three years later he found two sisters to be " mendaces et periuras, cum aliqua quesissemus ab eis sub iuramento suo." [5] There can be no doubt that many irregularities were never brought to the archbishop's notice.

Having found out failings, Rigaud was not always in a position to correct them. Other authorities might step

---

[1] See Appendix I. (B).
[2] Rigaud, 43, 48-9, 58, 100, 169, 206, 207, 268, 284, 338, 352, 383, 453, 500.   [3] Jenkins, *CQR*, 105.   [4] Rigaud, 538.   [5] *Ibid.*, 491, 598.

in. At the archbishop's visitation of Bacqueville in 1261, when for the eighth time he objected to the monks' meat-eating, the visitor of the Order was present " et dixit visitator quod hoc erat in dispositione abbatis sui, et quod super hoc dispensaverat cum ipsis." [1] Several important monasteries fortified themselves against the archbishop's severity with papal dispensations. In 1253 Abbot Robert d'Ételan of Jumièges received dispensation from observance of those Gregorian statutes which were not " de substantia regule." [2] Other houses in the province obtained the same privilege.[3] Bec sometimes granted dispensation for meat-eating to her priories, but did not always do so.[4] Rigaud encountered the papal authority on another matter when he found at Montivilliers in 1266 " ibi erant LXI moniales ; debent esse sexaginta ex numero statuto, sed legatus unam illic posuerat, videlicet, filiam Theobaldi Mauricii, servientis domini regis." [5] The archbishop tried to uphold the prohibition of solitary monks which Gregory IX had made. But when he found that a monk was living by himself in a priory of S.-Martin of Pontoise he was told that the bishop of Beauvais, its diocesan, had given his consent.[6]

In these ways the archbishop's power of correction was limited to some extent, but the indications of conflict of authority in practice are few. On the other hand a few rare passages point to co-operation. At S.-Wandrille, in 1265, Rigaud states a recent injunction of the visitor of the Order, and says " de ordinatione huiuscemodi aliquid noluimus immutare." [7] Likewise he seems to approve the visitor's injunction at Corneville in 1267,[8] and orders the nuns of Bival in 1256 to observe firmly the archdeacon's injunctions.[9]

---

[1] Rigaud, 409.

[2] *Ibid.*, 748 ; *Histoire de l'abbaye . . . de Jumièges* by [Dom J. Dubucq], ed. J. Loth (Société de l'histoire de Normandie, 1882), II. 12.

[3] Sauvage, *Histoire de l'abbaye de Troarn* (Caen, 1911), 396, 97 *n.* ; Porée, *Histoire de l'abbaye du Bec* (Evreux, 1901), I. 577 ; Matt. Paris, V. 380.

[4] Rigaud, 339 ; cf. *ibid.*, 411, 451.

[5] *Ibid.*, 564.

[6] *Ibid.*, 105, 504 ; cf. Grégoire IX, 3415.

[7] Rigaud, 516.

[8] *Ibid.*, 578.

[9] *Ibid.*, 268.

We have discovered two reasons why the archbishop's visitation was not thoroughly successful : he did not discover all offences, and other authorities sometimes prevented punishment. We must now consider how far he succeeded in having his injunctions obeyed when other authorities did not step in.

In the first place, it is worth remark that Rigaud himself frequently draws attention to the disregard of his orders. Time after time he states an offence, and adds some phrase such as " licet ipsos alias super his monuerimus." [1] These were not the only occasions when the archbishop had to repeat an injunction made at a previous visitation. Perhaps they seemed to the visitor the most flagrant cases, but it is not likely that they have much permanent significance. Generally speaking, we may assume that the repetition of an injunction means the repetition of an offence. We shall find exceptions, admittedly : in 1260 Rigaud forbade the nuns of S.-Saëns to veil any newcomers—he had made the same injunction in each of the three preceding years, and the number of regular inmates had decreased since the last time.[2] Again, at Montivilliers in 1262, the archbishop said: " Iocositates quas solebant facere in festo Innocentium penitus dimiserunt, ut dicebant ; item, precepimus omnino ab huiusmodi abstinere." [3]   In spite of these examples there can be little doubt that injunctions usually imply transgressions.

Here, then, we are dealing with positive evidence, and we may arrive at a result with a certain amount of precision.   Where the same sort of orders is being made by the same man over a period of twenty-one and a half years, we may fairly reckon the amount of improvement by the diminution of orders. The problem becomes a simple matter of statistics.   They cannot be more than

---

[1] Rigaud, 41, 42, 58, 59, 105, 111, 121, 132, 132, 166, 166, 167, 202, 206, 207, 227, 247, 264, 264, 265, 265, 265, 323, 326, 327, 327, 337, 353, 361, 362, 382, 383, 385, 396, etc.

[2] *Ibid.*, 380.   Vacancies through death may have been filled without the archbishop's consent.   [3] *Ibid.*, 431 ; cf. *supra*, 84 *n.*

approximately correct, and their presentation may involve some distortion ; nevertheless, the fullness of the evidence and the uniformity of the material suggest that the figures will repay examination.

The disadvantage of regarding in one mass a large number of houses is outweighed by the impossibility of forming any conclusion from the separate examination of each one's history. And the experiment involves scarcely as many risks as might be imagined. If the journal showed some religious houses to have rapidly declined while others struggled to the level path of virtue and security—then it might be a doubtful proceeding to strike an " average " of changes so diverse. But such is not the case. In the register, the history of individual houses seldom shows a regular decline ; few, also, were uniformly faultless. Most houses had some features to be reformed, and in most houses the archbishop did reform something.

Tables in the Appendix give the details of these statistics, which have been collected in three time-divisions : 1248-55, 1255-62, 1262-69. All the houses involved were houses of regulars. Since some writers have given statistics from the register which include cathedral chapters and colleges of secular canons, it is as well to emphasize their absence from the following analysis. The conditions of life of secular canons were so different from the conditions of life in religious houses proper that it seems scarcely fair to rank the two together.

IGNORANCE OF THE RULE AND STATUTES.[1]

The first fault to be remedied by any reformer of regulars must be ignorance of the Rule by which they live. Archbishop Rigaud had to deal with monasteries which did not even possess a copy of their Rule ; there were no complaints on this subject against Augustinian houses. In one nunnery a copy in the vernacular was wanting, " quia furata fuit in capitulo." [2] Equally important with the Rule, from the point of view of monastic discipline and

---

[1] See Appendix I. (A).   [2] Rigaud, 187.

administration, were the statutes of Gregory IX for the Black Monks. When Rigaud came to the see of Rouen they had been promulgated some twelve years, and there were still some monasteries in the diocese of Rouen which had no copy of them. In the first period of our tables there were twenty-one complaints. Even when Rigaud had ensured that a house possessed both Rule and Statutes he had sometimes to ordain that they should be read frequently. These injunctions, like the others, are less frequent in the last period than in the first.

Rigaud was, indeed, fairly successful in procuring copies of the Rule and Statutes and in seeing that they were read. After 1258 there was not a Benedictine house in his diocese which could plead ignorance of the Statutes. If he seems to have met with less success in ordering that the Rule should be obtained, it is partly explained by the bad state of Beaussault : here, after injunctions in 1254, 1256, and 1257, he remarked in 1259, " habebant regulam scriptam." But if this entry was not by error, the Rule was lost again ; for in 1261, 1263, and 1269 he enjoined that one should be procured.

DISCIPLINE.[1]

We may naturally pass next to the disciplinary methods of the monastery, as the Rule and the Statutes provided for them. Regular sessions of chapter were the usual safeguards of discipline and the method employed in them was that of proclamation. Thirteen times, in the early years, Rigaud complained that chapters were not regularly held ; but in this measure, preliminary to all reform, he seems to have gained his point. On the other hand, " unus non clamat alium " is one of the commonest charges, and clearly one of the most significant.[2] The capacity for mutual charity and forbearance which the custom of proclamation demanded and developed was undoubtedly essential to the common life of the monastery. St. Benedict had enjoined something of the sort, and a

---

[1] See Appendix I. (B).   [2] Cf. *supra*, 154.

celebrated preacher of Rigaud's day, Thomas of Chan-
timpré, urged with many arguments and examples, the
necessity of charitable fraternal correction. "When
accusations cease, excesses multiply," says Thomas.[1] But
a high spiritual standard was required if the practice
of accusation was to be valuable. Very easily it led
to slander,[2] or simply lapsed. Rigaud often complained
among monks and canons that it lapsed ; only once against
a nunnery did he lay the charge, " una non clamat aliam." [3]
The tables here show a marked improvement in the latest
period, but even in twenty years an essential defect of this
sort could not be obliterated. Against thirty injunctions
in the first period, we have forty-six in the second, and
nineteen in the third.[4]

"DE SUBSTANTIA REGULAE." [5]

The weakness of the communal spirit in human practice, which prevented mutual correction in chapter, is
illustrated in the attempts of the archbishop to abolish
private property from the cloister. Rigaud seldom noted
proprietary canons, but more frequently inveighed against
monks and nuns who keep chests and lock them, hoard
clothing, receive presents and sell for their own profit.

---

[1] *Rule of St. Benedict*, ch. xxiii. Thomae Cantimpratani, *Bonum
universale de apibus* (Douai, 1627), lib. II, c. xvi. ; cf. *ibid.*, II. xxxix.
" Quod rigor iustitiae et zelus correctionis in capitulis stricte sit seruandus."
Yet neglect of accusation was practically legalized in some places. Even
at Bec, almost a model abbey, " non consueverunt clamare se invicem,
nisi super infractione silentii " (Rigaud, 427 ; cf. *ibid.*, 389). After Rigaud
had been told this twice he made no more complaint.

[2] *Supra*, 85.   [3] *Ibid.*, 293.

[4] In these statistics, as in some of the other tables, a curious feature
may be noted. There are often many more injunctions in the second
period than in the first or last, suggesting that Norman monachism suffered
from a wave of depression between 1256 and 1262. This is obviously
unlikely. We may justly infer that as time passed the archbishop took
more notice of classes of offences which he had not at first recorded. As
an example, there is the injunction against hoarding in chests. Only one
mention of private chests occurs before 1255—at Bondeville in 1251
(Rigaud, 111). But the keeping of chests was no innovation.

[5] See Appendix I. (C).

Injunctions on this topic were as common in the last period as at the beginning of the archbishop's visitations. Incontinency among regulars does, however, decline under Rigaud's government. A fault which concerned comparatively few individuals could be dealt with more easily than the faults rooted in communities. The numbers of offenders in the three time-divisions of the register are 42, 17, and 9. One cannot but remark the inordinate proportion of peccant nuns. Their sin was easily discoverable, while the men could escape notoriety and punishment.

There is a number of other important points on which the archbishop issued injunctions, all of which echo the Statutes of Gregory IX. Gregory had enjoined silence in the church, the cloister, the refectory, and the dormitory—" pena transgressoribus secundum statuta regularia imponenda." He had forbidden monks to dwell alone in priories, ordering that they should be recalled or receive companions. Against the growing custom of using private rooms and wandering abroad the pope legislated and the archbishop gave injunctions. In all these matters, the observance of silence and the maintenance of the claustral life, Rigaud met with considerable success. He remarked less than half the number of offences in the last period than he had noted in the first seven years.

On the other hand, try as he would, the archbishop could not secure the observance of certain important injunctions. He repeatedly inveighed against the unlicensed eating of meat and the breaking of fasts, yet his success seems negligible ; the proportion of injunctions to visitations of monks is almost precisely the same in the first and the last periods. Injunctions against diminution of alms and the neglect of the infirm show an increase on the whole.[1]

The archbishop's attempts to restore discipline in connection with all these matters usually met with most success among the monks. The fact is conspicuous in the

[1] See Appendix I. (G and H).

statistics given. Among nuns and canons he has to repeat injunctions far more often. It may be that this was due to the better tone prevalent in the monks' houses from the first, and to their better financial position.

ADMINISTRATION AND FINANCE.

The regularity of Benedictine life depended in the last resort upon the heads of houses. " La prosperité ou la décadence de la discipline, aussi bien que de l'état économique, dépend du choix de l'abbé." [1] Rigaud on a few occasions suspended or deposed heads of houses in his diocese,[2] and at other times received the resignation of heads become incompetent through age or infirmity.[3] His control was thus brought to bear directly on the government of the house ; we see its effect in the decrease of injunctions for heads to join in the conventual life, and for the preparation and presentation of accounts.[4] There is a marked improvement in both matters. That prelates and obedientiaries were secretive or unbusiness-like in money matters is a fairly common complaint in the journal. There are many injunctions, as in Archbishop Pecham's register, that accounts are to be regularly presented in chapter, to the whole convent or to the *senior* or *sanior* part.

The statistics of monastic debt [5] seem more discouraging than any of the rest. These figures seem to show that however beneficial the archbishop's visitations were, they did not improve the financial position of the monasteries. Possibly without Rigaud's advice and action some would have sunk further into debt : but we cannot speculate on this. The fact remains that in the course of twenty-one years the general position became worse rather than better. This is incontestable. But we may doubt whether it has all the significance which at first it seems to possess. The table shows what it purports to show—but it does

[1] Berlière, *Innocent*, 149.
[2] Rigaud, 105, 133, 255.
[3] *Ibid.*, 380, 432, 513.
[4] See Appendix I. (I).
[5] See Appendix I. (J).

not reveal the fact that debts fluctuated violently from year to year. To illustrate this point we will take the case of Graville, a small house of canons, usually with eleven regular inmates. It is not an extreme case :—

In 1248 its revenues were stated as £300 (of Tours), and it had no debts.

1249   Debts £40, but £100 owed to the house.
1251   More owed to the canons than they owe.
1252   Debts c. £40.
1255   Debts c. £50.
1256   Debts £50.
1257   Debts £150.
1259   More owed to the canons than they owe by c. £60.
1260   Debts £46.
1262   Debts small—they can be cleared easily.
1263   Debts £100.
1265   Debts £240.
1266   Debts £250.
1268   No debts.
1269   Debts £60.

There is something rather surprising in the discovery that a house whose revenue is assessed at £300 can wipe out a debt of £250 in about fifteen months (between III. Non. Jan., 1266, and XI. Kal. Maii, 1268). We hear of no sale of property, no settlement with a debtor, no donation. The financial records must be incomplete. It is unlikely that the debts due to a house were always recorded, or that cash in hand always appears to counterbalance liabilities. Mont S.-Catherine had debts to pay for three years, but almost certainly had a large reserve of capital.

In view of this spasmodic indebtedness of houses we must assume that the business methods of monks were not those of modern days. If we agree with Dr. Coulton that " these debts did not spring from the unbusinesslike habits of men who were too charitable to press their legal rights,"[1] we are not bound to condemn the men for sheer incom-

[1] Coulton, *Five Centuries*, II. 226.

petence. For we do not know how the visitor obtained the figures he recorded. Was he each time presented with a full statement regarding the *status domus* as Gregory IX had demanded ? If so, was this statement complete ? And if it was complete how much of it did the visitor take into account when he wrote down " Debebant . . . libras ? " These questions are hard to answer, and without certainty on the matter we are not justified in treating the statement of debt as an infallible proof of the monasteries' insolvency.[1]

It was natural for the monasteries to suffer embarrassment from shortage of ready money. They apparently made great use of credit for big undertakings and found it advisable to lock up capital in various investments, and they borrowed in order to do so. The abbey of Le Tréport (its revenue was £1100), whose debt averaged about £220, was buying lands and rents fairly regularly during the period of Rigaud's visitations.[2] M. Génestal emphasizes the fact that there was nothing exceptional in such a situation. " On sait," he says, ". . . qu'un établissement religieux n'aliène pas, ne peut pas aliéner ses immeubles ; si donc une abbaye a fait des dépenses extraordinaires, par exemple, ce qui devait être le cas le plus fréquent, pour des constructions nouvelles ou des réparations, comme ces dépenses ne peuvent être couvertes que par les revenus mobiliers, il est possible que l'abbaye, d'ailleurs riche en capitaux immobiliers, soit endettée pendant quelque temps. Pour qu'il en fût autrement, elle eût dû quelques années avant d'entreprendre les travaux et en prévision de ceux-ci, économiser une somme suffisante sur ses revenus annuels. C'est précisément parce qu'elle ne le faisait pas, parce que tout capital

---

[1] For " fantastic methods of accounting " in a large monastic establishment, leading to this sort of understatement of resources, see H. W. Saunders, *An Introduction to the Obedientiary and Manor Rolls of Norwich Cathedral Priory* (Norwich, 1930), 23, 24, 29, 51, 110, etc.

[2] *Cartulaire de l'abbaye . . . du Tréport*, ed. P. Laffleur de Kermaingant (1880), table chronologique ; cf. the policy of Malton Priory in the same period in Graham, *Studies*, 256 (Trans. Royal Hist. Soc., N.S., xviii. (1904), 140).

mobilier, pour ne pas rester improductif, était aussitôt que possible placé en achats de terres ou de rentes, que toute dépense extraordinaire de quelque importance compromettait l'équilibre du budget. Mais il suffisait, nous l'avons vu, pour le rétablir, de quelques années de sage administration ; ce qui montre bien que la fortune de l'abbaye n'était pas sérieusement atteinte." [1]

In considering the import of these figures of monastic debt, we are justified in taking into account the visitor's attitude. It is worth noting that the archbishop sometimes remitted,[2] or partially remitted,[3] procuration fees because of a house's poverty. But the examples are not many in the diocese of Rouen. In the nunneries the archbishop continually inveighed against the veiling of new nuns, and gave the poverty of the house as the reason for his injunction on five occasions.[4] Such sidelights are rare, and, except in the more extreme cases, Rigaud recorded the amount of debt without comment. Dr. Power takes the nunnery of S.-Amand as an instance of incompetent management ; " here, in 1262, as much as £377 7s. seems to have been owing to the nuns at a time when they themselves were £142 in debt, and at the next two visitations complaint was made of debts (described in 1264 as ' bad ' debts, debitis male solubilibus) owing to them."[5] This does not seem a fair presentation of the facts. The Journal states baldly the amounts in 1262, in 1263 says " debebant circa centum libras, et aliqua debebantur eisdem," and in 1264 says " debebant V^c libras turonenses ; aliqua debebantur eis in debitis male solubilibus, ut dicebant."[6] It will be noted that no complaint was made. For S.-Wandrille in 1249 Rigaud gave the revenue as £4000 and then said : " debent circa M libras tantum."[7] At Bec, where the revenue is not stated, he said : " non debent nisi IIII^c libras,"[8] and at Beaulieu : " habent in redditibus CCCCL libras ; debent IX^{xx} libras.

---

1 Génestal, 163-4.
3 *Ibid.*, 241, 280, 427.
5 Power, 638.
7 *Ibid.*, 55.

2 Rigaud, 117, 193.
4 *Ibid.*, 44, 207, 207, 323, 361.
6 Rigaud, 456, 486, 512.
8 *Ibid.*, 8.

Omnia sunt in bono statu." [1] At S.-Pierre of Pontoise in 1253 he reported: " Omnia invenimus in bono statu, circa temporalia. Debent ducentas quadraginta libras abbati, et alibi, centum libras." [2] The average revenue of this house was £275. Perhaps it is peculiarly significant that at Graville in 1266 where (as has been seen) the debt was £250 and the revenue only £300, Rigaud prescribed to the prior : " quod numerum canonicorum residentium augeret." [3] He could only have made this injunction when he was thoroughly satisfied as to the solvency of the house. These indications, slight as they are, should prevent us from uttering hasty condemnations of the monastic economy. Admittedly, they cannot contradict the very widespread evidence of poverty of religious houses in the thirteenth century ; order visitors, popes and chroniclers witness to the embarrassment of monasteries in all parts of Europe. [4] But this evidence of Rigaud's register does not point to serious distress in the diocese of Rouen.

Closely allied to the question of indebtedness is that of the population of religious houses in the diocese. Did that decrease during the government of Rigaud ? If debt was extremely onerous we should expect to see a fall of numbers in consequence. There were empty priories from the first, and many times the archbishop refers to solitary monks who need companions. [5] But these irregularities did not increase in latter years : Rigaud's injunctions on this matter seem to have been very often obeyed.

We must look therefore for a decrease, if decrease there was, in the population of the larger houses (possibly depleted by the filling of dependent priories)—those in fact for which we have statistics of population. The figures for monks and canons in the three periods are 612, 631, 619. [6] It is clear from these figures, even if we cannot be

---

[1] Rigaud, 9. [2] Ibid., 166. [3] Ibid., 564.

[4] See e.g. Berlière, Honorius, 461 ; Recrutement, 3 ; Snape, 119-52 ; Pirenne, Polyptyque et Comptes de l'abbaye de S.-Trond (Gand, 1896), introduction ; Coulton, Five Centuries, I. 394.

[5] See Appendix I. (E). [6] See Appendix I. (C).

sure of their exact accuracy, that there was no notable falling off in numbers between 1248 and 1269. Rigaud frequently remarked in monasteries that they had not so many religious as used to be there,[1] but an injunction on this matter normally had effect : depletion, if there was depletion, had been at an earlier period. This evidence may be joined to other indications which suggest that monastic debt was rarely sufficient to damage a house permanently or to reduce the population it was capable of supporting.

The handling of this mass of various evidence, to twist about and compare, to resolve into an intelligible and significant whole, has resulted in a rather shapeless image with many little features and none predominant. But if from the handling one impression deeper than the rest has been left it is, surely, that the archbishop's chief obstacle was passive unspirituality in the cloister. Rigaud could enforce administrative reforms, he could have the Rule written and read ; but the little self-indulgences of the religious, their private stores, their meat for meals, he could not prevent. Stubbornness beat the strongest disciplinarian on these points. On the other hand, the recorded reduction of certain offences is too marked to be accidental. It is probable even that it underrates the tendency to improvement, for the archbishop's zeal did not abate, and oversights probably occurred most often in the earlier years. To the archbishop it is fair to give most credit for the change. The long persistence of the evils and the repetition of injunctions shows the opposition against which he contended. Only a strong external force continually returning could make an impression upon a

---

[1] Rigaud, 7, 47, 55, 57, 76, 99, 100, 103, 104, 106, 117, 121, 131, 132, 167, 192, 265, 319, 431, 442, 447, 475, 508. Dom Berlière has assembled a large amount of evidence on this matter, from several continental countries, in a study in the *Revue Bénédictine* (tome XLI, 1929), " Le nombre des moines dans les monastères au Moyen âge." In an article to follow we may expect Dom Berlière's conclusions on the mass of material which he has here accumulated.

disordered monastery, however zealous its head might be. To emphasize the amount of success with which Rigaud's efforts were rewarded is not to forget the limitations always operative. The archbishop could not make religion flourish : he could prevent its worse decay.

APPENDIX I.

STATISTICS RELATING TO NORMAN MONASTERIES, 1248-69.

Since the aim is to discover the extent of improvement from 1248 to 1269 it is obviously of little use to compare the first year's figures with the last year's; instead, we compare the statistics for three periods :—

From *XVI. Kal. Aug.* 1248 to *III. Non. Mart.* 1255.
From *II. Non. Mart.* 1255 to *Kal. Feb.* 1262.
From *IIII. Non. Feb.* 1262 to *XVII. Kal. Jan.* 1269.

The number of visitations counted for these periods are 228, 227, 227. An exact time division (equal periods of seven years and fifty days) would alter the number of visitations in each section to 212, 232, 238.

All the houses involved were houses of regulars : 29 houses of monks, 13 of regular canons, and 7 of nuns. Each was visited at least six times in all, and once at least in each of the periods specified above.

5 houses were visited 17 times   5 houses were visited 13 times.
10   „   „   „   16   „   „   „   „   „   11   „
9   „   „   „   15   „   1 house was   „   9   „
11   „   „   „   14   „   1   „   „   „   7   „
2 houses were visited 6 times.

(A) IGNORANCE OF THE RULE AND STATUTES.

	No Copy of Rule.		No Copy of Statutes.
	Monks.	*Nuns.*	*Monks only.*
1248–55	6	1[1]	21 (3[1])
1255–62	7	—	1
1262–69	3	—	—

	Rule or Statutes not Possessed or not Read.			No. of Visitations.		
	Monks.	*Canons.*	*Nuns.*	*Monks.*	*Canons.*	*Nuns.*
1248–55	46	1	1	142	59	27
1255–62	9	3	—	145	54	28
1262–69	11	—	—	134	58	35

[1] Denotes the lack of a copy in the vernacular.

(B) DISCIPLINE.

	Chapters Irregular.		
	Monks.	Canons.	Nuns.
1248–55	10	1	2
1255–62	1	—	—
1262–69	—	—	—

	"Unus Non Clamat Alium."			No. of Visitations.		
	Monks.	Canons.	Nuns.	Monks.	Canons.	Nuns.
1248–55	17	13	—	142	59	27
1255–62	22	23	1	145	54	28
1262–69	8	11	—	134	58	35

(C) " DE SUBSTANTIA REGULAE."

	Private Property.			No. of Visitations.		
	Monks.	Canons.	Nuns.	Monks.	Canons.	Nuns.
1248–55	10	3	8	142	59	27
1255–62	21	11	13	145	54	28
1262–69	14	7	13	134	58	35

	Incontinents.			Average Regular Population.		
	Monks.	Canons.	Nuns.	Monks.	Canons.	Nuns.
1248–55	7	18	17	461	151	221
1255–62	5	2	10	470	161	221
1262–69	—	1	8	465	154	222

The figures for incontinency reckon offences, not persons. They do not take into account the lapses of non-regular inmates—of these there were three in houses of monks, one in an Augustinian house and three in houses of nuns. The figures show a decrease of female offenders which is perhaps illusory, since it depends on one exceptional case. Rigaud's first visitation of Villarceaux found the nunnery in an apparently hopeless state of degradation ; this accounts for twelve of the cases in the first period. Though the archbishop visited Villarceaux ten times more he reported no more cases there.

(D) SILENCE.

	Silence.			No. of Visitations.		
	Monks.	*Canons.*	*Nuns.*	*Monks.*	*Canons.*	*Nuns.*
1248–55	9	5	5	142	59	27
1255–62	4	5	3	145	54	28
1262–69	3	4	1	134	58	35

(E) LONE MONKS.

	No. of Lone Regulars.			No. of Visitations.		
	Monks.	*Canons.*	*Nuns.*	*Monks.*	*Canons.*	*Nuns.*
1248–55	15	35	1	142	59	27
1255–62	12	10	1	145	54	28
1262–69	11	4	—	134	58	35

Besides solitary monks, the archbishop remarked three empty priories in the first period, fifteen in the second, and three in the last period. This was in addition to seven priories consistently empty throughout the twenty-one years of the journal (Rigaud: 5, 5, 9, 10, 99, 103, 250, and after).

(F) THE COMMON LIFE, AND CLAUSTRATION.

	Absence from Refectory.			Excursions.		
	Monks.	*Canons.*	*Nuns.*	*Monks.*	*Canons.*	*Nuns.*
1248–55	10	1	9	19	7	6
1255–62	5	—	4	8	7	9
1262–69	4	1	7	4	2	6

	Intrusions.			No. of Visitations.		
	Monks.	*Canons.*	*Nuns.*	*Monks.*	*Canons.*	*Nuns.*
1248–55	14	17	6	142	59	27
1255–62	11	11	8	145	54	28
1262–69	6	8	—	134	58	35

(G) FOOD REGULATIONS.

	Fasts.		Flesh-eating.		No. of Visitations.	
	Monks.	*Nuns.*	*Monks.*	*Nuns.*	*Monks.*	*Nuns.*
1248–55	55	—	82	5	164	27
1255–62	61	1	102	—	159	28
1262–69	45	—	69	—	137	35

In the foregoing table injunctions addressed to dependent priories have been included, and a visitation counted for each such injunction. The figures include cases where the monks stated that they had a clear conscience or else received licence from their abbot. They also include cases where the monks said that they ate flesh habitually.

There are no injunctions for houses of canons.

(H) INFIRMARY AND ALMS.

The complaints here are against inadequate accommodation, poor food, absence of medical attention and lack of services for the sick. Alms are to be increased or to be maintained at the normal level, and there are complaints of diminution.

	Infirmary.			Alms.			No. of Visitations.		
	Monks.	*Canons.*	*Nuns.*	*Monks.*	*Canons.*	*Nuns.*	*Monks.*	*Canons.*	*Nuns.*
1248–55	8	8	—	6	—	2	142	59	27
1255–62	9	8	2	11	3	4	145	54	28
1262–69	10	5	1	4	2	9	134	58	35

(I) ADMINISTRATION.

	Head at Fault.			Irregular Accounting.			No. of Visitations.		
	Monks.	*Canons.*	*Nuns.*	*Monks.*	*Canons.*	*Nuns.*	*Monks.*	*Canons.*	*Nuns.*
1248–55	5	1	6	32	12	6	142	59	27
1255–62	—	—	5	29	10	7	145	54	28
1262–69	1	—	1	14	10	5	134	58	35

(J) MONASTIC REVENUE AND DEBT.

The indebtedness of the religious houses in the province of Rouen has been analysed by Mr. Snape (pp. 178 *sqq.*), who has also provided some statistics for the diocese covering a few years (p. 150). He compares population with revenue and population with debt; but he does not compare revenue with debt except in the total amount of each. Consequently, while we see the average indebtedness of the average monk contrasted with his average income, we have no means of telling from Mr. Snape's tables whether, for example, the house with two inmates which owed above £100 had an income of "over £100" or "£20 or less" or any amount intermediate in the scale. It is rather important that we should have this comparison. It is also highly important for the purpose of the present inquiry to note such change as occurs in the course of the archbishop's visitations. The following table is constructed with these objects in view. There are only forty-one houses in the diocese of Rouen for which we have sufficient material (see *infra*, Appendix II.) for the purpose of this analysis.

The amount of debt reckoned in the tables is obtained in each case by subtracting what is owed to the monastery from what it owes. Where bad debts are mentioned, however, they are not reckoned in deduction of the monks' debt.

The payment of pensions by a monastery has been left on one side in reckoning the indebtedness of the house.

Where a monastery owes less than it is owed, its debt is taken as zero; it is not reckoned as a minus quantity for the reduction of the average indebtedness.

The *mark sterling* is reckoned at 2.4 *livres tournois*. The *livre parisis* is reckoned at 1.25 *livres tournois*. Where the text does not distinguish between the kinds of money, it is assumed that money of Tours is meant. There are a few exceptions where the contrary inference seems justified.

Considerable variations of revenue are left unexplained in the register: it may mean that the archbishop did not always learn the amount of a house's resources at his first visits. S.-Martin of Pontoise is first recorded as having a revenue of £1000. It rises to £1875. The nunnery of S.-Saëns had an income variously stated at £140, £270 and £450; but it is unlikely that the revenue fluctuated so much. Altogether, the financial statistics are the least comprehensible and the least trustworthy. It is impossible to obtain an aggregate of debt since many records of visitations contain no figures; and there is the possibility of considerable error in the statement of averages based on the insufficient (and sometimes ambiguous) material at our disposal.

If, as seems highly probable, the records of revenue disregard the amount of revenue *in kind*, the revenue tables given below provide nothing more than a rough average of money income, which would not necessarily be the chief item in a true statement of the total revenue. On this assumption, also, the expression of debt as a fraction of revenue exaggerates the significance of the monasteries' liabilities.

The last table, giving income *per head*, obviously bears little relation to the actual facts of monastic economy, but a theoretic statement of this sort may be of some use, and can be compared with Mr. Snape's figures in *English Monastic Finances* (p. 150).

ELEVEN HOUSES OF MONKS WITH MORE THAN TEN REGULAR
INMATES EACH.

Debt as Fraction of Revenue.	Number of Houses.			
	1248-55.	1255-62.	1262-69.	Average, Whole Time.
Under $\frac{1}{10}$ . .	4	4	4	4
$\frac{1}{10}$ to $\frac{1}{4}$ (inclusive) .	1	2	4	3
$\frac{1}{4}$ to $\frac{1}{2}$,, .	2	2	1	—
$\frac{1}{2}$ to $\frac{3}{4}$,, .	—	—	—	1
$\frac{3}{4}$ to 1 ,, .	4	3	1	3
More than revenue	—	—	1	—

FOURTEEN HOUSES OF MONKS WITH TEN OR LESS REGULAR
INMATES EACH.

Debt as Fraction of Revenue.	Number of Houses.			
	1248-55.	1255-62.	1262-69.	Average, Whole Time.
Under $\frac{1}{10}$ . .	2	1	1	1
$\frac{1}{10}$ to $\frac{1}{4}$ (inclusive) .	3	3	2	1
$\frac{1}{4}$ to $\frac{1}{2}$,, .	6	4	4	5
$\frac{1}{2}$ to $\frac{3}{4}$,, .	2	3	2	2
$\frac{3}{4}$ to 1 ,, .	—	1	1	4
More than revenue	1	2	4	1

FIVE HOUSES OF NUNS, EACH HAVING MORE THAN TEN
INMATES.

Debt as Fraction of Revenue.	Number of Houses.			
	1248-55.	1255-62.	1262-69.	Average, Whole Time.
Under $\frac{1}{10}$ . .	1	1	1	1
$\frac{1}{10}$ to $\frac{1}{4}$ (inclusive) .	2	—	1	—
$\frac{1}{4}$ to $\frac{1}{2}$,, .	1	2	1	2
$\frac{1}{2}$ to $\frac{3}{4}$,, .	1	1	—	—
$\frac{3}{4}$ to 1 ,, .	—	—	2	1
More than revenue	—	1	—	1

NINE HOUSES OF REGULAR CANONS WITH MORE THAN TEN
REGULAR INMATES EACH.

Debt as Fraction of Revenue.	Number of Houses.			
	1248-55.	1255-62.	1262-69.	Average, Whole Time.
Under $\frac{1}{10}$ . .	2	2	1	—
$\frac{1}{10}$ to $\frac{1}{4}$ (inclusive) .	1	2	2	4
$\frac{1}{4}$ to $\frac{1}{2}$,,	4	3	4	3
$\frac{1}{2}$ to $\frac{3}{4}$,, .	2	—	1	2
$\frac{3}{4}$ to 1 ,, .	—	2	—	—
More than revenue	—	—	1	—

TWO HOUSES OF REGULAR CANONS WITH TEN OR LESS
REGULAR INMATES EACH.

Debt as Fraction of Revenue.	Number of Houses.			
	1248-55.	1255-62.	1262-69.	Average, Whole Time.
Under $\frac{1}{10}$ . .	—	1	—	—
$\frac{1}{10}$ to $\frac{1}{4}$ (inclusive) .	—	—	—	1
$\frac{1}{4}$ to $\frac{1}{2}$,, .	2	1	1	—
$\frac{1}{2}$ to $\frac{3}{4}$,, .	—	—	—	1
$\frac{3}{4}$ to 1 ,, .	—	—	1	—
More than revenue	—	—	—	—

AVERAGE REVENUE AND DEBT PER HEAD OF REGULAR
POPULATION OF THE ABOVE FORTY-ONE HOUSES
(in livres tournois).

	Houses with More than Ten Regular Inmates.		Houses with Ten or Less Regular Inmates.		Average for all Houses.	
	Revenue.	Debt.	Revenue.	Debt.	Revenue.	Debt.
Monks	68·2	17·9	52·9	26·6	66·8	19·4
Canons	34·4	12·6	37·2	14·1	34·6	12·9
Nuns	23·0	3·5	—	—	23·0	3·5

APPENDIX II.

NAMES OF HOUSES INCLUDED IN STATISTICS IN APPENDIX I.

*Names marked with an asterisk are omitted from the finance tables.

MONKS.

Alba Mallia (Aumale).
Altifagus (Auffay).
Basquevilla (Bacqueville).
*Beccus Helluini (Le Bec-Hellouin).
Bellus Saltus (Beaussault).
*Burae (Bures).
Calvus Mons, Beata Maria (Chaumont-en-Vexin).
Evremodium (Envermeu).
*Gaaniacum (Gani).
Gemeticus (Jumièges).
Gisetium (Juziers).
Leonis Curia (Liancourt).
Noion (Charleval).
Novum Marchesium (Neufmarché).
Pennes (Parnes).
Pratum iuxta Rothomagum (Rouen, Le Pré).
*Sanctus Audoenus Rothomagensis (Rouen, S.-Ouen).
Sanctus Georgius de Bauquiervilla (S.-Georges-de-Boscherville).
Sancta Katherina in Monte Rothomagensi (Rouen, Mont-Ste.-Catherine).
Sanctus Laurentius in Cornu Cervino (?).
Sanctus Martinus in Warenna (S.-Martin-en-Garenne).
Sanctus Martinus Pontisarensis (Pontoise, S.-Martin).
Sanctus Petrus Pontisarensis (Pontoise, S.-Pierre).
Sanctus Sidonius (S.-Saëns).
Sanctus Victor in Caleto (S.-Victor l'Abbaye).
Sanctus Wandregisilus (S.-Wandrille).
Serancium Boticularii (Serans-le-Bouteiller).
Ulterior Portus (Le Tréport).
Walemont (Valmont).

CANONS.

Augum (Eu).
*Aula Puellarum iuxta Rothomagum (S.-Julien, Petit-Quevilly).
Bellus Locus (Beaulieu).
Burgus Echardi (Bourg-Achard).
Cornevilla (Corneville).
Guerardi Villa (Graville).
Mons Duorum Amancium (Les Deux-Amants).
*Mons Leprosorum (Rouen, Mont-aux-Malades).
Novum Castrum (Neufchâtel).
Ovilla (Ouville).
Salicosa (Sausseuse).
Sanctus Laudus Rothomagensis (Rouen, S.-Lô).
Sanctus Laurentius in Leonibus (S.-Laurent-en-Lions).

NUNS.

Bondevilla (Bondeville).
*Buievilla (Bival).
Monasterium Villare (Montivilliers).
*Sanctus Albinus (S.-Aubin).
Sanctus Amandus Rothomagensis (Rouen, S.-Amand).
Sanctus Sidonius (S.-Saëns).
Villa Arcelli (Villarceaux).

APPENDIX III.

BIBLIOGRAPHY AND ABBREVIATIONS OF REFERENCES.

Abingdon Chron. *Chronicle of the monastery of Abingdon, 1218-1304,* ed. and trans. by J. O. Halliwell (Berkshire Ashmolean Soc., Reading, 1844).

Alexandre IV. *Les registres d'Alexandre IV (1254-61),* (Écoles françaises d'Athènes et de Rome, 1895-1907).

Ann. Mon. Annales Monastici, ed. H. R. Luard, 5 vols. (Rolls series, 1864-9).

Augustinian Chapters. Chapters of the Augustinian Canons, ed. H. E. Salter (Oxford Hist. Soc. and Canterbury and York Soc., 1922).

Autun Cart. Cartulaire de l'évêché d'Autun, ed. A. de Charmasse (Autun, 1880).

Baluze-Mansi. *Miscellanea,* by Etienne Baluze, revised by J. D. Mansi (Lucca, 1761-4).
The *Acta* of Archbishop Simon of Bourges occurs in volume I., pp. 267-310.

Beaunier et Besse. *Abbayes et Prieurés de l'ancienne France,* tome 7, Province ecclésiastique de Rouen (Ligugé et Paris, 1914).

Benedictine Chapters. Documents illustrating the Activities of the General and Provincial Chapters of the English Black Monks (1215-1540), ed. W. A. Pantin, 3 vols. Camden 3rd series, 1931-7.

Berlière, *Elections. Les Elections Abbatiales au moyen âge,* Dom U. Berlière (Mémoires de l'Académie Royale de Belgique, 2e série, tome 20, 1926).

Berlière, *Honorius. Honorius III et les monastères bénédictins, 1216-27,* Dom U. Berlière (Revue Belge de Philologie et d'Histoire, tome 2, 1923).

Berlière, *Innocent. Innocent III et les monastères bénédictins,* Dom U. Berlière (Revue Bénédictine, tome 32, 1920).

Berlière, *RB. Les chapitres généraux de l'Ordre de Saint Benoît,* Dom U. Berlière (Revue Bénédictine, tomes 8, 18, 19, 22 (1891, 1901, 1902, 1906).

Berlière, *Recrutement. Le recrutement dans les monastères bénédictins, aux XIIIe et XIVe siècles,* Dom U. Berlière (Mémoires Acad. Roy. de Belgique, 2e série, tome 18, 1924).

Boniface VIII. *Les registres de Boniface VIII (1294-1303),* (Éc. franç. d'Athènes et de Rome, 1884-1939).

Bronescombe. *The registers of Walter Bronescombe (1257-80) and Peter Quivil (1280-91), bishops of Exeter*, ed. F. C. Hingeston-Randolph (London, 1889).

Cantilupe. *Registrum Thome de Cantilupo Episcopi Herefordensis (1275-82)*, ed. R. G. Griffiths and W. W. Capes (Canterbury and York Soc., 1907).

Clément IV. *Les registres de Clément IV (1265-8)*, (Éc. franç. d'Athènes et de Rome, 1893–1945).

Corbridge. *The register of Thomas of Corbridge, lord archbishop of York (1300-4)*, ed. Wm. Brown, 2 vols. (Surtees Soc., 1925-8).
  Volume II. has a lengthy introduction to the whole register by Prof. A. Hamilton Thompson.

Coulton, *EHR*. *The interpretation of visitation documents*, G. G. Coulton (English Historical Review, vol. 39, January, 1914).

Coulton, *Five Centuries*. *Five Centuries of Religion*, G. G. Coulton. Vols. I. and II. (Cambridge, 1923-7).

CPR. *Calendar of entries in the Papal Registers, relating to Great Britain and Ireland*, Vol. I. (1198-1304), ed. W. H. Bliss (London, 1894).

Decretales. *Corpus Iuris Canonici*, ed. Friedberg, Vol. II. (Leipzig, 1881).

Decretum. *Corpus Iuris Canonici*, ed. Friedberg, Vol. I.

Dugdale. *Monasticon Anglicanum*, Wm. Dugdale, ed. J. Caley, etc., 6 vols. (London, 1817-30).

Durandus, *Constitutiones*. *Les Instructions et Constitutions de Guillaume Durand le Spéculateur* (Académie des Sciences et Lettres de Montpellier, 2e série, tome 3, 1900).

Durandus, *Speculum*. *Speculum Iuris* Gulielmi Durandi (Basle, 1574).

Evesham Chron. *Chronicon Abbatiae de Evesham, ad annum 1418*, ed. W. D. Macray (Rolls series, 1863).

Fournier. *Les Officialités au moyen âge*, Paul Fournier (Paris, 1880).

Frere. *Visitation Articles and Injunctions of the period of the Reformation*, Vol. I. Historical Introduction, W. H. Frere (Alcuin Club Collections, vol. 14, 1910).

Gandavo. *Registrum Simonis de Gandavo Episcopi Sarisbiriensis (1297-1315)*, ed. C. T. Flower and M. C. B. Dawes (Canterbury and York Soc., 1914–34).

Génestal. *Le rôle des monastères comme établissements de crédit étudié en Normandie du XIe à la fin du XIIIe siècle*, R. Génestal (Paris, 1901).

Gesta Dunelm. *Gesta Dunelmensia*, ed. Prof. R. K. Richardson (Camden Miscellany, Vol. XIII., 1924).

Giffard, *Worc.* (1) *Register of Bishop Godfrey Giffard (1268-1303)*, ed. J. W. Willis Bund, 2 vols. (Worcestershire Historical Soc., 1899-1902).
  A calendar of the entries, in English.
      (2) *Original MS. of the register*, Worcester Diocesan Registry.

Giffard, *York.* *The register of Walter Giffard, lord archbishop of York (1260-79)*, ed. Wm. Brown (Surtees Soc., 1904).

Glorieux. *La Littérature Quodlibétique de 1260 à 1320*, abbé P. Glorieux (Bibliothèque Thomiste, vol. 5, 1925).

Gloucester Cart. S. Petri Gloucestriae Historia et Cartularium Monasterii, ed. W. H. Hart, 3 vols. (Rolls series, 1863-7).

Graham, *Studies*. *English Ecclesiastical Studies*, Rose Graham (London, 1929).

Graham, Dr. Rose. *The Administration of the Diocese of Ely, sede vacante, 1298-9 and 1302-3*. (Trans. R. Hist. Soc., 1929, series IV, vol. XII.)

Gravesend. *Rotuli Ricardi Gravesend Episcopi Lincolniensis (1258-79)*, ed. F. N. Davis, with an introduction by A. H. Thompson (Canterbury and York Soc., 1915-25).

Gray. *The register, or rolls, of Walter Gray, lord archbishop of York (1225-56)*, ed. James Raine (Surtees Soc., 1872).

Grégoire IX. *Les registres de Grégoire IX (1227-41)*, (Éc. franç. d'Athènes et de Rome, 1892-1955).

Grégoire X. *Les registres de Grégoire X et Jean XXI (1271-7)*, (Éc. franc. d'Athènes et de Rome, 1892-1906).

Grenoble Visitations. *Visites pastorales et ordinations des évêques de Grenoble de la maison de Chissé (14e-15e siècles)*, d'après les registres originaux, ed. Abbé C. U. J. Chevalier (Docs. inédits sur le Dauphiné, 4e livraison, Montbéliard, 1874).

Grosseteste. *Rotuli Roberti Grosseteste Episcopi Lincolniensis (1235-53)*, ed. F. N. Davis (Canterbury and York Society, 1910-13).

Grosseteste, *Epistolæ*. *Epistolæ Roberti Grosseteste*, ed. H. R. Luard (Rolls series, 1861).

Halton. *The register of John de Halton, bishop of Carlisle* (1292-1324), ed. T. F. Tout (Canterbury and York Soc., 1913).

Hartzheim. *Concilia Germaniae*, ed. J. Hartzheim (Cologne, 1757-75).

HMCR. Historical Manuscripts Commission Reports (England).

Honorii III. *Regesta Papae Honorii III*, ed. P. Pressutti, 2 vols. (Rome, 1888-95).

Honorius IV. *Les registres d'Honorius IV (1285-7)*, (Éc. franç. d'Athènes et de Rome, 1888).

Hostiensis, *Comment. Henrici de Segusio Cardinalis Hostiensis in Primum* [. . . etc.] *Decretalium Librum Commentaria* (Venice, 1581).

Hostiensis *Summa. Henrici de Segusio . . . Summa Aurea* (Lyons, 1588 and 1597).

IAD. Inventaires des Archives Départementales (France).

Innocent III. *Regesta Innocentii III* (Migne's Patrologia Latina, vols. 214-7).
    The letters are numbered in books according to the pontifical years. There is a supplement in vol. 217.

Innocent IV. *Les registres d'Innocent IV (1243-54)*, (Éc. franç. d'Athènes et de Rome, 1884-1921).

Innocent IV. *Comment. Innocentii IIII Commentaria in Primum* [. . . etc.], *Decretalium Librum* (Venice, 1578).

Jaffé. *Regesta Pontificum Romanorum . . . ad annum 1198*, ed. P. Jaffé, 2nd edition by Loewenfeld, etc., 2 vols., Leipzig, 1885-8.

Jean XXI. See Grégoire X.

Jenkins, *CQR. A Thirteenth-Century Register : Odo, Archbishop of Rouen*, Prof. Claude Jenkins (Church Quarterly Review, vol. 101, October, 1925).

Jocelin. *The Chronicle of Jocelin of Brakelond*, trans. Sir E. Clarke (King's Classics, 1903).
The latin text was edited by J. G. Rokewood for the Camden Society, in 1840.

Lacger, *RHE. La primatie et le pouvoir métropolitain de l'archevêque de Bourges au XIIIe siècle*, L. de Lacger (Revue d'Histoire Ecclésiastique, vol. 26, January and April, 1930).

Lanercost. *The Chronicle of Lanercost (1272-1346)*, trans. Sir H. Maxwell (1913).
Chronicon de Lanercost (1201-1346) was published complete by the Maitland Club, vol. 46, in 1839.

Leclercq-Hefele. *Histoire des Conciles*, C. J. Hefele, ed. Dom H. Leclercq (Paris, 1907, etc.).

Linc. Visit. *Visitations of Religious Houses in the Diocese of Lincoln*, Vol. I. (*1420-36*); Vols. II. and III. (*1436-49*); ed. A. Hamilton Thompson (Lincoln Record Society, 1914, 1918, 1929; Canterbury and York Society, 1914, 1919, 1929).

Lyle, *English Bishop. The Office of the English Bishop in the First Half of the Fourteenth Century*, by E. K. Lyle (Philadelphia, 1903).

Mansi. *Sacrorum conciliorum nova et amplissima collectio*, by J. D. Mansi, 31 vols. (Venice and Florence, 1759-98).
The *Acta* of Archbishop Simon of Bourges occurs in vol. 24, cols. 649-766.

Martin IV. *Les registres de Martin IV (1281-5)*, (Éc. franç. d'Athènes et de Rome, 1901–35).

Matt. Paris. *Matthæi Parisiensis Chronica Majora*, 7 vols. (Rolls series, 1874-89).

Nicolas III. *Les registres de Nicolas III (1277-80)*, (Éc. franç. d'Athènes et de Rome, 1898–1938).

Nicolas IV. *Les registres de Nicolas IV (1288-92)*, (Éc. franç. d'Athènes et de Rome, 1886–1905).

Pecham. *Registrum Johannis Pecham Archiepiscopi Cantuariensis (1278-92)*, (Canterbury and York Soc., 1908–1969).

Peckham. *Registrum Epistolarum Johannis Peckham Archiepiscopi Cantuariensis*, 3 vols. (Rolls series, 1882-6).

Poitiers Cart. *Cartulaire de l'évêché de Poitiers*, ed. L. Rédet (Archives Historiques du Poitou, Vol. X., 1881).

Pommeraye, *Concilia. Sanctæ Rotomagensis Ecclesiæ Concilia, ac Synodalia Decreta*, ed. F. Pommeraye (Rouen, 1667).

Pommeraye, *S.-Ouen. Histoire de l'Abbaye Royale de S.-Ouen de Rouen . . . et celles des Abbayes de Ste.-Catherine et de S.-Amand* [by F. Pommeraye], (Rouen, 1662).

Pontissara. *Registrum Johannis de Pontissara Episcopi Wyntoniensis* (*1282-1304*), ed. C. Deedes (Canterbury and York Soc., 1915-24).

Potthast. *Regesta Pontificum Romanorum* (*1198-1304*), ed. A. Potthast, 2 vols. (Berlin, 1874-5).

Power. *Medieval English Nunneries c. 1275-1535*, Eileen Power (Cambridge, 1922).

Quinq. Compil. *Quinque Compilationes antiquæ necnon collectio canonum Lipsiensis*, ed. E. Friedberg (Leipzig, 1882).

Rabanis. *Clément V et Philippe le Bel*, M. Rabanis (Paris, 1858). Pp. 152-99 contain a 16th-century summary of the visitation acts of Bertrand de Got, Archbishop of Bordeaux, in his province, 1304-5.

Ramsey Cart. *Cartularium Monasterii de Ramseia*, ed. W. H. Hart and P. A. Lyons (Rolls series, 1884-94).

Rigaud. (1) *Regestrum Visitationum Archiepiscopi Rothomagensis ; Journal des Visites Pastorales d'Eude Rigaud, Archevêque de Rouen* (*1248-69*), ed. Th. Bonnin (Rouen, 1852).

(2) *Original MS. of the register*, Bibliothèque Nationale, MS. Latin 1245.

Rockinger. *Briefsteller und Formelbücher des elften bis vierzehnten Jh.*, L. von Rockinger (Quellen zur bayerischen und deutschen Geschichte, IX., 1863-4).

Romeyn. *The Register of John le Romeyn, lord archbishop of York* (*1286-96*), ed. Wm. Brown, 2 vols. (Surtees Soc., 1913-17).

Schmalz. *De instituto Officialis sive Vicarii Generalis Episcopi*, C. Schmalz (Breslau, 1899).

Script. Tres. *Historiæ Dunelmensis Scriptores Tres*, ed. James Raine (Surtees Soc., 1839).

Sext. *Corpus Iuris Canonici*, ed. Friedberg, Vol. II. (Leipzig, 1881).

Snape. *English Monastic Finances in the Later Middle Ages*, R. H. Snape (Cambridge, 1926).

Swinfield. *Registrum Ricardi de Swinfield Episcopi Herefordensis* (*1283-1317*), ed. W. W. Capes (Canterbury and York Soc., 1909).

Thomassin. *L'Ancienne et la Nouvelle Discipline de l'Eglise*, L. Thomassin 2e édition, 3 vols. (Paris, 1679).

Urbain IV. *Les registres d'Urbain IV* (*1261-4*), (Éc. franç. d'Athènes et de Rome, 1901–58).

VCH. *Victoria County Histories* (of England).

Vendeuvre. *L'Exemption de Visite Monastique*, J. Vendeuvre (Dijon, 1906).

Welles. *Rotuli Hugonis de Welles Episcopi Lincolniensis* (*1209-35*) ed. W. P. W. Phillimore and F. N. Davis (Canterbury and York Soc., 1904-9).

Wickwane. *Register of William Wickwane, lord archbishop of York* (*1279-85*), ed. Wm. Brown (Surtees Soc., 1907).

Wilkins. *Concilia Magnæ Britanniæ et Hiberniæ*, ed. David Wilkins, 4 vols. (London, 1737).

Winchelsey. *Registrum Roberti Winchelsey Archiepiscopi Cantuariensis (1294-1313)*, ed. Rose Graham (Canterbury and York Soc., 1917–56).

Worcester Liber Albus. [Selections translated] by J. M. Wilson (London, 1920).

York Visitations. *Documents relating to Diocesan and Provincial Visitations from the Registers of Henry Bowet (1407-23) and John Kempe (1425-52), Archbishops of York,* ed. A. H. Thompson (Surtees Soc. Miscellanea II. (1916), pp. 133-334).

INDEX.

Bishops are indexed under the names of their dioceses, and Popes under that title. The following abbreviations are employed : Aug. (Augustinian), Ben. (Benedictine), Cist. (Cistercian), Clun. (Cluniac), Prem. (Premonstratensian). A place-name in parentheses indicates the diocese of a religious house.

ABBEVILLE, Gérard d', 88
Abingdon, Ben. abbey (Salisbury), 142
Agropoli, bishop of, 20
Alba Julia, Hungary, bishop of, 41
Albi, diocese of, 11 n., 127
Alien priories, 102.
Almenèches, Ben. nunnery (Séez), 116, 130, 145
Amalfi, archbishop of, 134
Amiens, bishop of, 25
Anagnano, priory (Arezzo), 27
Anchin, Ben. abbey (Arras), 45, 47
Angers, bishop of, 81
Angles, Aug. abbey (Poitiers), 58, 113
Antioch, patriarch of, 142
Aosta, bishop of, 146 ; San Orso, Aug. priory, 146
Appleton, Cist. nunnery (York), 96
Aquitaine, primate of, 11, 134
Arbury, Aug. priory (Coventry), 50
Archdeacon, 46, 128
Ardennes, Prem. abbey (Bayeux), 39 n.
Ardington, Ben. nunnery (York), 58
Arezzo, bishop of, 27
Ariano, bishop of, 20
Arles, archbishop of, 27, 134
Armagh, archbishop of, 139-40
Arras, bishop of, 41 n., 45, 47
Arroasian canons, 50
Articles of inquiry, 13, 56, 72-5
Arundel, alien priory (Chichester), 102
Auch, archbishop of, 126
Auffay, Ben. priory (Rouen), 153
Augustinian canons, General Chapters, 36, 51-2
Aurillac, Ben. abbey (Clermont), 126
Autun, bishop of, 43, 107, 114, 123, 130 ; S.-Martin, Ben. abbey, 107, 123
Auvergne, Guillaume d', bishop of Paris, 31
Avranches, bishop of, 41 n.

BACQUEVILLE, Ben. priory (Rouen), 155
Bangor, diocese of, 143

Bannister, Canon A. T., 10
Bar (Langres), archdeacon of, 110
Bardney, Ben. abbey (Lincoln), 35, 101
Bari, archbishop of, 41 n.
Barking, Ben. nunnery (London), 146
Basel, bishop of, 26
Basilian monasteries in Sicily, 28
Bath and Wells, Bishop Jocelin (1206-42), 33 ; Bishop William Bitton (1248-64), 123 ; visitation of diocese, 143.
Battle, Ben. abbey (Chichester), 6, 34, 41-2, 123
Bayeux, bishop of, 107, 122, 130 ; cathedral chapter, 130 ; custumal of the cathedral, 39 ; Hiémois archdeaconry, 10 ; official, 130 ; S.-Vigor-le-Grand, Ben. priory, 107, 122
Beaubec, Cist. abbey (Rouen), 153
Beaulieu, Aug. priory (Rouen), 164
Beaussault, Ben. priory (Rouen), 158
Beauvais, bishop of, 110, 131, 155
Bec-Hellouin (Le), Ben. abbey (Rouen), 92, 115, 155, 159 n., 164
Beckford, alien priory (Worcester), 109
Benedictine monks, General (Provincial) Chapters, 36, 48-51, 85, 92, 98, 138
Benevento, archbishop of, 142
Berlière, Dom Ursmer, 17-19, 48-50, 52 n., 149, 161, 166
Bermondsey, Ben. General Chapter at, 138
Billinkem, Ben. nunnery (Würzburg), 40
Bishop, general powers over monasteries, 19-25 ; rights in exempt houses, 37 ; told to help reformers of exempt houses, 25-6 ; and see Visitation
Bival, Ben. nunnery (Rouen), 8 n., 145, 155
Blyth, alien priory (York), 5, 102
Bologna, Santa Margarita, nunnery, 86
Bolton in Craven, Aug. priory (York), 56, 75, 81, 88
Bondeville, Cist. nunnery (Rouen), 159 n.

(183)

Exeter, Bishops: Walter Bronescombe
(1258-80), 6, 96, 124; Peter Quivil (1280-
91), 124, 126; Thomas Bitton (1292-
1307), 14; visitation of diocese, 143
Extravag. Commun: I. vii. 1, 69

FAVERSHAM, Ben. abbey (Canterbury), 51
Fécamp, Ben. abbey (Rouen), 40, 43
Fees, *see* Procuration
Felley, Aug. priory (York), prior of, 75
Feret, l'Abbé, 12 *n.*
Fermo, bishop and cathedral chapter, 82
Fleury, Ben. abbey (Orléans), 102
Florence, bishop of, 28
Fontevrault, nunnery (Poitiers), 40
Fountains, Cist. abbey (York), 50-1, 68
Fournier, M. Paul, 128
Frere, Dr. W. H., Bishop of Truro, 39 *n.*,
75, 98 *n.*, 99, 124-5
Friars and visitations, 35, 83, 138 *n.*
Frivolous accusations, 84-5

GAILLAC, Ben. abbey (Albi), 86-7
Gaillard de Roche, 131
Gaillonnet, Aug. priory (Rouen), 116
Gaul, diocesan government in, 19
Génestal, M. René, 163
Gisors, S.-Martin, Ben. priory (Rouen), 100
Glandèves, bishop of, 132
Glastonbury, Ben. abbey (Bath), 39 *n.*, 41,
122
Gloucester (Worcester), St. Oswald's, Aug.
priory, 33; St. Peter's, Ben. abbey, 34, 74
Graham, Dr. Rose, 51, 73, 144
Grandcourt, Eustache de, 88 *n.*
Grandmontines, 26, 40 *n.*
Gratian, 20, 24
Graville, Aug. priory (Rouen), 162, 165
Graystanes, Robert de, 64, 77, 79, 140 *n.*
Great Malvern, Ben. priory (Worcester),
42 *n.*, 63, 101
Grenoble Visitations, 10, 55 *n.*, 127 *n.*
Guisborough, Walter of, 64 *n.*, 68 *n.*

HADENHAM, Edmund of, 82 *n.*
Hastings, Aug. priory (Canterbury), 79
Hauck, Albert, 32, 128
Hauréau, Bernard, 16 *n.*
Hayles, Cist. abbey (Worcester), 109, 138 *n.*
Henry E. Huntington Library, MS. at, 42 *n.*
Hereford, Bishops: Thomas de Cantilupe
(1275-82), 63, 69, 80, 96, 146; Richard
de Swinfield (1283-1317), 63, 69, 102;
visitations of the diocese, 10, 84 *n.*, 130,
143
Hez, S.-Martin, Ben. priory (Rouen), 112
Hiémois (Bayeux), archdeaconry, visitations
of, 10
Hildesheim, bishop of, 27
Hincmar of Reims, *see* Reims

Hostiensis, Henry of Susa (Cardinal bishop
of Ostia), 2, 21, 31-2, 45-6, 48-50, 77-8,
93, 104, 117, 122, 127, 142
Hyde, Ben. abbey (Winchester), 120

INCONTINENT regulars, 160, 169
Infamia, see Defamation
Injunctions, 8 *n.*, 14, 96-9; to be displayed
to visitors, 15, 73, 97; to be read often,
72, 98; penalty for breach, 98; sealed,
97; occasionally superfluous, 84 *n.*, 156
Ivry, Ben. abbey (Evreux), 145

JENKINS, Professor Claude, 8 *n.*, 9, 89, 94,
150
Jessopp, A., 10 *n.*
Jumièges, Ben. abbey (Rouen), 70, 84, 153,
155

KENILWORTH, Aug. priory (Coventry), 67,
103
Keynsham, Aug. abbey (Wells), 33

LACGER, M. L. de, 47, 144
Lagny, Ben. abbey (Paris), 31
Lanercost, Aug. priory (Carlisle), 64
Langres, bishop of, 43 *n.*
Lanthony by Gloucester, Aug. priory
(Worcester), 14, 63 *n.*
Laon, bishop and cathedral chapter of, 146
Launceston, Aug. priory (Exeter), 14
Leclercq, Dom H., 40, 44
Leighlin, diocese of, 117
Leominster, Ben. priory (Hereford), 15 *n.*,
63, 69, 96, 103, 146
Leon, Kingdom of, 28
Lérins, Ben. abbey (Grasse), 27
Lesne, M. E., 133
Lesnes, Aug. abbey (Rochester), 147
Lessay, Ben. abbey (Coutances), 102 *n.*
Letterbooks, as evidence for visitations, 14,
63 *n.*
Liancourt, Ben. priory (Rouen), 112
Lichfield, *see* Coventry
Liége, bishop of, 28
Limoges, bishop of, 27, 110; S.-Augustin,
Ben. abbey, 27; S.-Martial, Ben. abbey,
27
Lincoln, Bishops: St. Hugh I (1186-1200),
98; Hugh de Welles II (1209-35), 4,
14, 33, 34, 59, 69, 98, 128; Robert
Grosseteste (1235-53), 5, 12 *n.*, 34-6,
41 *n.*, 59, 69, 73 *n.*, 79 *n.*, 81, 95, 98,
102, 106; Richard Gravesend (1258-79),
4, 124; Oliver Sutton (1280-99), 15, 58,
103, 147; William Gray (1431-6), 3;
William Alnwick (1436-49), 5, 6, 9;
diocese, extent of, 127-8; number of
exempt religious houses, 39 *n.*; visitations of, 142-3